COUNTRY COMFORTS

THE NEW HOMESTEADER'S HANDBOOK

by
Christian Bruyere
and
Robert Inwood

DRAKE PUBLISHERS INC.
NEW YORK • LONDON

Published in 1976 by
Drake Publishers Inc.
801 Second Ave.
New York, N.Y. 10017

Library of Congress Cataloging in Publication Data

Bruyere, Christian, 1944-
    Country Comforts—The New Homesteader's Handbook.
      1. Homesteading. 2. Construction.

Country Comforts
GV   75-
ISBN 0-8473-1031-0
ISBN 0-8473-1138-4 pbk.

Book Club Edition
Printed in The United States of America

CONTENTS

Introduction

As a follow up to *In Harmony With Nature, Country Comforts* describes several aesthetically pleasing and quite efficient designs for the homestead. *In Harmony With Nature* dealt mostly with the main structures. *Country Comforts* deals with the necessary secondary structures and many of the other essentials of a well designed, working homestead. It follows the seasons in presenting information provided by the homesteaders and designers themselves. These men and women proudly explained their noteworthy achievements and unselfishly shared their researched ideas with me. They are all people just like you and me who are very alive and are energetically trying to learn to develop the earth instead of destroy it. Their designs have been proven from experience and are not just theorized brainstorms that might work if all the variables are in their favor. Our only research, except in a few cases, was just the first-hand experience of folks who have to live with their creations. Sure, a lot of the designs have some structural or efficiency mistakes in them, but so does

most everything around. These fine folks were honest enough to reveal their past oversights, and through using their greenhouse, root cellar, or other structures they have developed ways to improve the primary designs of these. As many as possible of the advantages and difficulties of each are mentioned in the text to give the future designers guidelines in which to follow when they are developing their conveniences. This is not a book which snobbishly states a one-and-only answer to a certain problem but gives alternatives and explains in detail all that is familiar to the author-homesteader's and illustrator's realm of experience about a given design. It compares designs in some cases, describing the highlights and short-comings of each. It's up to the reader to decide what would work in his or her case, because everybody's particular needs and availability of materials are different. So read and enjoy the book. I'm sure it will prove to be entertaining and valuable no matter what your situation. It's a book for all people who enjoy experiencing life.

Christian Bruyere

Chapter One

Stretching The Growing Season

I built this cold frame to have more control at the beginning and end of the seasons, since the optimum growing period is so short in our northern valley. I wanted to be able to transplant in early May, getting a sufficient head start with the tomatoes, cucumbers, and peppers, and have it all extend longer into fall, so that most of the fruit could properly ripen on the vine. My original design called for a concrete enclosed frame which slopes slightly to the south. This frame was to be covered by a glass-paned roof. But I didn't have any old windows around that I wanted to use for the job, so I used 1 x 2″ lath sticks as frames and covered them with plastic. This of course didn't work very well because the plastic ripped too easily and the thin wood strips didn't hold their shape. The whole mess was too flimsy but it made it through the first season, barely. The next season we tried the present design which has been working very well.

A concrete frame was used primarily to create a barrier against the rapidly growing couch grass which plagues all the gardens in the area. Also concrete is very solid and permanent. It allows moisture in as it sweats to produce humidity within the frame. The plants love this warm, wet environment. I constructed forms around the 14 x 5′ perimeter of the frame using 1 x 8s with 2 x 4 stakes to hold them in place and thin braces spaced out along the sides, inside and out. Holes were drilled into the tops of these braces for the wire spacers to go through. A nail was placed at the outside of the form to hold the doubled wire and another nail was twisted between the inside ends until the forms were held exactly 6″ apart. They were then leveled with a carpenter's level. These forms were built high enough so they would be above the couch grass, 4″ above the surface at the low end and 8″ above at the high end to create the slope. The enclosed area was dug out 8″ deep for added protection and the inside form was extended down to that level. The 6″ wide space between the forms was then dug out for 18″ under the outside surface so the concrete pour would go well below the roots of the surrounding couch grass to prevent them from working their way into the cold frame (plates 1 and 2).

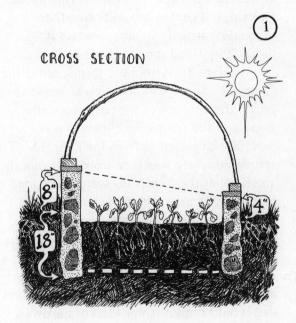

CROSS SECTION

WIRES ARE TIGHTENED BY TWISTING NAIL

6"
1"x8"
6"
1"x4"
1"x8"

2 x 4 Stakes
1x4
1"x8"
5'
1"x8"
14'

CONCRETE FORM

The concrete was mixed in a wheelbarrow and was poured into the forms. An additional horizontal brace was put in, extending between the inside forms of the two sides. The wet concrete was then tamped rigorously to make certain it thoroughly filled the space between the forms (plate 3). Within the forms, along the ends, a 1″ board was set in on an angle to create the contour of the north-to-south slope and the remaining concrete was carefully shoveled in from the high side. The setting concrete was then troweled smooth and level at the top. Nails were embedded around the frame with their pointed ends sticking out long enough to accommodate the 2 x 6″ sills and to bend down over them (plates 4, 5).

I didn't want to get into a lot of nailing and constructing of individual frame covers that would require some kind of hardware hinges for easy lifting. Hardware hinges seem to have a tendency to screw up in such outdoor type uses. And no other flat type covers seemed suitable. Finally, I started thinking about bent-pole "hoop" construction that I've seen around. The

arched poles seem to provide a strong support with gravity and downward pressure working against the tension of the arch. Anyway I wanted a high, arched type roof over the top to allow the plants plenty of room to grow and still be protected within the cold frame during the fall frost periods.

To get the poles, I went out into the woods where the second growth is really thick. In between the medium-size trees were a lot of little guys that would grow up to be no more than 10′ tall, and not get any thicker than 1½″ to 2″ at the butt. I searched for trees with a 1½″ butt that had very little taper—less than ½″ from top to bottom. This is about as small as you'd want to work with. If they were any fatter they would be hard to bend over into an arch the size I wanted.

I was finding only fir trees for the job. Most other species tapered too much, even at that tiny size. They were cut in early spring when the trees were just getting the new sap (plate 6).

To figure out the length I needed I found a piece of black plastic pipe and arched it between the sides of the frame. I liked the

(3)

height of that arch, approximately 3′ above the concrete sides in the center, and decided to work with that length. In order for the poles not to break, there has to be a true arch. It can't be too shallow. I cut the saplings to the proper size and peeled strips of bark off with a knife. Then I drilled holes into the sill boards on the north and south sides, making a larger 1½″ hole at the top side for the butt and smaller 1″ holes on the bottom side. The poles were bent into position and their ends were diagonally nailed with thin finishing nails to keep them in place (plates 7 and 8).

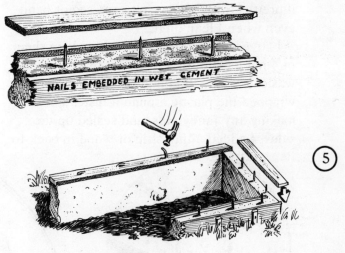

NAILS EMBEDDED IN WET CEMENT

(5)

(4)

SLANTED BOARD IS NAILED BETWEEN THE FORM WALLS. CEMENT IS PRESSED INTO FORM WITH A SHOVEL.

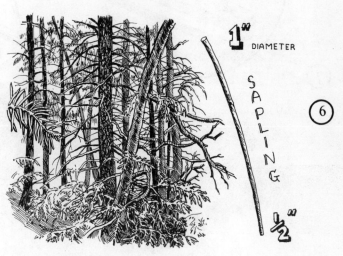

1″ DIAMETER

SAPLING

½″

(6)

This process worked great. Almost all the poles took shape immediately as I bent them. When finding poles for this job you should use green instead of dried-out or dead saplings. The greener they are, the more spring and durability they have. Actually, a couple of the poles cracked while being bent in place. I guess this could be attributed to the fact that it was so early in spring and the sap hadn't really had a chance to flow yet. But I could tell which ones were going to break through because they had knots in the wrong places and were less solid than the others. Once all the arched poles were in place, I lashed a long horizontal pole across the framework to provide it with greater lateral stability (plate 9). Diagonal braces would probably even keep it in place better, but actually the tension of the arches makes it pretty strong. It doesn't even sag or bend even when I lean on it.

I covered the framework with a long sheet of 4-mil plastic. It worked out that the arch was exactly the width of the plastic. I just wrapped the plastic around it instead of making any fancy cuts, and sealed up the sides. I added a thin strip of wood in back to protect the plastic for nailing through and wrapped it all around, with the higher plastic outside of the lower so that the water wouldn't fall down into the cracks where the folding occurred. Then it was tacked with broad-headed roofing nails at the top or north side. The ends were just tucked in with boards. At the more exposed, lower south side, I ran a couple of layers of 2″ masking tape along the front edge of the plastic. I cut slits like button holes into this protected edge at regular intervals, to correspond to the roofing nails, which were then nailed along the outside of the front sill. The whole thing buttons down really fast (plates 10, 11, 12). Having it this way is nice

⑧

⑦

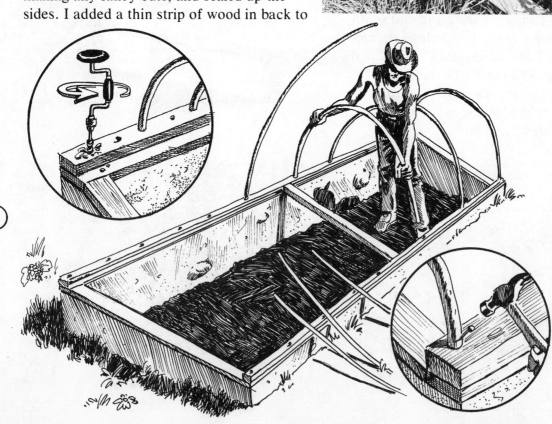

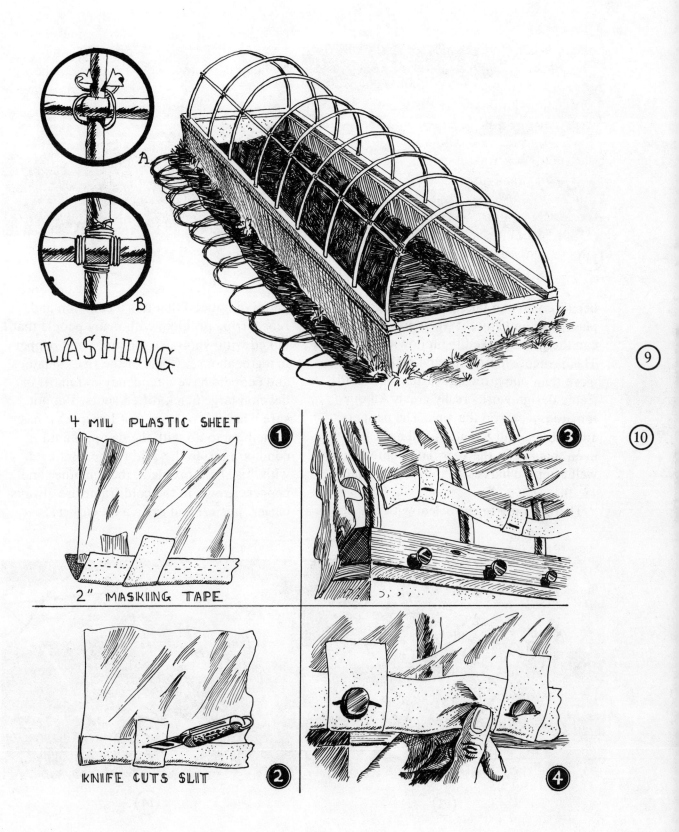

LASHING

A

B

4 MIL PLASTIC SHEET

2" MASKING TAPE

①

KNIFE CUTS SLIT

②

③

④

⑨

⑩

7

⑪   ⑫

because you can take the unaltered sheet of plastic off and store it when not in use. It can then be retacked the following spring. This protects the plastic and makes it last more than one growing season. This cold frame design works really great. All our tomatoes ripen on the vine. The peppers, cucumbers, and tomatoes still have fruit even this late in the year (late September), well after we harvested the garden (plates 13, 14).

There is only one problem with this setup,

and I've noticed that it is a common and reoccurring problem with many people that I talked with who raise tomatoes and peppers in a greenhouse. Some of the ripe tomatoes and peppers have a tendency to fall off or develop large black rotten spots. I'm not sure what this is from, but I suspect it has something to do with the damp, humid condition inside the cold frame. But even with this slight problem, the tomatoes and peppers grown in the cold frame are always bigger, juicier, and ripen a lot earlier.

⑬   ⑭

Chapter Two

Solar Greenhouse

It was pretty obvious to me 5 or 6 years ago that money was not going to even be able to purchase food in the near future. The quality of food that will be available for purchasing will soon be so substandard anyway, because wholesalers and distributors have been milking the food dollar with increasing ruthlessness. The grower is getting less and less percentagewise for his efforts, thus the production of high quality produce gets neglected since monetary greed leaves no room for this type of incentive to flourish. The syndrome of city living is such that people in large urban centers spend all their work energy making money to purchase their necessary food items. Consequently, these people have no training in developing their own crops in case the food is not shipped in. What an utterly helpless situation to be in. If food shipments were cut off, all the money in the world probably couldn't purchase those simple little items which we've learned to take so casually for granted. In fact, just lately a friend of mine told me about a farmer near Albuquerque, New Mexico who, during a recent food shortage, was assaulted by about twenty carloads of people, who drove right into his fields and ripped him off for a good deal of his crops.

And so we made the inevitable move from the city, built a temporary shelter to house our large family and began developing a piece of raw land. Of course, one of our first major concerns was to prepare an area for a garden that would feed us; 10 to 12 adults. This wasn't an easy task since the ground we were working with was 50 percent gravel and 50 percent light sand, with not enough soil to stain your hands when wetted down. We had a shredder so we went to all the

neighbor's yards and collected their leaves and shredded them. The leaf shreddings decomposed well. Soon we didn't even notice them in our garden, except for the presence of a new fiber in the ground. We also searched and scrounged the nearby hillsides for topsoil, and within a few months we developed the garden plot into workable soil.

An indispensable item that we have had a great deal of success with is the compost bin. We built a square frame out of poles, about 4' in height, 8' on each side, to hold leaves, manure, garbage, and other organic substances which will quickly decompose. In such a small, square pile the decomposing process works extremely fast from the bottom center, outward. Within a year, most of the organic substances in this pile break down into rich humus, which we spread over the garden and till in to build up the soil (plate 1).

①

COMPOST PILE

The first year on our land was one of unpredictable weather. It was rainy and cold all spring, and even in summer there wasn't enough direct sunlight to sustain a lot of our crops—especially since the soil needed so much attention. Due to this factor, and instead of dealing with the direct weather, we wanted to expend our energies into developing a controlled-environment greenhouse. Here we could bring up most of our vegetables in flats and then transplant them after they had a proper start. This way we'd also have more than a month jump on the other people in the area. It is risky to start most crops in the ground until June in our area because of late spring frosts which annually take their toll. We just start them in the greenhouse, thin them out right in the flats, and then transplant them into the ground. There wasn't anything that just didn't take off right away in the greenhouse. This was very encouraging. If it grew half as well outside we'd have excellent crops. We didn't lose any of the greenhouse-started plants. It was not like having hit and miss rows of plants, we controlled exactly what we wanted. We put in 137 tomato plants last year without losing one plant. And that was true of all our transplants—they went right on growing rapidly. It was definitely worth the effort in putting our energies into this type of controlled environment. I wouldn't do it any other way except maybe add a greenhouse to an already existing dwelling house so that the greenhouse could get the heat exposure from the dwelling all year round.

The site for the greenhouse was an electrical power line clearing with good southerly exposure. It gets the morning sun as well as an uninterrupted exposure throughout the day. We leveled off the top of the clearing and dug corner holes outlining the 12' x 16' area. Other holes were

DIAGONAL BRACING OF 1" x 4" LUMBER IS INSET ON THE EDGES OF 2" x 4" UPRIGHT STUDS

DOOR

CREOSOTED CEDAR POSTS 12" ABOVE GROUND

2" x 6" LAMINATED SILL

dug at 4′ intervals along these periphery lines. We creosoted cedar posts which were then put into the ground in them. We chose a size that would allow us to keep fragile plants, such as peppers and cucumbers, in it throughout the entire growing season. Fortunately, I had a transit to make sure these posts were really level. Cedar sills were then cut and placed above these posts. They were just above ground level. I figured that creosoted cedar on porous soil such as this is good for at least 40 years, so why worry about a concrete foundation for such a light weight structure.

A conventional stud wall was built over the sill in front and on the sides up to about 30″, to the bench height, leaving a space on the west wall for a door. We're short people, so we prefer that height. The windows and glass began at this level. Cedar was also used for the sheathing inside and out, with 3″ *batons* between each of the vertical boards. 3½″ of fiberglass insulation was put in between the studs with an 18-pound building paper backing on either side. A 4-mil plastic vapor barrier was then stapled in over the building paper.

The high 12′ back wall was constructed in the same manner. This tall back wall provided us with the necessary pitch and gave us total exposure to the whole greenhouse by making it possible for us to use a shed-roof design rather than a hip design. If the roof went up and back down as it would in the hip-roof design, the storage space on the walls would have been cut down considerably. You need a lot of storage space in a greenhouse for fertilizer and soil preparations, such as bone meal, and peat moss. Also, the high north wall provides protection against the cold northern winds and weather (plates 2-4).

Even with the sheltering north wall and the shed-roof design, there has been no problem with plants leaning toward the south, not even in early spring, when the arch of the sun is furthest away. The deflection seems to be pretty even in the greenhouse throughout the growing season. If this problem should arise, it can be easily remedied, just by turning the flats around. This will force the plants to grow back the other way.

The spaces between the side wall studding depended upon the width of the glass used. We scrounged around and finally found a

ROUGH CUT CEDAR SHEATHING WITH 1″ × 4″ BATTEN BOARDS

18 POUND BUILDING PAPER

18 POUND BUILDING PAPER

4 MIL PLASTIC VAPOUR BARRIER

INTERIOR CEDAR SHEATHING

3½″ FIBREGLASS INSULATION

3

man who wanted to sell all his used glass pieces. We made him an offer for the whole lot and brought the assortment home. We found the widest width we could use, saving the most glass. We cut all the glass to that 21-inch width. The height didn't matter. It could be as long as possible. Our pieces ran between 2″ to 20″. The longest pieces were saved for the roof because of the greater spans.

We were dealing with double pane and thicker glass which was really a hassle to cut, but before long we became quite proficient in glass cutting. Some of the glass had extreme tensile strength and didn't cut properly. To cut such miscast glass at absolute right angles was nearly impossible because it has a tendency to break away on your line, undercutting itself (plates 5, 6). If you stack glass with this kind of break it leaves a small opening between panes, causing weather to come through. Where I made good cuts I just stacked the glass vertically, edge to edge between the grooved

studs, then nailed and puttied them in. Where the cuts weren't so straight we put a ¼″ to 3/8″ lap on it just like a shingle. We put in one finishing nail on each side underneath the glass being lapped, one part way up to hold it in place and one just below the top of that piece to accommodate the above lapped piece and set in the putty. There was no leakage on the side walls and only a small amount of leakage from the overhead glass where the putty has cracked.

The side wall 2 x 4 studs were rabbeted on the outside end to give them a ¼″ tongue, just enough to keep the pieces of glass from touching each other on either side of the tongue to accommodate the glass. These laps were set in deep enough to allow a little space between the outer edge of the studs and the glass so nails could be driven in and putty could be spread (plates 7, 8). A space narrower than 21″ was left near the end of each side wall to take the smaller pieces which we had left over. This prevented wasting our resources and allowed us to not

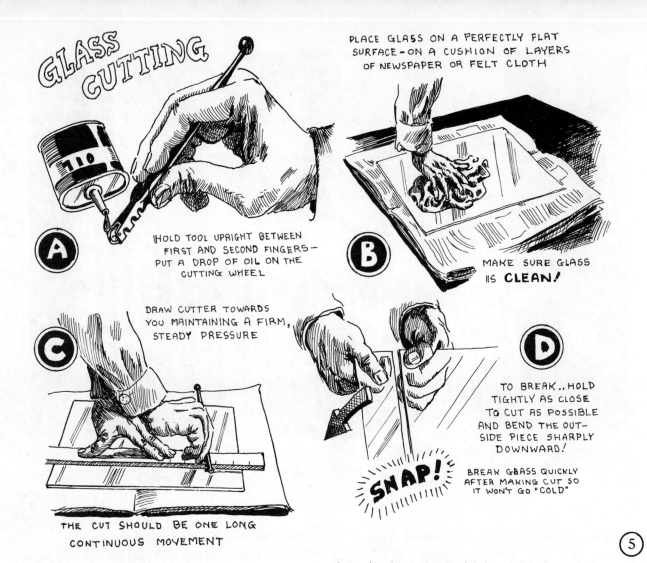

GLASS CUTTING

PLACE GLASS ON A PERFECTLY FLAT
SURFACE - ON A CUSHION OF LAYERS
OF NEWSPAPER OR FELT CLOTH

A HOLD TOOL UPRIGHT BETWEEN
FIRST AND SECOND FINGERS —
PUT A DROP OF OIL ON THE
CUTTING WHEEL

B MAKE SURE GLASS
IS **CLEAN!**

C DRAW CUTTER TOWARDS
YOU MAINTAINING A FIRM,
STEADY PRESSURE

THE CUT SHOULD BE ONE LONG
CONTINUOUS MOVEMENT

D TO BREAK.. HOLD
TIGHTLY AS CLOSE
TO CUT AS POSSIBLE
AND BEND THE OUT-
SIDE PIECE SHARPLY
DOWNWARD!

SNAP!

BREAK GLASS QUICKLY
AFTER MAKING CUT SO
IT WON'T GO "COLD"

⑤

⑥

"UNDERCUT"
BREAKS
IN HIGH TENSILE
MISCAST GLASS

have to compensate for the exact size of
panes plus the distances between each panel
in figuring out the overall length of the side
walls (see plate 6).

For a necessary artistic touch, I made a
stained glass window for the upper section
of the dutch door. The door provided the
greenhouse with a softness that it wouldn't

otherwise have had with its rigid glass and
wood framed composition. This was also an
excellent way of using some of the scrap
pieces of glass we had left over. It further
tested my skill in cutting glass. But the *came*
around the pieces was too small—a mistake.
Consequently, I had to back it with unsightly
welding rod for additional support. This door
was hung on hinges to the double 2 x 4″ stud
which bordered it (plates 9, 10).

A dutch door is an excellent door design
in a structure such as a greenhouse where
you want to allow the maximum ventilation
on hot days, but without letting animals in.
The dutch door keeps the dogs out, but since
there is no screen protection, the cats still
come in, walking across the flats, seeing
how all the little plants collapse underneath
their feet. They also have a tendency to use
the flats as kitty boxes, scraping the soil,
disrupting the seedlings, and doing their
thing in it.

Screens are a necessity in our greenhouse because of the fly problem, caused by having our compost bin so near it. At this point we seem to be propagating as many flies as plants, but screens should eliminate this problem and also keep the cats out.

For the front windows I constructed light-weight frames, 21″-square, out of 1½″-wide by 1″ material. I wanted to keep them narrow so they wouldn't throw off too large a shadow. In doing so I sacrificed strength for transparency—which was a mistake. The frames should have been

ventilation because I didn't want to have to white wash all the glass in the greenhouse to prevent the plants from burning on hot, dry days. As long as the soil in the flats is kept moist, the ventilation prevents the plants from burning. We watered first thing in the morning and an hour before the sun set each day, saturating the plants until a puddle formed. Then as soon as the temperature dropped, we closed off the greenhouse so it would retain the heat.

Directly above the window spaces we put in a wallplate of double 2 x 6s laminated

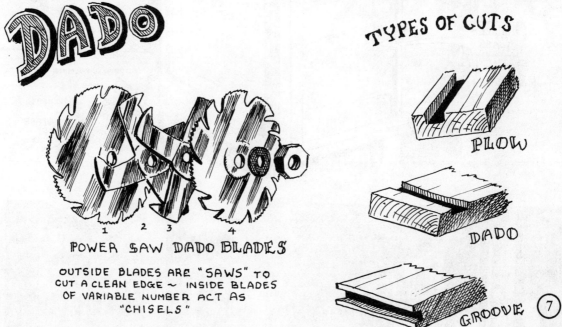

DADO

POWER SAW DADO BLADES

OUTSIDE BLADES ARE "SAWS" TO CUT A CLEAN EDGE ~ INSIDE BLADES OF VARIABLE NUMBER ACT AS "CHISELS"

TYPES OF CUTS

PLOW

DADO

GROOVE ⑦

stronger to hold the heavy glass. They were grooved on the inside all around to snugly accommodate the glass pieces and were tenon-jointed at the ends. Handles were put on the lower sill pieces for ease in closing and eye screws were fastened for locking. I also installed locks at the bottom to hold the windows open so they wouldn't bang shut during a gust of wind. Thin cull cedar strips were then attached as stops, leaving the area between the ends of the sill open to conserve on materials (plate 11).

There are eight windows along the front wall going from one end to the other (plates 12, 13). I used a lot of windows here for

together (see plate 13). The lower rafter ends were cut flat at the bottom to meet this plate. These rafters extend from the front wall to the back wall, spanning 14′ with a double-laminated 2x beam supporting them in the center of their span. This beam is held in place above the center studs at the opposing side walls. Here too, I feel the construction should have been more solid. This supporting roof beam should have been heavier and also be braced in the center by an upright of some type. But we were running out of material and wanted to finish the greenhouse for use. Perhaps the additional reinforcement will be put in later.

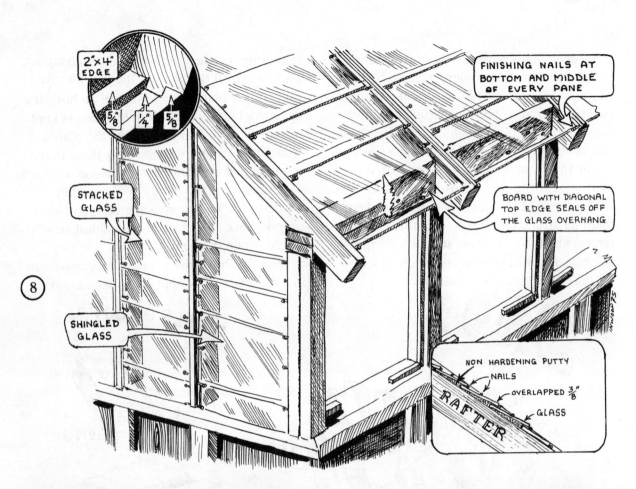

2"×4" EDGE

5/8" 1/4" 5/8"

STACKED GLASS

8

SHINGLED GLASS

FINISHING NAILS AT BOTTOM AND MIDDLE OF EVERY PANE

BOARD WITH DIAGONAL TOP EDGE SEALS OFF THE GLASS OVERHANG

NON HARDENING PUTTY
NAILS
OVERLAPPED 3/8"
GLASS
RAFTER

9

10

Even the way it is now the 33-degree pitched roof held a load of almost 3½′ of snow at one point last winter without sagging.

The tops of the rafters where the glass panes seat into them were rabbeted in the same manner as were the upright studs. All the roof panes were shingled above the rafters, starting at the bottom of each panel and working upwards with each just like you'd shingle a roof. They were held in

place at the bottom with finishing nails and putty, the same as were the shingled wall panes (plate 14).

Square glazing nails would be ideal for this job but we could work only with what we had. In fact, the roof leaked because the putty I used soon got brittle and cracked. I couldn't find any non-setting putty, but I advise the use of this kind of putty for sealing in this type of roof. It remains soft

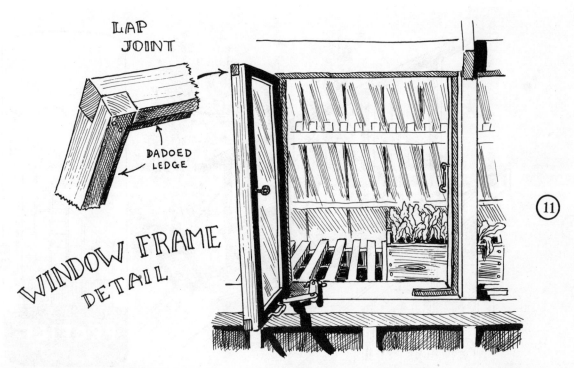

LAP JOINT

DADOED LEDGE

WINDOW FRAME DETAIL

⑪

and pliable instead of hardening and cracking with age.

I would have used cedar for the rafters because it is by far the most weather resistant of the local woods but clear cedar in 14′ lengths would have cost a fortune. I used fir instead, and coated it with urethane to help preserve it. Hopefully, this coating will allow it to last about as long as the cedar but the urethane has to be replenished at least every other year for full protection.

Next, we made the three top vents which allowed the hot, rising air to escape as the cool, low air entered to circulate. These vents were framed in the same manner as were the front windows and were fastened to the top wall plate with hinges. The glass

used was a heavy rippled, opaque shower door glass. I used this heavy glass mainly to test my skill at cutting. Four long upright braces were then constructed above the high back wall and a 2 x 4 cross piece was nailed in above to connect them. Three pulleys were suspended from this top piece for the cords which are connected to the bottom of the vent on one end to one of a series of hooks on the other. The hooks were spaced at different levels; the highest closed the vent; the one below it allowed the vent to be held half way open; and the bottom one allowed the vent to be opened all the way. This lower hook was another mistake, because it held the vent open too far. Consequently, a wind came by and broke

⑫

⑬

one of the panes (plates 15-17).

The interior of the greenhouse was also designed to fit our needs and was constructed out of the materials we had left, mostly cull cedar. The benches are 30″ high along the front and side walls. They were very simple and economical to build, utilizing a lot of scrap. The inner ledges were nailed to the wall at the 30″ height. Several 2 x 4 upright braces were then set up 24″ from the walls to accommodate a front cross piece at the same 30″-level. 1″ slats were then ripped with a power saw and nailed at 1½″ intervals across the two ledges. These racks held the starter flats which were filled with prepared soil. The flats were also made from the scrap cedar. They were 14″ x 21″ and 4″ in height. Their bottoms were slatted with from 1/8″ to ¼″ space between each slat to allow them to drain down onto the dirt floor (plate 18).

The plants are started in the flats on the front and side wall racks until they are developed enough to take care of themselves, then they are shifted to the back shelves and more seeds are started, taking their place on the rack. The back shelves are also slatted for drainage and economy of materials. They are braced against the back wall with diagonal supports which extend from that wall to the front crossing piece (plate 19). The higher shelves are for the more self-sustaining plants like the maturing cantaloupes and cucumbers. To water them we just bring a ladder and spray them with a fine mist spray from a hose attachment. The cucumbers are set in deep flats along the top of the back wall. They just drape over the shelves and vine down. They were an excellent crop last year. The cantaloupes didn't really make it through, because there wasn't much direct sun to nourish them. They got to the size of baseballs and that was it.

(17)

(18)

SEED FLAT
CONSTRUCTION

An excellent attraction of our greenhouse is the hot box which enables us to start plants as early as February or March. We keep the primary flats in here until the plants sprout their true leaves, then they can go out to the racks. This gives us a great jump on the season. This hotbox is 2′ wide by 4′ long and is 34″ deep. It is powered by a series of

19

four 60 watt bulbs which are located at the bottom. This is a pretty minimal source of heat so the box was built as tightly as possible. It has two doors; a drop door on bottom hinges to feed the lower slatted shelf; and a lifting lid on top, with framed glass to allow sunlight into the top shelf (plates 20, 21, and 22).

Even when the temperature outside was just below freezing (26 degrees F) the hotbox maintained a good 70 degrees F. It got us over that early spring fluctuation of cold spells that keep snapping in, threatening to wipe out all the flats even though the plants have pretty well started. Now, in the warmer months, we just use it at nights for the beginning flats. We put the flats in, then turn it on. It holds the temperature at about 75 degrees F to 80 degrees F. It's almost a better environment than is the whole greenhouse. In the greenhouse you have to keep watching the temperature, while the

(19)

(20)

LAP JOINT

GLASS

LAYER OF ROUGH CUT CEDAR BOARDS

4 60 WATT LIGHT BULBS

hotbox always maintains a pretty constant temperature.

The hotbox will take 8 flats, but we get a better circulation of the heat when we use just 7; 3 in the bottom and 4 on top. The top ones are double tiered, two above the other two. As long as the plants are young the top flats won't interfere with the growth of the lower tier.

To get rid of the snow on the greenhouse roof we just turn on the hotbox and within

24 hours the whole building gets warm enough for the snow to start melting. The only problem then was that the greenhouse is so low in front that we had to do a lot of shoveling to get rid of all the accumulated snow.

Another necessity in a greenhouse is a large, central mixing box where you have plenty of room to set your flats and mix your soil. We have a large box in the center of the floor for this purpose, with a shelf built in below it for storage (plate 23). Here

we prepare the soil. Our proportions are about 40% soil which comes from the bottom of the compost. It was set out on plastic for 6 months to air out and was used the following year. The remaining 60% is mostly peatmoss with about a hand full of finely crushed bonemeal in each 14″ x 21″ flat. This mixture works great. I haven't done a pH test on the soil but from the way things are growing in it I'd say it is more acid. Most plants can take a soil that is more acid than alkaline.

When we close the greenhouse off it retains moisture so well that we get humidity vapor on every pane. I don't think I need to introduce another source of humidity or else it might begin producing mold. I sometimes get some surface scale, mainly because the soil is rich with compost and bone meal. But a little scale can't really hurt.

For our needs, this greenhouse is proving to be perfect. The only flaw I really want eventually to correct is the cracking putty, but that's minor. In an area such as the one when we live where the spring weather is so doubtful and unpredictable, and when you know several people have to eat from the crops that are grown, a greenhouse such as this one is indispensable, to ensure that those crops will be substantial. I wouldn't want to risk being at the mercy of the elements after witnessing the loss of crops by several people last year because of the late frosts.

Sure, I suppose we could have gotten by with several outdoor hot frames and cold frames but it's not that pleasant in the spring to be working outside, doing your bedding plants and what not.

And in the middle of winter the greenhouse is a pleasant, peaceful space to just go into and relax, it's always warm enough in there even if it is below freezing outside.

Chapter Three

A Ground Type, or Sunken Greenhouse

Life's too short to be trading it for money. I did just that for 25 years. But for the last 13 years I've spent a lot of energy working hard on a worthwhile project—our homestead. I used to work on long jobs like constructing the Alaska Highway, back in 1947. I saved up my money, and by the time I got around to spending it, it had devaluated so much that it just didn't seem worth the trouble of accumulating it. Nevertheless, I spent a few more years traveling around, working where work was available, until one day I found a place I wanted to call home. It was a beautiful spot, secluded, at the end of a road, with an old house on it. We bought the land very reasonably and immediately began fixing up the place. Soon we got the feeling we didn't want to move again. With that acknowledgement we were inspired to make lasting improvements and to develop the land to accommodate our needs. We became compulsive homesteaders, building and planting and raising and hunting. The resources were all ours to make do with as we wanted. We could waste them through ignorance and idleness or learn about what we had to work with, producing what we needed right on our own homestead. Now we have nearly everything we need in case there comes a time when we couldn't just go out and buy it. We have good soil with gravity water which comes down the mountainside to irrigate our place. We have fruit trees and pasture to feed our livestock. There are many wild animals which we hunt, and here is timber for constructing the necessary buildings. And we have some good neighbors who are also conscientious homesteaders. We do a lot of trading with them. Some years they have crops that are excellent when some of ours fail, so we trade with them. You can't go it alone—there's just too much that needs to be done. You have to cooperate with your neighbors, each concentrating on particular tasks.

This last year we decided we needed a greenhouse so we could have some control over our crops. Depending on good weather may work in some milder area but in our region we are constantly threatened with late frosts and long periodic stretches of foul weather. Some years we lose a lot of crops. Several times I watched my wife's

frustration after she labored over her little plants, transplanting and weeding them, just to see them get destroyed by a late frost or get flodded by a long, heavy spring rain which interrupted their growing cycle. It frustrated me in other ways too, knowing we wouldn't have enough of a harvest to last us through the long winters without having to go out and buy a lot of produce.

We figured that the best place to build a greenhouse would be in a clearing with plenty of sourthern exposure, preferably with some protection from the cold north. With good exposure to the sun, the greenhouse could capture the solar heat and retain it, providing nourishment for the plants. Protection on the north side would help keep in the warmth and cut down on the energy needed to heat the structure.

Another way we could economize on energy and hold in the heat is to build the greenhouse into the ground. So, we dug a two foot hole for the structure so that it would be protected by ground mositure and by its warmth. Even when the temperature above the ground level is -20 degrees, it will remain only 40 degreesF. below the frost level. Everything in the ground keeps warmer, less fuel is needed to protect the starting plants through the early spring. We would have gone even deeper but we encountered huge boulders (plate 1). As an added precaution, to prevent periodic cold spells from destroying our early efforts, we also heated the greenhouse with an efficient wood-heating system.

Such a heater should be foolproof. It has to be able to give off continuous heat through the late winter and into the early spring danger period, when a momentary frost could wipe out all your preparation work. It should be located somewhere along the north wall, so that plants to the north, furthest from the sun, can get the most heat. Our heater burns dry cottonwood very efficiently. You put a stick in and it burns to the last ash, going 24 hours or more without

reloading. I designed it using an old wood heater door, welded onto an old sawdust burner firebox. It has a 12″ galvanized "smoke pipe" which is connected to the firebox, extending the length of the greenhouse. This smoke pipe acts as a heat exchanger unit, radiating the heat throughout the greenhouse with the help of an aluminum reflective shield that reflects it into the room. This unit is on a slight incline pitch from the firebox to the east wall, 4″ in 14″, so the smoke can properly travel through it and out the stonework flue chamber and stove pipe chimney located outside the east wall. This incline also allows the creosote to run back into the firebox instead of accumulating in the smoke pipe; but an even greater incline would have been better. The loading door is outside to prevent drastic temperature changes when refueling and to provide the oxygen from the outside instead of depleting the moisture content from the greenhouse (plates 2-4).

3

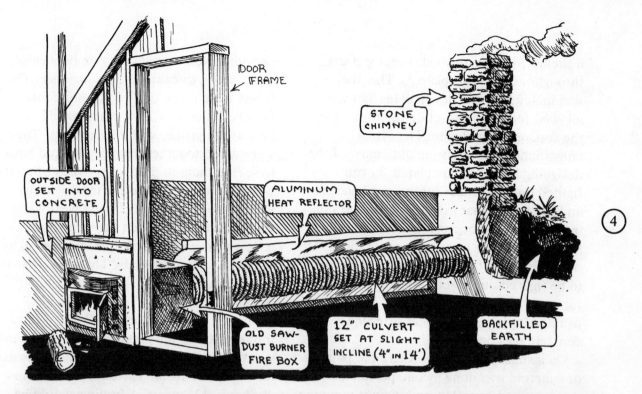

DOOR FRAME

STONE CHIMNEY

OUTSIDE DOOR SET INTO CONCRETE

ALUMINUM HEAT REFLECTOR

④

OLD SAW-DUST BURNER FIRE BOX

12" CULVERT SET AT SLIGHT INCLINE (4" IN 14')

BACKFILLED EARTH

⑤

The outside dimensions of the greenhouse proper are 7′ wide by 14′, 4-3/8″ in length. The length was determined by the width of the glass panes, plus space between glass (tongue of rafters) plus ⅛″ allowance for each pane (to be explained in detail later). It was important to me that the building be laid out so the glass would come out evenly—because the glass had been precut. This greenhouse has an outside porch area which extends to the west. The outer dimensions of the porch are 7′ x 7′, making it a 6½′ x 6½′ enclosure for protection from the weather when stoking the fire. It is also a shelter for the firewood, keeping it dry throughout the year (plate 5). This shelter was included in the design plans and was allowed for when we set up the forms for the concrete foundation. The actual construction did not begin until most of the designing had been completed. I even figured out the braces for interior benches and shelves so that iron pegs could be sunk into the setting concrete, instead of drilling holes into it later to accommodate them. All openings and interruptions in the walls had to be figured out exactly when building the forms, otherwise changes might have forced us into altering these spaces after the concrete was poured.

On a small job like this where the pouring of concrete was done by one person alone, the pour was very slow and did not require a solid form, especially since a lot of stones were used. Stone is harder than any manmade material. You can save money by using all the stones the walls will take, providing you've put concrete between every stone to cement them together. The forms were made of 1″ x 10″ horizontal boards, braced by 2 x 4 uprights which were held at the proper width by spacers. They were wired together near the top and bottom to secure them in place. The wires of course were left in the concrete after the forms were removed. The south and west walls were poured first. Then the same form panels were used for the other walls, so as to conserve on materials. The whole job was more than I wanted to pour at one time, working by myself.

I began the concrete work by pouring a footing around the greenhouse. This footing was the height of the 1 x 10″ which was used for the inside form. The outside form was dirt bank, 12″ away. A footing should be at least twice the width of the walls. My walls were to be 6″ in width. The height of each wall depended on the slope of the land. The front, south wall needed to be 24″, so a form

CEMENT FOUNDATION

TWO PILASTERS BUTTRUSS THE BACK WALL

BOLTS SUNK IN CONCRETE

DOTTED LINE INDICATES LEVEL OF DIRT AFTER BACKFILLING

⑥

was built to that height. This form extended from the east wall to 3′ beyond the greenhouse proper to allow for a stepway at the center of the south porch wall. The west wall was the same height and the north porch wall was stepped up a few more inches, making it level with the ground. It had to be stepped up again to 48″ at the beginning of the greenhouse to compensate for the sloping ground. It remained this height until after the northern half of the east wall. It was then stepped down to 24″ to allow the southern light in. Here the form was built around the smoke pipe as the inner west wall form was built around the firebox, both already being in place. Two pilasters were added at equal distances of 7′ along the back wall to protect it against eventual back pressure from the expanding ground in winter. These pilasters were 10″ wide, diagonaling from the top of the north wall to 3′ beyond it at the base. Each pilaster was reinforced with cross-welded metal rods for added support. Holes were then drilled into the forms to accommodate the bolts and pegs for the shelves and tray before the cement was poured (plate 6).

I used a 1.5 mix of Portland cement and sand, putting in as many stones as possible. Cement was used instead of concrete blocks because cement allows moisture through the walls and concrete blocks have air spaces which cause the moisture to evaporate within them. Moisture is necessary to create

humidity and should be allowed in whenever possible. I tamped the freshly poured concrete slightly with a stick to press it down and then hit the bracing studs really hard several times with a hammer to make it settle. You can see the air bubbles come up and the top of the concrete just level right off as you rap on the studs. After the concrete was tamped and leveled, bolts were sunk into the setting concrete to accommodate the 2 x 6 sills which will be resting above these walls (plate 7).

I used rough-cut material throughout the greenhouse to get the full 2″ out of the board instead of losing ½″ with the planing. The front sills overlap the concrete by about 2″, shielding it from direct runoff. These sills are tapered 12 percent on the outside edge to prevent runoff from entering into the greenhouse. The taper enables the runoff to drain down into the dirt outside (plate 8).

Instead of working with the usual 16″ to 24″ center spacing with the wall studs and the roof rafters, I calculated the spaces so the distances between all the studs and rafters would be equal. I had to do this because all the glass I used was salvaged ¼″ glass that was already precut at 12″ widths. The glass was salvaged from a plate glass company. I got a great price on it, 50¢ per foot, because most people can't use small ¼″ pieces, since sashes are not made for them. I bought all the plate they had from which 12″-width pieces could be cut—length

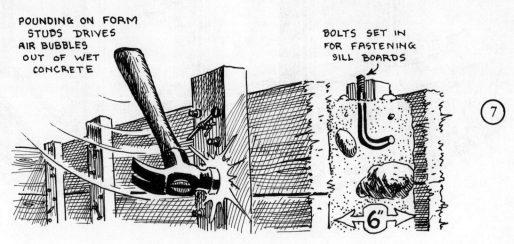

POUNDING ON FORM STUDS DRIVES AIR BUBBLES OUT OF WET CONCRETE

BOLTS SET IN FOR FASTENING SILL BOARDS

7

6″

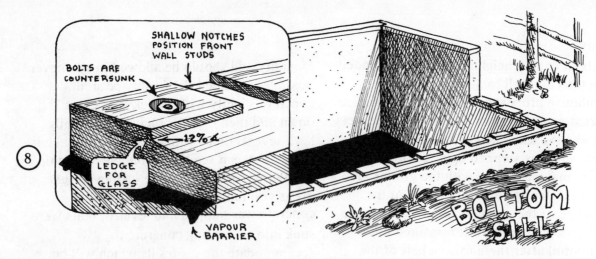

SHALLOW NOTCHES POSITION FRONT WALL STUDS

BOLTS ARE COUNTERSUNK

⑧

←— 12% ◁

LEDGE FOR GLASS

VAPOUR BARRIER

BOTTOM SILL

did not matter. The company had to do all the cutting because ¼″ is too difficult to attempt to cut without the proper facilities. I figured out 13 panels each with 12″-wide panes. This meant that each panel had to be 12″, plus the space between the glass taken by the 1″ stud or rafter tongue, plus ⅛-inch allowance for clearance on either side of the glass, plus 2″ on each wall for the width of the corner 2 x 4, making the total wall length 14′, 4-3/8″. Each of the studs and rafters were cut out of the rough-cut 2 x 6 stock, making them plenty strong at such narrow centers to hold any snow load, even if

single-weight glass was used. I wanted these rafters to be strong because within 10 years the rot will weaken them. It's best to prepare yourself in the beginning for eventual rotting instead of having to do the job over again in a few years.

The pitch of a roof that is comprised of only rafters and glass should be quite steep, having at least a ½′ or 3½′ in each 7′-pitch, so as to allow the accumulating snow to slip down off the panes.

The studs between the short wall windows were cut slightly over 24″ in length to accommodate the 24″ windows. They were

LAP JOINT

⑨

¾″ UPPER STOPS ARE NAILED IN

TONAILED

DADOED STOPS ON 2″ x 6″'s TO HOLD GLASS

28

rabbeted on the outside end so all the protruding tongues between the window laps were centered 1″ high and 1″ across. The widths of the laps were each approximately ½″ depending on the exact width of the 2x stud. The studs were placed at slightly over 12″ centers and were capped with a 2 x 6 wall plate which was lap notched into the crossing sidewall plates at either end. The glass was then set in and framed with the ¾″ strips left over from rabbeting the studs (plates 9 and 10).

Next came the rafters. I cut them in such a way that I got two out of every 10′ board, using the same angled top cut for both sides. they provided the necessary pitch. These rafters were rabbeted in the same manner as were the front studs and were cut at angles top and bottom to allow them to seat as much as possible at the 2 x 8 ridge beam and the top wall plates. Since the rafter tongues between the panels were ¾″ higher than the glass, planks could be put across them,

⑩

⑪

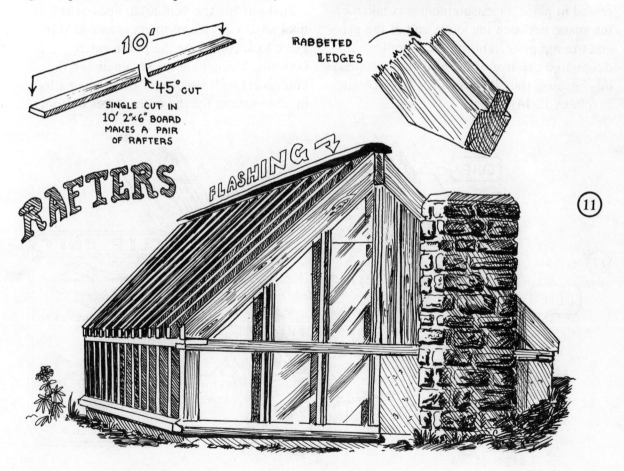

10′

45° CUT
SINGLE CUT IN
10′ 2″x6″ BOARD
MAKES A PAIR
OF RAFTERS

RABBETED
LEDGES

RAFTERS

FLASHING

resting on the wood instead of coming in contact with the glass and possibly shattering it (plate 11).

The glass was now ready to be set in as shingles would be, starting from rafter bottom up. Before laying in these lapped panes, I first set a bed of putty down, using black caulking compound for this job, because it does not dry and crack as readily as does normal putty. Small metal S clips were then nailed into the rafter bottoms on either side of the glass. The length of the bottom pane was then measured and another set of clips were nailed in where the top of this pane meets the rafters. The bottom pane was then seated into the putty between the clips and the above piece was lapped about ½" to ¾" over it. At this overlapping a tapered wedge was set in above the rafter seats to compensate for the lap, allowing the glass to set snug into the putty. This wedge was feathered with a hand plane until it was the proper size.

After the bottom panes in each panel were seated in place a measurement was taken of the space between the lower end of the glass and the top plate. This measurement designated the size of the bird stops, called this because they do stop birds from coming in (plates 12-14).

It is important to have a roof that allows the source of light to come straight overhead because plants will reach toward the light. If light comes in from overhead, plants will grow straight.

The north side of the east wall and the west wall, where the front door is located were sheathed in on both sides with 1" cedar because these areas get very little direct sunlight. The front door has 6'4" of vertical clearance, and was constructed of rough cut vertical 1xs held together with a Z brace. Thin baton strips were nailed on over the board junctions to seal them off. Above this door I installed a vent. The vent cover was hinged at the bottom with a strip of rubber, allowing it to open to the inside (plate 15). Greenhouses should have good vents high up where the plants don't get the direct draft. High vents also help circulate the air and prevent hot air from collecting at the top, which eventually gets the greenhouse warm enough to burn the plants on warm days.

Just outside the vent area, above the doorway, a 2 x 8 crosspiece was nailed in place to accomodate the porch rafter bottoms. Uprights were set up above the outer west wall and a wall plate was nailed in across them for the outer rafter bottoms.

The opposing rafter tops then met at the ridgebeam. *Stringers* for the *shakes* were nailed in place and an inverted V-shaped plate was attached where this roof separated from the greenhouse roof. A small ridge cap was extended from the apex of that inverted V to the greenhouse roof peak. This area between the roofs was sheathed in and capped with aluminum flashing to prevent leakage into the porch area. Shakes were then split and put on the proch roof. Another piece of aluminum flashing was nailed in above the shakes at the peak, to seal the roof (plates 16-18).

The wood heating system previously described works excellently in heating and producing humidity for maximum growth in the late winter and early spring. In fact, the plants closest to it and furthest away from the southern sun grew much faster and healthier then those closest to the direct sunlight (plate 19). This could be attributed to the hazy, overcast early spring weather during which time the direct sun seldom came out. For humidity, we simply set a kettle of water on the firebox and let it steam into the greenhouse. And if we wanted more moisture content in the air, we just hosed down the dirt floor and let is circulate throughout. Plants thrive on humidity and should always be supplied with plenty of it.

The bottom shelf along the back wall for the plant flats is supported over two pipe rails which were bracketed to the east wall

VENT

HINGE IS OLD INNER TUBE RUBBER WITH SHEET METAL STRIPS

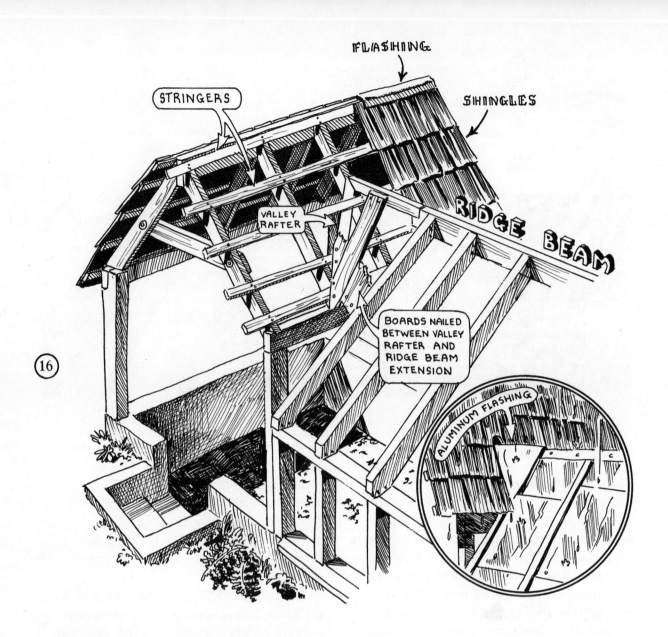

STRINGERS

FLASHING

SHINGLES

VALLEY RAFTER

RIDGE BEAM

BOARDS NAILED BETWEEN VALLEY RAFTER AND RIDGE BEAM EXTENSION

ALUMINUM FLASHING

16

and held up with a wire support at the west wall. The pipes are also braced in the center by upright pipes resting on concrete footings. 2 x 4 blocks are spaced along these pipes and notched over them to hold the crossing shelf boards (plate 20). Another narrower shelf, also for the starter flats, was suspended above this lower shelf. It is held with blocks nailed to the side walls at either end and supported in the center by a wire bracket hanging from the above rafter (plate 21).

The flats were made from the cedar shake scraps. They are 13″ long, 4¾″ wide and 3″ deep. The plants are transferred to these flats shortly after they are started in the front

17

tray, then they are transplanted into the garden. There are never more than two rows of plants in each flat—to avoid crowding (plate 22).

The front tray is used for starting the plants, mixing the soil and growing plants which will not be transplanted into the garden until well after the last frost threat, if at all. This tray extends from one end of the south wall to the other, held on brackets attached to peg bolts (plate 23). It is supported at the center by a crossing pipe rail which is encircling a peg bolt at the

some metal roofing you can buy nowadays. Everything is made so stinking thin and cheap—except the prices; there's nothing cheap about the prices.

We added only cow manure to the soil. Even without the use of chemical fertilizers all the plants grew very well in the greenhouse. We definitely wanted to stay away from the use of any such inorganic conditioners because they quickly deplete the soil by speeding up the growing process beyond natural limitations, thus exhausting it prematurely.

(24) BRACKET BOLTED TO PINS SET IN CEMENT

CORRUGATED METAL FORMS TRAY BOTTOM. EDGES ARE BENT OVER AND NAILED TO SIDE BOARDS.

BRACKET WELDED TO SUPPORT PIPE

BOLT SUNK INTO CEMENT HOLDS MIDDLE BRACE PIPE

3/4" PIPE

STRAP IRON

south wall end and is held up on an upright welded to it on the inside end. The tray bottom is of corregated galvanized roofing which lines the boards on either side and is turned up 1″ at the ends to hold water. I had to split the ends every few inches on the ribs with a pair of shears to make the bend, otherwise it would just widen itself and go out of shape (plate 24). I didn't want to use wood for the tray bottom because it would just rot out after a couple years and need replacing. I was lucky to have an old piece of galvanized roofing. It is good, heavy stuff, not like the crap you buy today. A cigarette wrapper would be stronger than

The leaf lettuce just shot right up, tasting as good as if it were grown in the garden. The peppers were enormous. They really benefitted from the heating system. Even the peppers closest to the sunlight were dwarfed compared to the ones nearest the heater. We started them in late February and by May 1st they were already flowering. Some plants didn't do as well, but I attribute this to the soil. It was a bit too hard, which does not allow for good drainage. It also seemed to be in need of lime, which is a deficiency in most of the soil in this area. Lime deficiency also makes sour weeds grow well, and we had plenty of them. Ashes are a

cheap, excellent source of lime. They are
also a good mulch and help keep worms and
pests out of the soil. Squash was by far the
fastest growing greenhouse crop. It grew so
huge even early in spring that we had to take
out a few panes and add a temporary plastic
shelter to the greeenhouse to contain it way
before it was safe enough weatherwise to
transplant it (plates 25 and 26).

Because the greenhouse is a closed
shelter, not allowing bees in to naturally
pollenate the plants, we help them along by
rubbing the blossoms from one plant with
the end of a feather and transferring the
pollen to another unfertilized plant with it
(plate 27).

All and all we are extremely pleased with
the greenhouse and feel that our efforts were
well justified. Even with the slightest fire
from the wood heating system we can keep
the tomato plants going until December 1,
getting several quarts of ripe tomatoes. We
even have enough to give to neighbors.
Outside, most years, the frost kills the
tomatoes before the first ones get a chance
to really ripen.

㉕

㉖

HAND POLLINATION
WITH
FEATHER

27

Chapter Four

Tender Loving Care—Biodynamic Gardening

A *Biodynamic garden* is one that incorporates the principles of companion planting, planned yearly crop rotation, and replenishment with natural composting. A well managed biodynamic garden should be well composted and replenished with large supplements of fresh manure every year. The gardener layers well decomposed cow manure 4″ thick throughout the whole garden and tills it in well. A few of the fundamentals of companion planting are:

a. Try to put plants that require plenty of light near those that prefer partial shade.

b. Alternate shallow-rooted plants with deeper-rooted plants, because they get their nutrients from different areas of the soil.

c. Protect plants that have few flowers and a largely exposed terminal bud (e.g., cabbage) with plants that have many blossoms (e.g., nasturtiums).

d. Do not grow heavy feeders together. These include cabbage varieties, leaf vegetables, celery, squash, cucumbers and corn. Interplant them with light feeders, such as carrots, beets, and turnips (specific cases excepted).

e. Use plenty of aromatic herbs and flowers that repel insects and otherwise aid in the production of the garden without taking away from the health-giving qualities of the plants.

Yearly planned crop rotation. This should take into consideration the following principles:

a. Heavy feeders should be followed by nitrogen-rich legumes, such as beans, peas, clover, or alfalfa to replenish the soil.

b. Light feeders such as bulb and root vegetables (carrots, beets turnips, etc.) should follow on the enrichened soil provided by the legumes.

c. Plants that do not stand up well against competing weeds should follow those that were well mulched or relatively free of weeds.

d. Any plant that is prone to disease or malformation of the roots should not be put in the same place two years in succession.

e. Root plants should follow plants that loosen up the soil and aerate it.

Another important and helpful measure is keeping a record of the garden from year to year to make sure the same vegetable is not replanted in the same bed and to properly plan the crop rotation. A good practice is to use the same garden layout and planting plan each year. The sections of this plan are divided and numbered. Each section represents a bed. Each area of the plan representing sections of the garden are filled in with the names of the plants which were planted in that section or bed (plate 1).

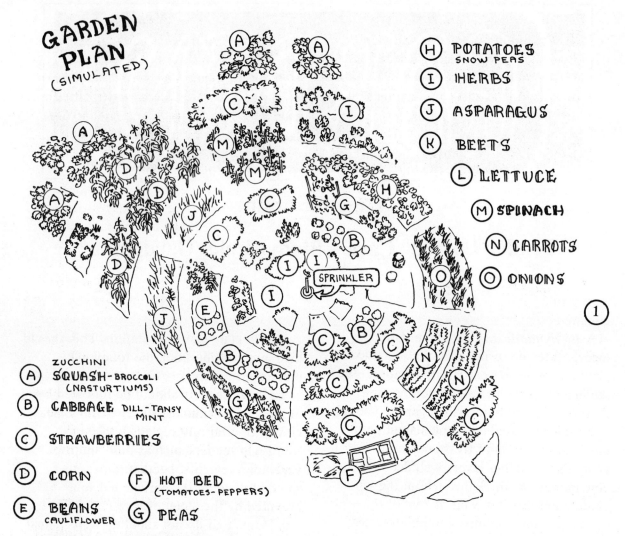

GARDEN PLAN
(SIMULATED)

H POTATOES SNOW PEAS
I IHERBS
J ASPARAGUS
K BEETS
L LETTUCE
M SPINACH
N CARROTS
O ONIONS

1

SPRINKLER

A ZUCCHINI SQUASH-BROCCOLI (NASTURTIUMS)
B CABBAGE DILL-TANSY MINT
C STRAWBERRIES
D CORN
E BEANS CAULIFLOWER
F HOT BED (TOMATOES-PEPPERS)
G PEAS

There is a particular biodynamic garden we know about. This garden is the best example we could find of a working biodynamic garden. It truly reflects the tender loving care of the lady who owns it.

This gardener believes in the principles of crop rotation because she realizes that otherwise the plants would utilize the same nutrients year after year and consequently soon deplete the soil.

For example, if you planted potatoes in a particular bed, you don't want to replant potatoes because they carry diseases and the second time around they are much more susceptible. If peas were grown in one area, something else that likes a whole lot of nitrogen will get a lot of goodies from that pea bed in the next season—nutrients that the peas don't need again. Plants that are really bulbous such as beets and carrots, can

use a set of nutrients that are different from those of spinach or cabbage.

One exception—tomatoes happen to like being planted in the same bed year after year. They thrive on a compost made with their own stalks and leaves.

The planting method that she uses divides up the garden plot into beds instead of rows. It is known as "The French Intensive Method". The beds are narrow enough to permit easy weeding and harvesting. Bed, lengths vary with crop and location and do not have to be confined to any set measurement. Within the beds are combinations of from one to four plants. She claims that all do well under the principles of companion planting. Planting thickly within the beds is an important aspect of this method.

Plant thickly and thin by harvesting as

needed. Eventually the plants will displace the weeds. This biodynamic gardener had virtually no weeding to do and nothing was hurt by it as long as there was enough manure.

Generally, this gardener has extremely good success with her garden, considering the variables of the climate in her location. The garden is in a northern location with a very short growing season. The last spring frost occurs as late as June 10th and the first heavy fall frosts come as early as mid-September. The garden is in a frost pocket and gets frost earlier than most surrounding areas. Since this particular climate is better for potatoes and cabbages, she grows an abundance of these and trades them with a friend down the valley who grows ''terrific'' corn, beans, and squash. She has a hard time growing these latter crops in the variables she has to deal with.

Up until the time that she planted the asparagus behind them, the potatoes were doing very poorly. They were really weak plants. She dug in a lot of manure and planted the asparagus in the same bed. She obtained a prime crop of asparagus and had incredibly huge potatoes last year.

She had great success with cabbage too. She planted two rows of cabbage, one row of dill in the center and then tow more rows of cabbage. The cabbages were planted close enough so that they wree almost touching. That way less time was spent weeding because the leaves shaded the ground and didn't permit the weeds to grow.

In the first years a lot of her cabbages were lost to root maggots and cutworms. She finally had to use a chemical to control the maggots and got rid of the cutworms with cardboard collars. These collars are 1½" to 2" high and 6" long. They are bent into a circle around the young newly transplanted cabbage's stems and stapled twice to hold them in place. The collars are pushed firmly into the ground to create a barrier around the plants. Cutworms have to come up to the surface for any great lateral movement. When they hit the cardboard they can go no further. She also used similar collars on tomatoes and peppers (plates 2 and 3).

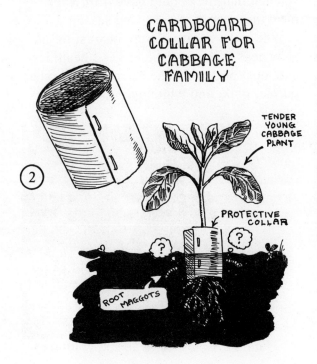

CARDBOARD COLLAR FOR CABBAGE FAMILY

TENDER YOUNG CABBAGE PLANT

PROTECTIVE COLLAR

ROOT MAGGOTS

②

③

Cutworms live on dying weeds in fall, and if the garden is completely cleaned out so that there is no dying refuse, then there is less likelihood of the cutworms living through fall.

Members of the cabbage family are prone to rapid decay because they have been developed to an enormous bud and their flowering process has become insufficient to protect them. They are helped by plants that have many blossoms and those which are strongly aromatic. These characteristics compenstat for the cabbage's weaknesses. This gardener added tansy and dill to the bed to maintain a balance (plate 4).

In this biodynamic garden, the carrots were almost surrounded by strawberries. Both crops did very well. The carrots were great.

The beans and cauliflower did exceptionally well, too. She planted purple Royalty Beans from Dominion. They do not rot on cold ground and mature quickly. By August 1st she had beans for dinner.

She planted nasturtiums and dill with the zucchinis and broccoli. The zucchini didn't do too good because one zucchini plant was shaded by a huge broccoli plant. She maintains that nasturtiums should always be planted with zucchini. Certain things are beautiful together. The purple beans and the white cauliflower are beautiful together—complimentary in color—and beautifully balanced. One is a long, purple pod and the other is the chunky white cauliflower. And it is aesthetically pleasing to see the huge heads of cabbage with long shoots of dill right in the middle. Likewise, in the middle of the enormous squash plants are the brilliant, bright red, orange, and yellow nasturtium flowers. Nasturtiums balance the squash flowers. Part of planting is seeing how you can make a bed look its prettiest. According to the biodynamic gardener, if you make it as beautiful as you can, you'll want to be there amongst it.

Unless they are tied, cauliflower will *bolt* and go to seed early. Tying protects them with shade cover and prevents the rain from entering and rotting them in their final stages of growth (plate 5).

Our biodynamic gardener planted New Zealand spinach this year and was very pleased with it. She said that it did not bolt at all like the other types. Its growing season is from June to frost. There was so much spinach that they could have it for every meal throughout the growing season.

Where the potatoes were nearest to the snowpeas they were the biggest, healthiest, and most plentiful. The surrounding brilliant purple, pink, and white pyrethrium daisies

(4)

(5)

were planted for protection against the bugs. This is based on the theory that if the powder made from the plant is an insecticide, then the plant itself must be good to give protection.

The garden is set up with herbs in the center and around the sides. These plants are beautiful and many are believed to discourage various detrimental insects. Mint was planted in the cabbage bed one year to discourage the cabbage moth. It seemed to do the job. Mint should be planted in small cans within the bed to prevent this plant from overtaking the bed with its tremendously fast spreading growth.

Garlic in a bed discourages insects that do not like strong smells (nasturtiums and garlic repel aphid). Garlic is also easy to grow and is a very useful plant. The original settlers in this region are said to have taught that garlic should be planted in really rich chicken manure—planted in October, before winter. Leave them until late summer when they lop over. When they lop over they are ready.

Then harvest them, pulling them up with the stock still on them, and tuck them in underneath that stock. For best results in preserving garlic, just take a bunch of them and roll the stock back over them in the garden for a couple of days while its sunny, than take them out, rub them down (to clean them) and braid them. According to our dynamic gardener, braiding them is the only way to keep them for any length of time. It keeps them in the air and they don't gather moisture. She says that if garlic is kept in a dry place (but not a root cellar), they will last about a year (plate 6).

Tomatoes and peppers had to be kept in a hotbed because the season is too short to allow them proper development time in the biodynamic garden. In the hotbed the tomatoes and peppers can be started as early as May 1. Ordinarily, they couldn't be put into the ground in this garden until June 10.

The protective frame around the hotbed is approximately 3 x 8′. The size of the opening was determined by the dimensions

GARLIC

HARVEST IN LATE SUMMER WHEN TOPS HAVE FALLEN

DRY IN SUN A BIT

HANG IN COOL DRY PLACE

6

CHECK TEMPERATURE

8" TOPSOIL

STRAW
LIME
MANURE
STRAW
LIME
HOT MANURE

STRAW

2'

⑦

of the three windows which comprise the top of this enclosure. The hotbed itself is merely a pit, dug about 2' deep. This pit is filled to a height of 1' or 18" with hot compost, consisting of half cow manure and half chicken manure, mixed in layers with quite a bit of straw or other organic material that would allow air into the mixture when stacked. The mixture is left beside the pit for 2 or 3 days before it is put into it. During this period it is turned once. After this initial

turning the center of the pile is checked for temperature. Do not just stick your hand into the center to check because it is sometimes hotter than you would want to touch. Put a thermometer into the center of the pile. If the reading is 90 degrees or higher, then put the pile into the pit. If it isn't, either turn it again and wait another three days, loosen the mix with more straw, or get some fresh manure (plates 7 and 8).

Sprinkle a little lime over the mixture to

⑧

HOTBED

42

help keep it cooking, then throw in an 8″ layer of loose dirt. You want the dirt to be quite porous for aeration to allow the heat to rise to the plants. Check the temperature of that dirt after leaving it for a while under the glass cover. If daily weather temperature remains a constant 80-85 degrees throughout the low and high of the outside temperature it is ideal. But if the weather temperature gets to below freezing, which it sometimes does in this area, even in May, the hotbed should never go below 45 degrees or else it isn't functioning properly. To efficiently check the temperature of the hotbox during the low and high temperatures outside a high-low thermometer should be used. This device has a magnetic registering system that holds the low and high throughout a given period with two black indicators. If the low indicator goes below 40 degrees the hotbed isn't working, consequently the young plants will not be adequately protected against the frost (plates 9 and 10).

TO KEEP TOMATOES OFF THE GROUND

CHICKEN WIRE RING

CARDBOARD TUBE PROTECTS STALK

⑨⑩

⑫

⑪

⑫

The hotbet of the biodynamic garden has a 3′-high rail in front of it for the plastic covering to drape over when protecting the mature plants from an early autumn frost (plate 11 and 12).

The new blossoms off the tomato and pepper plants should be pruned in fall to keep them from forming any late fruit. The late fruit wouldn't have a chance to ripen anyway and the blossoms take juice away from the existing fruit.

Her cucumbers are also grown separately from the garden. They are grown in a cold frame with a protective wall behind it that blocks off the chilling north wind. There is a network of string trellises that go up the wall for the five hills of cucumbers to climb.

She lets her cucumber plants climb up like beans. They are easy to pick and there is considerably less chance of rot when they are up off the ground. They remain fresh. (plate 13).

⑬

These examples were the only ones described as being successful combinations for biodynamic gardening. However, other logical and obvious suggestions have been made by Helen Philbrick and Richard Gregg in *Companion Plants*.* It takes years of experimentation and study to develop workable combinations, and an equally long time to test the ones which are available. Several variables have to be taken into consideration and each garden plot has to be tested individually. Only through tried and true personal experience can any gardener really know for certain, beyond the obvious companion plant combinations and helpful hints, what will really work in their garden.

⑭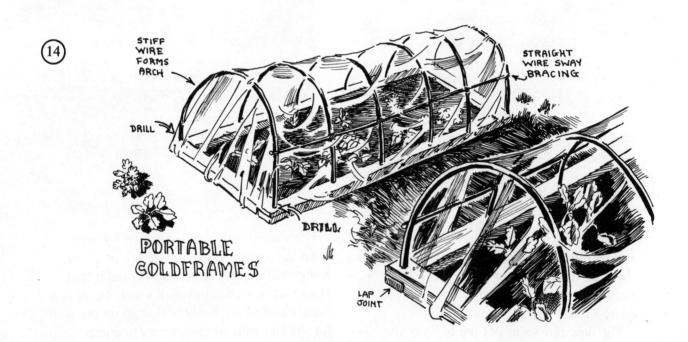

STIFF WIRE FORMS ARCH

STRAIGHT WIRE SWAY BRACING

DRILL

DRILL

PORTABLE COLDFRAMES

LAP JOINT

PHILBRICK, HELEN and GREGG, RICHARD B.: COMPANION PLANTS AND HOW TO USE THEM. The Devin-Adair Company, Old Greenwich, Conn . . . 1966.

Chapter Five

Building a Squatter-type Outhouse

①

After traveling around in the Middle East and North Africa for a year I got used to squatting instead of sitting when eliminating and began liking that position much better. It makes a lot of sense, too. Elimination is more automatic when your torso is in a straight line. When sitting, your body is sort of squeezed together in a rather unnatural position, making it more difficult to perform the natural function. When squatting there is less pressure on the intestines and things usually happen very quickly. There is a tendency, when sitting, to take time to relax the constricted muscles for awhile, before eliminating, thus sometimes dragging out the performance longer than should be necessary and also making it needlessly laborious. A previous hemorrhoid sufferer

once told me that his problem went away shortly after he began squatting.

A squatter-type outhouse is rather simple to build. It is post-and-beam construction with diagonal bracing and is set on skids to make it portable when the hole becomes filled (plate 1). The hole was dug first. Its size was relative to the average approximate cubic footage per year per person. Supposedly the average person eliminates a cubic foot per year of compressed waste (3 cu. ft. not compressed). The hole was dug out about 7 cubic feet, so the squatter would not have to be moved very often.

The cedar half-log skids were placed about 4′ apart, with the hole centered between them. Two cedar sill logs were nailed across them at front and back and a 2x flooring was laid across the sills, leaving a long narrow opening in the center. 1x boards were then nailed across the outer ends of the 2xs, narrowing down the hole to the approximate size I saw in the Arab countries, about 6″ wide by 12″ long, slightly wider in front then back. This size seems to be adequate for both men and women, but it may be a little short for women if they don't squat right back on the foot boards when urinating, since they tend to hit the front boards.

The foot rests were set up to my measurements. They were adjusted back and forth until I found the right position that would be the most comfortable and would allow me to miss the wood. This design is a hassle for little kids but is quite comfortable for most people. The way it is now, kids get on it and are afraid they might fall in. I'm not sure how I'd adjust it for little kids—maybe a removable seat would be the answer.

I wanted the floor space to be rather large and up off the ground. There is enough room on it for some storage and for a container of ashes that get thrown into the hole every couple days. The ashes help cover the odor of the excreta and enrich the decomposing waste with lime and other minerals. This large platform also provides the base to the loft storage area above. I believe in having as much as possible under one roof. The 4″ floor sills allow for an air circulation space under the platform to prevent odors from building up in a stagnant space and seeping up through the platform hole (plate 2, 3). Also, I ask my visitors to avoid using the squatter for urinating whenever possible, because urine mixed with excreta promotes foul odors. Another preventative measure against unpleasant odors is a hole cover which I shaped to fit snugly into the platform hole (plate 4, 5).

I believe that the more open you have an outhouse, the better. A closed building brings on the insect and odor problems. It attracts flies and other insects because it lacks proper air circulation and also traps these pests inside. An open outhouse allows a person to feel as one with the surrounding beauty instead of being closed off from it. To keep the squatter open yet protect it from chilling winds I set up posts at each of the four corners and supported them with 45-degree diagonal braces. A 3′ railing was put up around three sides and the sections

below the railings were sheathed with vertical slabs (plate 6, 7). The posts were notched out a bit where the diagonal braces met them to provide a small shelf under the brace as a ledge for it to rest so it isn't entirely relying on the nails to keep it in place. (plate 8, 9).

The squatter was then roofed with a gable roof to allow for storage of wood and other materials. The end rafters were extended out at slight angles at the peak to give the building more overhang on the ends and the eaves were gradually brought out with an

increasing thickness of nailers to give the roof a slight sweeping affect for aesthetics. The roof was then finished with the leftover number four grade shakes which would be plenty good enough for this small building (plates 10-12).

I'm very pleased with this squatter and consider it a very healthful alternative to the conventional seated outhouse. Surprisingly enough even my folks who are in their mid-fifities enjoyed using it as a refreshing

⑫

⑬

change from what they were accustomed to. And any type of temporary outdoor set up is far more efficient than the indoor toilet system that empties into a closed off cesspool or sewer, because the compost that is being produced can be used for many purposes after it has been given the proper time for anaerobic decompostion to ensure the destruction of pathogens and insect eggs. This takes at least 8 months of undisturbed decomposition. To speed up this process while the excreta is accumulating I run a hose into the hole about once a year and throw in a bunch of lime to help it spread out and break down. Instead of collecting this as compost to be taken elsewhere, I cover the almost filled hole with good soil, wait the proper period for decomposition and plant a tree over the hole. Where I've done this the outcome has been amazing. I have mint and rhubarb growing over a few of the previous holes. These plants just take right off every year.

(14)

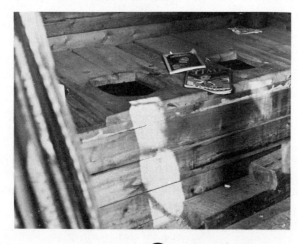

(15)

(16)

Chapter One

Beat The Heat

Like most people, we find ourselves outdoors a great portion of the time in the hot summer. Since this season is so short and good weather is such a treat in our area, we take every chance we can to enjoy the sunshine and make several excuses to be out in it. We are constantly building on to our homestead and working the garden and fields, so we are outdoors much of the time. But there are many indoor chores that we began to dread during this season. You can guess them; cooking, baking, and canning: all involve starting up the old wood cookstove (since we don't have any other fuel source). With this old stove at full-blast we had to remain indoors in the stiffling heat. We needed to remedy this situation.

Upon visiting friends we found some alternatives to tending the indoor cookstove. One group had an old rusted stove that they had set outside. They did their cooking on it. What a great idea. We thought about it and decided that we definately needed an outdoor cooking set up, but wanted something more permanent—more protected. We built a large porch area outside our cabin and roofed it to protect whatever heating device we would use. This porch would also shelter us from the weather when we cooked outdoors during the not so desirable seasons, and as a change of pace from being cooped up in the cabin.

We decided to be creative and also add another aesthetic touch to our home. A design for a rock stove was roughed out and materials were soon gathered up. The gathering process became quite interesting. Our design changed to fit the materials available. We found old discarded wood cookstoves and ripped them apart, taking the oven doors, dampers, and grates. One stove had a top that was in excellent shape so we removed that for the top to our stove (plate 1).

2

12" WIDE

18 INCHES BELOW AND ABOVE GROUND

Before long, we trucked back a quantity of possible junk which could turn out to be vital organs for our creation.

Being a plentiful commodity on our homestead, we brought in several loads of angular, granite rocks. Angular rocks were preferred to round ones because they were easier to stack and adhere to one another. Granite was favoured over a softer type, since granite rock doesn't chip or crack as easily. These were to be the facing rocks for the stove.

Up to this point all the materials were free. All we really needed to buy was about five bags of Portland cement, type 1, two bags of lime, and a few fire bricks. The lime was added to the cement to give it a sticky consistency. But we had to go sparingly with it, because lime tends to weaken the cement. I mix my own Portland cement rather than buy premixed masonry cement. Portland cement is far stronger for the purpose, and if by chance you end up with any extra lime it can go into your compost or be used in the outhouse. Nothing should ever be wasted.

I will explain the procedure of building our stove, but I will give only the measurements

that are structurally necessary to make for an efficient unit. All other dimensions should suit the individual taste of the builder and should not be copied from mine.

We began construction by first digging an 18" deep U-shaped trench for the footing. The open part of the U faced the direction we wanted the front of the stove to be. This footing can be deeper or shallower, depending on the frost level in the area, but should always be at least 6" to 8" in thickness below ground to properly carry the heavy rock load. It should also be at least 12" wide to support these mortared rocks.

The use of a form depends upon the ground. If the soil is clay-like, no form is needed. If the ground is rocky or otherwise porous and loose, build a form out of 2x material and brace the outside with stakes. Have this form extend up past the surface another 18". If you do not use a form below the surface start the 18" form at ground level, just outside the poured footing (plate 2).

At this point the inner form boards and stakes are removed and a short front form piece is added. The height of that piece is dependant on how thick the ash pit is to be.

54

At the open end, hinges were sunk in the soft cement to accommodate an old oven door which I used as the ash pit door.

On top of the U footing I laid a rectangular firegrate into a bed of fresh mortar. This grate rests 2″ into the side walls of the footing for sufficient support. Our grate is a solid piece of ¼″ plate steel, 2′ x 4′ wide, leaving a space at the closed part of the U for ashes to drop down to the ash pit. The ashes will remain there until there are enough of them to put on the garden or compost pit. The grate has no holes to supply the fire, so all the air comes from the front opening above the grate (plate 3).

A more of an airtight stove can be made if the grate has holes in it allowing air to come up from a controlled ash pit door, and if the firebox were supplied with a tight door. Our firebox does not as yet have a door. But we are thinking that one would be a good idea because it would make this a more efficient stove. But since we've been burning pieces of wood that are longer then the firebox (and which stick out from it), we wanted to leave that space open for the time being.

After the grate was set in we put in the firebox. We began with a collapsable wooden mold. The size of this mold form could be up to 4″ less than the width of the grate and just as long as the grate, depending on the size of stove top to be used. The height is determined by the size of wood burned. This form will temporarily take up the area of the firebox. A course of form boards was then built around the top of the footing. This form does not have to be strong because it is just a guide for the rock face. All the rockwork can be done without a form, but I prefer to work with one to help me develop the proper taper for the stove. I wanted it broader at the base to carry the weight and narrow at the top where it didn't need as much support. These forms consisted merely of long 2 x 4 stakes set at the corners of the stove which accommodated the horizontal form boards as they were nailed on. The boards were raised as I laid the courses of rock. This prevented having to deal with a high clumsy form when setting in the rocks.

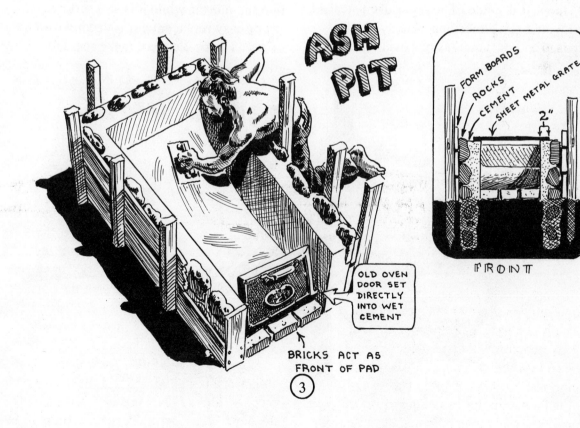

ASH PIT

OLD OVEN DOOR SET DIRECTLY INTO WET CEMENT

BRICKS ACT AS FRONT OF PAD

③

FORM BOARDS
ROCKS
CEMENT
SHEET METAL GRATE
2″

FRONT

The collapsable wooden form acted as the inside mold for the firebox area. A layer of firebricks stacked to the height of the mold was placed on either side of it. Then mortar and rock was set in to fill the gap between the outside forms and the firebrick. I used 1″ firebricks, and can see now, after several years of stove use that a few are already cracking. It would have been better to have used 2″ brick. They last much longer. Also, I omitted using any type of mortar of fire clay between the firebricks. The firebricks should have been glued together with fire clay for optimum heat radiation. This would also have kept them secure.

Fire brick is the best of all possible materials and can be removed easily for replacement, because it is not interlocked into the structural work of the fireplace as rocks are (plate 4).

In our chimney base we installed an oven drum just behind the firebox. It has a door on the left side of the stack base. It is made from a cut off section of a water heating tank bottom and is 14″ in diameter and about 30″ long. It is made of heavy-gauged steel and would last almost indefinitely if not exposed to hot flames as our oven drum is.

If we were to do this drum over again we would put it higher into the stack—about chest height. This would make it last much longer because it would not be directly exposed to hot flames. This would also allow the heat to circulate around it more evenly. Now we have to watch it very carefully to get good results when baking with it.

To create the space for the oven, just make a temporary inside form box that is the size of the drum diameter, plus 8″ in width, and the same length of the drum. This form should be set on short legs, suspending it between the grate and the wall of the closed end of the U footing. It should extend through to the outside left side to allow an opening for the drum door. Then build the rockwork up to the top of that box, using an outside form as suggested before.

When the mortar has set, take the inner form box out and replace it with the oven drum. You can improvise a homemade door to this oven which would be hinged to the rockwork opening. The hinges can be sunk into the mortar while it is still setting.

For easy replacement, if drum wears out or needs to be cleaned, make the door

④

FIRE BOX

CEMENT BETWEEN ROCK AND FIRE BRICK

FRONT

1″ THICK FIRE BRICK LINES BOX

ROCK GUIDE BOARDS

SHEET METAL FIRE GRATE

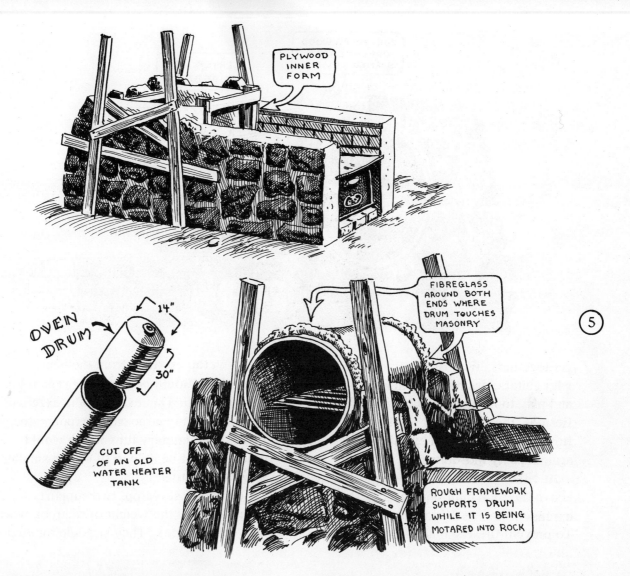

PLYWOOD INNER FORM

OVEN DRUM

14″

30″

CUT OFF OF AN OLD WATER HEATER TANK

FIBREGLASS AROUND BOTH ENDS WHERE DRUM TOUCHES MASONRY

5

ROUGH FRAMEWORK SUPPORTS DRUM WHILE IT IS BEING MOTARED INTO ROCK

opening large enough so the drum can slip out. It is also a good idea to sink a bolt support somewhere at the middle of the drum, above the firebox, so a bolt from the drum can be secured to the stove, keeping the drum in place. The drum must have a backing of 2″ fiberglass insulation or other material wherever it directly comes in contact with the mortar and rock. This will prevent the heat expansion of the drum from cracking the mortar and rock and also make for easy removal of the drum (plate 5, 6).

As you build the stack, be sure to leave at least 4″ of space between the top of the drum and the mortar and rocks so the smoke can easily draw up through the chimney. This space can be easily allowed for by improvising two small removable forms that fit into the areas to the front and rear of the drum. (plate 7, 8).

Above the firebox, about ½ way up the drum, I placed a damper which regulates the smoke around the drum. When in closed position the smoke and heat travel only around behind it. This damper could be omitted if the oven was further up the chimney. I strongly recommend the higher drum placement, as opposed to my present design.

Before building the smokestack and chimney we prepared the area above the firebox for the stovetop and set that piece in. A fresh bed of mortar was poured over the rock sides around the firebox for the long edges fo the old wood stovetop to be sunk into. This cast iron stove top is 32″ long by 24″ wide and has four removable plates. The plates are covers for the 2-9″ holes and 2-8″ holes. This stove top can be completely taken apart. Its hole covers and all the crosspieces that hold them can be removed, leaving only the outlining rim as a stationary piece. It is the ideal stovetop, allowing us to enjoy an open fire for evening

get togethers. We just sit around the fire pit with guitars, drums, and other instruments and play to its energy-giving inspiration. Besides, the flames and smoke from an open fire such as this are an excellent deterrent against pesty mosquitoes.

At either side of this stovetop, directly above the rock mansonry, is a 4″ shoulder extension to give the top more surface area. To prevent these shoulders from cracking as the stovetop expands from the heat, V-grooves should be made between it and the metal top. This extra area is excellent for accommodating large canning pots, steeping kettles, and laundry tubs which would otherwise not be able to fit on the smaller stovetop (plate 9).

Behind the stovetop, two supports were put in to carry the weight of the rock work above the firebox. They straddle the two

⑦

⑧

sides and were set into fresh mortar. These supports were made from an old chainsaw bar and an old leaf spring. The leaf spring is still holding up fine after several years but the chainsaw bar got soft from the heat and consequently drooped down into the firebox area, not doing any harm, in fact preventing large pieces of firewood from being shoved down into the ashpit. So you could very well either use expensive 3″ to 4″ angle iron or the leaf spring as alternatives for this support (plate 10).

The mortar and rocks were then set up to approximately the 6′-level, leaving a flat platform at the top. The inside should be a fairly square flue hole, 10″ to 11″ in width. The rock work has to be at least 6″ to 8″

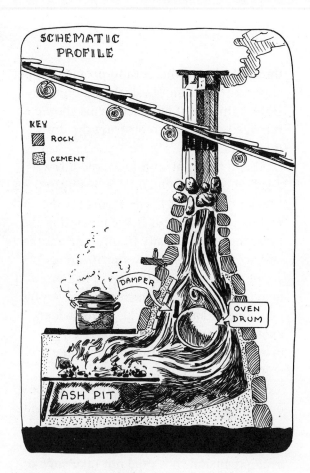

thick all around this area to provide proper support for the smokestack and chimney. Before this point all inner forms should be removed so as not to obstruct the draw. (plate 11).

Above this platform I stacked a few 5-gallon oil cans which I use as improvised flue linings and as inside forms for the rock and mortar chimney. Being tapered at the tops, these cans easily fit into one another and are held in place by a protruding lip about 4″ down from the top. They are of a heavier gauge than commercial stove pipe and have a diameter of 11″. This wider diameter is instrumental in providing a proper draft for the firebox since the chimney is so short.

When using a metal flue lining I suppose one should take the precaution of allowing an airspace the width of 2″ fiberglass insulation or another material to absorb the heat expansion, but I did not take such a precaution. Yet, in the several years of use the chimney has only developed a few

hairline cracks.

At this point, I stopped using awkward forms and laid the rocks around the cans as they fit. I inserted strips of doubled-up chicken wire between the oil can flue and the mortared rocks to reinforce against cracking or loosening. Since we didn't have a form over this area we had much more freedom to be creative with the rockwork. We made little shelf ledges for matches, thermometers, and other equipment that we would be using regularly. We also were able to clean the rocks as we laid them, providing a much more aesthetic finish to our labours (plate 12, 13).

This chimney extends up through the roof of the porch about 2′, giving it an overall length of 11′. It shouldn't be much shorter than this or it might cause draft problems. It could have been capped with 4″ concrete top for protection against the weather. We omitted that precaution. But one precaution that should always be taken is to add a spark screen. We set in a piece of ½″ hardware

11

12

cloth above the chimney to protect the roof, the cabin, and nearby woods from any hot sparks which might otherwise jump out and cause a fire. This cloth should be shaken out often since it collects a lot of soot and ash (plates 14-16).

As a finishing touch, fill in all the cracks between the rockwork. This does not provide any more structural strength but improves the looks of the stove. Actually, you can do this pointing as you build if you devise a removable form system that would enable you to clean off the setting mortar and work around the freshly laid rocks.

Be sure to let the rockwork season at least five to six weeks before starting your first fire. The mortar should be dampened at least once a day during this period so that it will cure properly. When starting your first fires make them rather low instead of roaring until you are certain that the mortar has seasoned long enough. And clean the chimney often, paying particular attention to

⑬

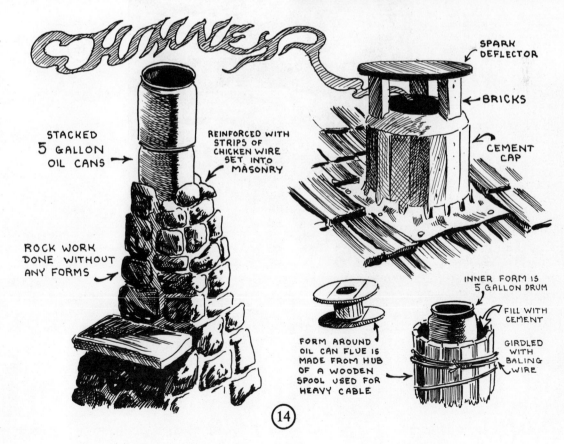

CHIMNEY

STACKED 5 GALLON OIL CANS →

REINFORCED WITH STRIPS OF CHICKEN WIRE SET INTO MASONRY

ROCK WORK DONE WITHOUT ANY FORMS →

SPARK DEFLECTOR

← BRICKS

CEMENT CAP

INNER FORM IS 5 GALLON DRUM

FILL WITH CEMENT

GIRDLED WITH BALING WIRE

FORM AROUND OIL CAN FLUE IS MADE FROM HUB OF A WOODEN SPOOL USED FOR HEAVY CABLE →

⑭

the area surrounding the oven drum because creosote will have a tendancy to build up more in that area than the straighter areas.

So, we have developed an outdoor stove that enables us to heat and bake and cook all in one unit. It is a beautiful addition to our homestead and is invaluable during the hot summer months. Plus—we don't have to worry about spillage and keeping the floor clean. We can be as messy as we want, letting wood chips pile up and dirty feet go wherever they want.

⑮

⑯

Chapter Two

Water is Life

The very first consideration on any homestead should be setting up a water system. We unfortunately bought an existing homestead which had been neglected for several years. The orchard was neglected for over 15 years, with sucker branches as big as main limbs. The huge logs which comprised the barn were so rotten that when I walked on a side wall the bottom logs caved in. The house roof leaked and the floor was on enough of a slant from age that a ball placed in the middle would quickly roll toward the south wall. And when the winter came the snows caved in the utility shed roof and the old water system froze, forcing us to haul water for ourselves and two cows. So we were compelled to leave our warm, sheltering retreat and battle the elements until we successfully thawed out the water system. This sometimes took days of sitting by the waterbox in subzero weather, chipping ice and burning through rusted galvanized pipe with a propane torch until the ice melted enough for the water to begin again to flow. I remember one time sitting up there, cursing the cold as my frozen fingers gripped the wrench, to disconnect an old galvanized fitting, only to have it freeze to the fitting before I could loosen it. Those are days I'd rather forget.

In the following spring, as soon as thaw set in, we dug up much of the old water system to find out why we were having so many problems with it. First, it wasn't put deep enough into the ground. A waterpipe should always be put in well below the frost level to prevent it from freezing. The frost level in our area is 18", but most of the pipe was only buried from 3" to 6". No wonder it froze.

As we were digging out the old makeshift system we came upon a few 6' lengths of fir logs. They were connected to each other by a tapered male end fitting into a female end which was bored out larger than the hole that ran the length of the logs. The hole was 4" wide in diameter, continuing through the pipes. A wire was wrapped around the outside of the female end to keep it from expanding as the male end swelled from the water running through it. This sealed the lengths together. Most of this pipe was badly rotted, but I could tell that this must have been the original water system of the homestead (plate 1). I searched around for more traces of it and came across a few old crisscross trellises which once held sections of flume (plate 2).

Curiousity soon got the best of me. I searched the neighboring farms for some of the homesteaders who had been around for a long time. My search led me to one extremely friendly pioneer who settled here long ago. He knew the people that originally farmed our land and explained the water system to us. It consisted of two systems that began at the same source. One system was of the buried fir wood pipeline for

6 ft.

WRAPPED
WITH WIRE FOR
HIGHER PRESSURE
SYSTEMS

JOINT DETAIL

4"

BURIED
WOODEN
PIPE

①

FLUME

②

year-round domestic use and the other was a series of trellises which carried a long flume across several hundred feet to the irrigation ditches of the farm's pasture. The flume came directly out of the creek on a slight decline, all the way to the pasture. The underground system began at a nearby collection box (plate 3). The homesteader I talked with told me of the days, some 40 years before, when he and his partner used to make these pipes. They rigged up a drilling device made from a 1927 Chevy overhead valved engine and transmission with a sliding carriage. Auger heads of various diameters were made from large thick-walled pipe-like truck drive shafts and whatever other material was available. The end cutters were ground and sharpened hard steel bits and the blades were simply ½″ bar stock, spiraled down the entire length of the auger body. They were periodically screwed into the body to hold them secure. The smaller augers were made from the drive shaft that originally fit into the plate of the transmission to avoid excessive play while boring the holes (plates 4-5). The sliding carriage was made from an old sawmill carriage mounted on angle iron bed rails which guided it straight into the stationary engine and direct drive auger. The carriage

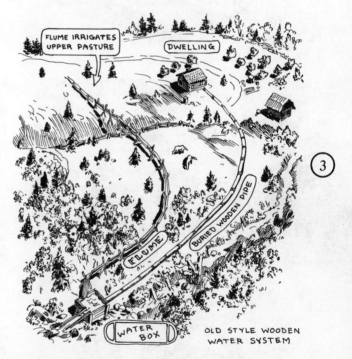

FLUME IRRIGATES UPPER PASTURE

DWELLING

③

FLUME

BURIED WOODEN PIPE

WATER BOX

OLD STYLE WOODEN WATER SYSTEM

was at a nice height so the workers didn't have to bend over. The 6′ length of log was placed on the carriage and held with two wood levers. These levers consisted of a wooden crossbar with a rounded notch on the underside that had two short spikes coming from it to hold the log in place. A spring was attached to the opposite end of the handle to allow the crossbar to remain horizontal over the log, thus providing equal pressure on the log. There were two of these

HAND FORGED
WOODEN PIPE
AUGER

OLD TRUCK
DRIVESHAFT

FILED

$\frac{3}{8}$" SQUARE STOCK
FORGED INTO
SPIRAL SCREW

FORGED
CUTTERS

④

TINES OF
DRIVESHAFT MESH
WITH TRANSMISSION

ADJUSTABLE
CHISEL BLADES
CUT JOINTS INTO
LOG BUTTS

BOLTED
ONTO
TRANSMISSION

⑤

⑥

levers, one for each of the workers.

The hole was bored through in several stages, going about 1′ at a time. The auger was brought out each time and the shavings were cleaned off. This operation was

repeated until the shaft was in 3′ or more. The log was turned around and was brought through again until the hole was completed. The female end was then augered out a bit larger to accomodate the tapered male end which was chiseled out conical shape on a revolving lathe, also attached to the motor. The male end was checked with calipers to make sure it would be a good, tight fit and the wire was put around the female end. All the left-over shavings were used for kindling; nothing was wasted (plate 7).

The pioneer told us that he made very little money from selling the pipe, but he didn't need much money in those days

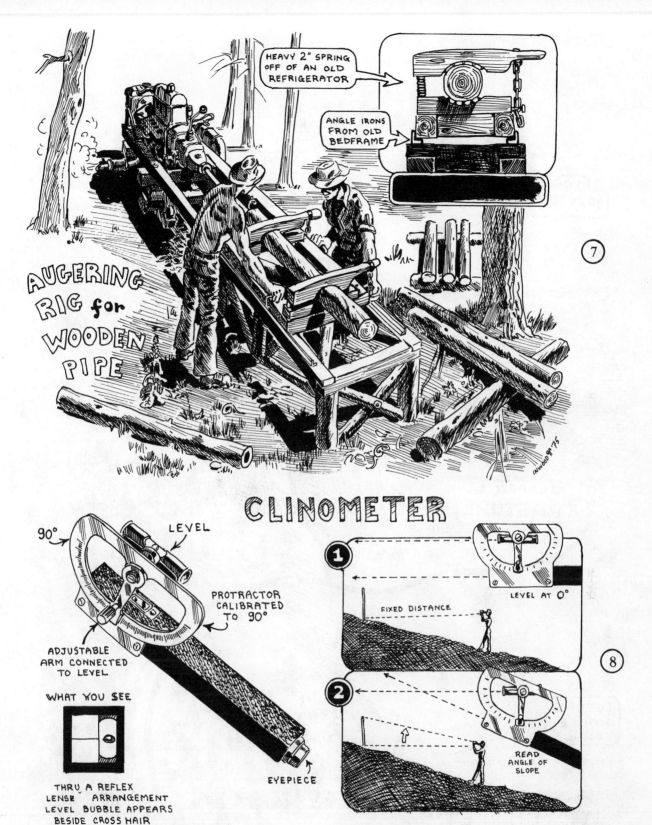

HEAVY 2" SPRING OFF OF AN OLD REFRIGERATOR

ANGLE IRONS FROM OLD BEDFRAME

⑦

AUGERING RIG for WOODEN PIPE

CLINOMETER

90°

LEVEL

PROTRACTOR CALIBRATED TO 90°

ADJUSTABLE ARM CONNECTED TO LEVEL

WHAT YOU SEE

THRU A REFLEX LENSE ARRANGEMENT LEVEL BUBBLE APPEARS BESIDE CROSS HAIR

EYEPIECE

① FIXED DISTANCE   LEVEL AT 0°

② READ ANGLE OF SLOPE

⑧

because there was nothing to spend it on.

Getting back to our water system. In realizing that our present water system was inadequate for our purposes, we bypassed the old system and started a new one at a higher elevation. We needed approximately 26 outlets for the fields, the house, the orchard,

the garden, and the barn. This meant that we needed more volume and more *drop*. The drop would be provided by constructing the intake collection box much higher up the hill than it had been and the volume would be supplied by larger diameter water pipe, over a longer distance.

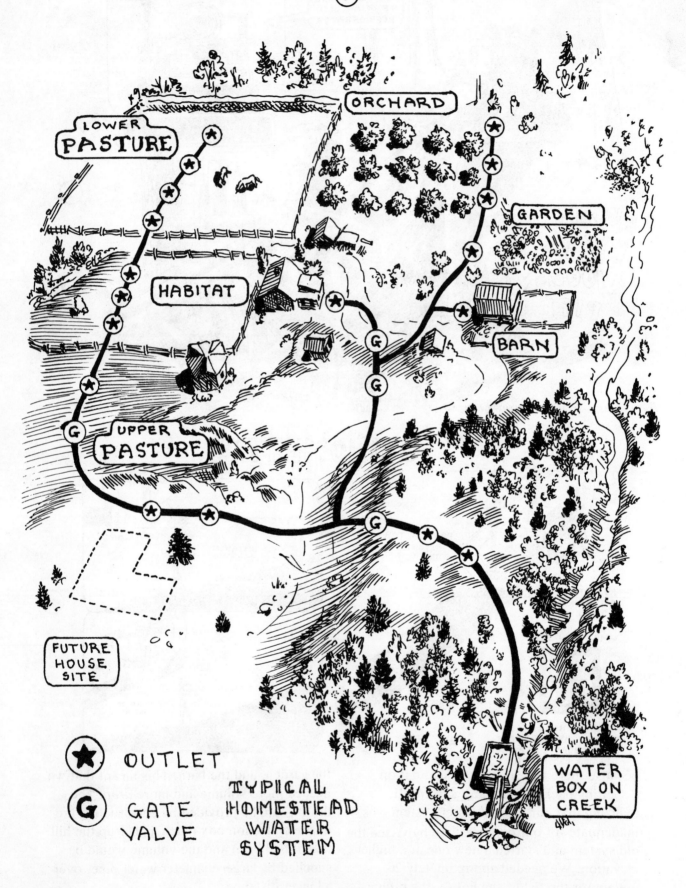

LOWER PASTURE

ORCHARD

GARDEN

HABITAT

BARN

UPPER PASTURE

FUTURE HOUSE SITE

WATER BOX ON CREEK

★ OUTLET

Ⓖ GATE VALVE

TYPICAL HOMESTEAD WATER SYSTEM

Our water source is a substantial year-round creek that comes gradually down the mountainside at approximately a 7½ percent grade. Even in the driest years when many of the surrounding water supplies had dried up, this creek kept flowing. A proper drop needed for our situation would be at least 50 feet, working with a constant volume supplied by a 2″ pipe. In order to obtain that 50-foot drop the water line had to be run well over 1000 feet down the slope before the first outlet. In other words, with an average gradient of 7½ percent, we get about a 50′ drop in 1000 feet, supplying the pressure we need. Each 2.31 feet of head or vertical drop produces about 1lb./sq. inch (p.s.i.) of pressure. When using most brands of low friction plastic pipe (check with manufactor's specifications for exact friction loss) there will be approximately 40 percent pressure loss to friction if the gradient is an average of 5 percent. At 25 percent gradient the loss will be only 8 percent. The steeper the gradient the less the overall loss by friction. This means that if you are running a length of pipe 1000 feet at a 5 percent gradient, instead of getting a total of more than 50 feet of drop you will only be getting 30 feet of head or a loss of 40% by friction.

You can figure your own gradient with a *clinometer* by taking several readings of equal distance no longer than 50 feet each. Add up the readings and divide them by the amount of readings to get the average slope over a given area. Then figure out the average percent. That is your drop (plate 8). The amount of drop required depends on your particular situation. Check with your local water rights branch for that information.

We required a large drop but were careful in our calculation not to have too much pressure in our system or we would be constantly repairing broken pipe. With all the outlets turned on, we have enough pressure to keep the 18 to 20-pound pressure sprinklers going and still have enough flow for the house and barn. Yet the total p.s.i.

pressure is not greater than 60 p.s.i. at any point. The reason for this is that we compensate for pressure by supplying volume. For the first 1000 feet or so the line is a 2″ plastic pipe, which provides sufficient volume for the entire system. From this one 2″ line we gradually *tee* off to four 1″ lines without losing any of the volume, because the volume of one 2″ line is equal to the volume of four 1″ lines. Figure it out. In other words, we can tee off to two 1½″ lines, one going to the pastures and the other going to the pastures and the other going to the house, barn, garden, and orchard, without losing any pressure because two 1½″ lines have the same volume as the 2″ line. If we wanted to, we could then reduce the 1½″ lines to two 1″ lines and still have the same pressure. But we decided to reduce the pipes differently because we wanted the greatest amount of pressure in the pastures. For the pastures we began with a 1½″ pipe and gradually reduced it down to 1″ at the bottom, thus providing it with ½ of the entire volume. When that volume is forced into a smaller diameter pipe you get much more pressure. For the house, barn, garden, and orchard we didn't need quite as much pressure. So these usages could share the other 1½″ line, ¾″ pipe going to each. (plate 9).

"Type 2" plastic pipe, varying between 50 p.s.i. for the 2″ line and 80 p.s.i. for the 1″ and ¾″ was used. Since the 2″ pipe is closest to the source and higher up the slope it doesn't require the pressure rating required by the smaller diameter pipe. Because of the expense of plastic or any other pipe, you don't want to purchase any thicker gauge than necessary. We chose to use type 2 plastic pipe because it is durable, long lasting, and is flexible. It requires no maintentance and is easily taken apart when it has to be. It has plastic fittings with stainless steel clamps to keep them in place. The fittings are very versatile and inexpensive compared to any other type fitting. For instance, you can make a tee from a 2″ line to a ¾″ line with only one fitting. With galvanized steel you need several fittings to gradually reduce down to the ¾″ size. Also, this material rusts in time, making it nearly impossible to separate the lengths short of using a blow torch. It is very rigid, requiring fittings at every bend. Special tools are also needed for cutting and threading. I guess another alternative could be the wood pipe but I doubt that you'll be able to find anyone who is making it. If you want it bad enough, maybe you should try making it yourself. If could actually be done with a hand auger set up without the use of a motor driven machine (plate 10).

Then again there are other easy ways to bypass the tremendous expense of a water system such as the one we put in. The pipe and fittings cost only a total of about $80. We simply applied for a retail license and bought in quantity for several families, charging all of them just slightly more than the wholesale cost of the pipe. This saved us all a considerable amount of money, but it got a few of the local merchants a little perturbed—because in doing so we found out their profit margin . . . uhgghh . . . oh well, we all have to get by the best we can I guess.

So, getting back to our water system—the first thing we did was locate the intake and collection box site. Next, we acquired a

⑩ HAND AUGERING WOODEN PIPE

PICTURED AS PRACTICED IN ENGLAND AS LATE AS THE 1920's

FAVOURABLE WOODS
EAST COAST ⚬⚬⚬ WEST COAST
ELM   DOUGLAS FIR

Inwood 75

⑪ 1½″ PIPE REDUCED TO ¾″ PIPE   BELOW FROST LEVEL

GATE VALVE ⑫   FULL OPEN   HALF OPEN

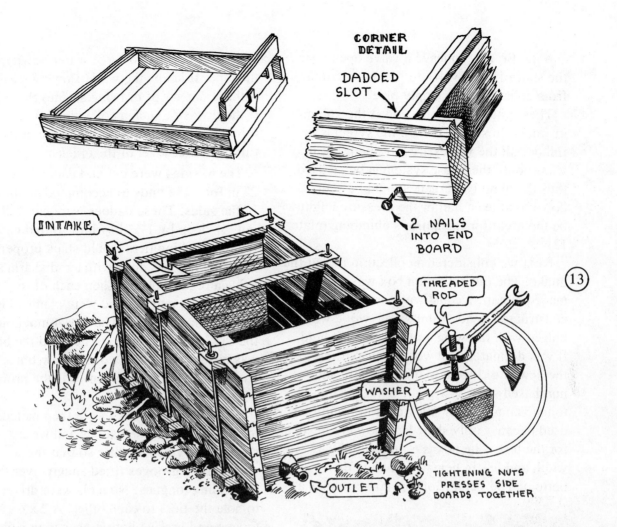

CORNER DETAIL

DADOED SLOT

2 NAILS INTO END BOARD

INTAKE

THREADED ROD

WASHER

OUTLET

TIGHTENING NUTS PRESSES SIDE BOARDS TOGETHER

(13)

backhoe operator to dig the trench for the system. Be sure to take a lot of time to clearly think out the route because this job is expensive and should never have to be redone. Then we laid our pipe into the ditch, carefully thinking out all the outlets, tees, and gate valves.

Our outlets for the pastures were simple tees above the main line, each ¾″. Above that tee we added a short length of ¾″ pipe that brought the outlet above ground level for the hose valve. This hose valve then takes a regular ¾″, wide thread, standard female coupling for the irrigation pipe to the sprinklers (plate 1).

The barn, garden and orchard, outlets are done in the same manner. The pipe for the house is simply coupled to the male end of a galvanized steel nipple made to receive plastic pipe.

Gate valves should be installed throughout

the system where ever there are any major tees. We have one before the first 1½″ tee, one after the second 1½″ tee, and one after the tee to the house and the tee to the garden and orchard. The first gate valve can shut off the entire system in case there is trouble anywhere along the line or in case the line has to be drained for some reason. The second gate valve shuts off the water to the pasture for the winter. You don't want to chance water in the lines throughout the winter when the system is not going to be in use. Water could go up the short, vertical pipes and freeze, bursting the pipes. This gate valve is located just after the tee because a 1½″ gate valve is half the price of a 2″ gate valve. The third valve shuts off the water to the house and the fourth shuts off the water to the garden, barn and orchard for the winter.

Note; Be sure to leave a valve open near the shut-off gate valve to prevent vacuum from collasping the empty pipe.

These gate valves also adjust the volume of water. In summer when the sytem is in full use all the valves are left open, but in winter only the house system is being used, thus the main (first) gate should be shut down to at least half or the pressure might be too great for the house's plumbing (plate 12).

Next we considered a collection box at the intake. The old collection box was inadequate in size and was poorly constructed, made from ½″ plywood which bulged with the weight of the water it held. It was definately not worth transporting to the new site. I went to the local mill and purchased some low-grade 2 x 6 cedar tongue-and-groove. A lower grade could be used because only short lengths were needed for the box. The box is 6′ in length by 42″ in width and 38″ in height, including the bottom. The volume of this box provides a

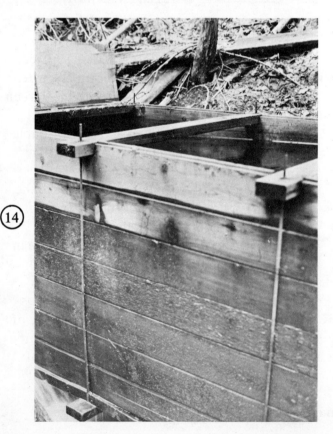

constant pressure to force water down into the pipe. It keeps the water flowing steadily without danger of drawing air into the line. If there wasn't such a collection box there would be the problem of dealing with the varying water level of the creek.

The 6′ sides were cut and dadoed exactly 2″ in form the ends to accommodate the ends of the sides. These dadoes were carefully cut ½″ deep by 1½″ in width so that each of the interlocking tiers would stack properly. The dadoing was done with a radial arm saw, using a regular blade. Then each of the boards were marked and were clamped in place along the table. The horizontal hold of the saw carriage was loosened and the blade was brought over the wood, a few times back and forth until the cut was the proper width.

Each of the box tiers were then nailed together through the dadoes and were stacked above each other so that the surrounding grooves fitted snugly over the protruding tongues. No nails were driven in to hole the tiers to each other. A 2 x 6 tongue-and-groove bottom was then nailed to the bottom tier.

Six 48″ long 2 x 4s were cut and placed along the length of the box, one at top and bottom at either end and at the center. Holes were drilled into these boards just outside

(16)

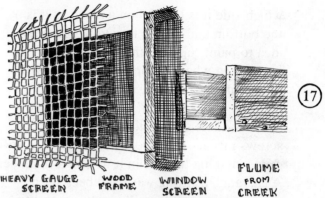

(17)

HEAVY GAUGE SCREEN   WOOD FRAME   WINDOW SCREEN   FLUME FROM CREEK

(18)

the 42″ width of the box to accommodate the 48″ long threaded ready rods which hold the tiers together. The rods were pushed through the holes, then nuts and washers were screwed on to both ends of the vertical rods. These nuts must be tightened very securely to press all the tongues deeply into the grooves. At least 2″ of ready rod was left sticking up from the box to accommodate the overlapping 48 x 76″ plywood top. This top prevents leaves and other organic matter from dropping in, consequently clogging and contaminating the water box and outlet (plate 13 and 14). It is also a shelf in winter allowing snow to stack on it. Snow is an excellent insulator, usually building up to a substantial height before the sub-zero cold spells of mid-winter really hit.

With this construction the cedar sides swell enough when the water was put in so that no water leaks out from the box. Some water does leak out from the bottom however, carrying out accumulating silt which comes in through the intake screen. In the last three years only 6″ of silt has accumulated at the bottom and I've had to shovel it out for the first time only this season. The only maintenance problem we do have with this design is cleaning off the leaves and rocks that collect around the intake. I don't know of anyone who has been able to successfully alleviate this problem (plates 15 and 16).

Our intake consists of a double-screened 16″ x 16″ framed opening and a second double screened opening, 24″ long by 4″ wide. The 16 x 16 opening is the actual intake from which water enters the collection box. It is located at the upper corner, closest to the creek. It is screened on the inside with a heavy-gauge, wide-mesh screen which protects a lighter gauge, narrow-mesh outer screen from collapsing under the pressure of the water. These screens prevent large matter from eventually clogging the outlet. They are framed with 1½″ x 2″ strips of cedar, as is the other opening (plates 17 and 18).

The long, narrow opening is located at the bottom left of the intake, allowing the water table to reach that height and spill out without interfering with the inflowing water. If I were to redesign this intake, which I might do in the near future, I'd rig up a framed slot for a removable intake screen so that it could be easily replaced periodically.

The outlet is located at the lower left front corner, buried below the ground outside to protect it from freezing. It doesn't matter which side it is located on as long as it is at the bottom and can be buried. It is a good idea to paint, tar, or otherwise protect this outlet area where it comes in contact with the ground to preserve it from premature rot. The outlet has a 2″ circumference to accommodate a galvanized fitting which screws into it. The threads twist into the soft cedar, making threads in it to seal it in place. A galvanized fitting was used because a plastic fitting would never make a good tight fit. If the area around the fitting began to leak, this would cause a slight loss of pressure to the outlet and would eventually cause it to work loose from the box. A short piece of plastic pipe, just long enough to attach an elbow to was clamped to it and another 2′ length of pipe was attached, bringing the outlet line down so it could be buried sufficiently deep into the ground. Then another elbow was added. Sure it would be wiser to bring the whole front side deeper into the ground, but we were confronted with a rock problem which didn't permit it.

The outlet is protected inside the box by a perforated milk can which is suspended around the opening from a nail above (plate 19). The weight of the milk can holds it in place. Anything lighter, like a screened box for example, should be weighted down from

the inside with a good sized stone or something, or else it might float up, leaving the outlet opening unprotected. It is extremely necessary to protect this opening, otherwise large particles could pass through and collect at the outlet valves, clogging them. I once had a problem of wood particles collecting where pipe cupplings reduced the line. I had to search for the connection, digging several holes into the ground until the problem area was located. That type of aggravating chore I could do without.

To control the flow of water to the newly installed collection box, I built a dam, using whatever branches, rocks, and logs I could find in the immediate area. This dam diverts a more than adequate flow into the flume (plate 18). A 2 x 8 three-section, flat-bottomed flume comes from the dam at a slight downhill slope to carry the creek water into the intake. A flume such as this one is usually necessary when bringing water from a higher area to a lower intake which is not directly in the creek itself (plate 20). This flume should be kept free from accumulating rock and matter so it can continue to unobstructedly bring in a sufficient volume of water to the box. Try not to allow the

OUTLET

(19)

METAL NIPPLE SCREWED INTO CEDAR BOARDS

MAIN LINE

2″ PIPE

OLD MILK CAN PUNCHED FULL OF HOLES

water level in the collection box to go down past the outlet screen, otherwise air will get in your lines, sputtering and causing compression. This disturbance shortens the life of your irrigation system. It is wise to periodically wander up to the collection box and check that leaves and twigs haven't clogged the screen.

Finally, a neighbor came down to help me *shade* the pipe in our trenches. This pipe should be filled with water prior to shading and backfilling, so as to lessen the chance of it collapsing. We checked all the connections to make certain they were very tight because once the ditch is backfilled there is no way, short of digging down 3', to tighten a loose connection. We fill in the trench 6" by hand to protect the pipe from large, sharp rocks that might cut or crush it when the machine

back fills. The "cat" came and did its thing.

The water system has proven to be excellent, supplying us with all the irrigation and domestic water we need for our homestead. Without such an efficient system many of our projects would not have been possible. The pastures are producing good hay, the garden is flourishing, and the orchard is filled with huge, succulent apples. To a homesteader cutting out his or her place in an undeveloped forest the water system should be the first consideration. With it you can begin living on your land, developing the necessities, and irrigating the newly planted trees which will someday provide shade for your future dwelling. Water is life.

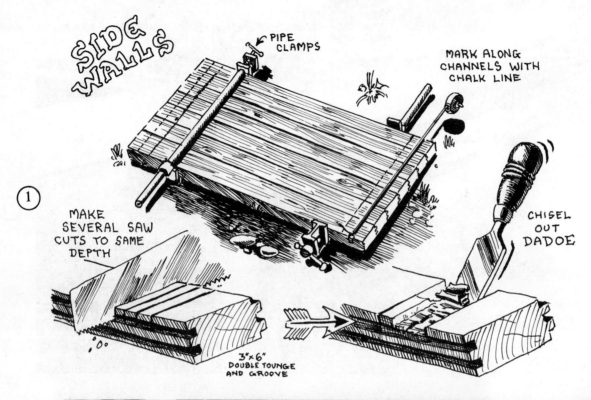

① SIDE WALLS

PIPE CLAMPS

MARK ALONG CHANNELS WITH CHALK LINE

MAKE SEVERAL SAW CUTS TO SAME DEPTH

CHISEL OUT DADOE

3"x 6" DOUBLE TOUNGE AND GROOVE

②

Chapter Three

Even From a Trickling Brook

About 75 vertical feet above the flat where our houses are situated, the water from a tiny brook emerges for a final time on the mountain, then runs down a gully until it eventually sinks back into the ground. Technically, this flow is considered a brook since the water comes to surface at several places on up the mountain, but for the purpose of taming the supply, it is treated as a spring and has been called such. And because we were the first people to settle on the surrounding land, the local water rights branch dubbed our source with our name.

At the point where the brook makes its final emergence we constructed our water system. It consists of a dam to catch the flow and a box to store it for volume, thus allowing it to be pressure-released to the outlet pipe. The box, built first, holds approximately 800 gallons of water and is located at the first level spot below the spring, about 36′ below the dam site. This location must have a substantial draining capacity and be large enough in size so that the stability of the box will not be threatened by eventual erosion. The size of the box was determined by our need for storage capacity and pressure since the spring reduces to a trickle in late summer. The dimensions of this box are 8′ in length by 42½″ in width and 46½″ in height. It is constructed out of 3 x 6″ double tongue-and-groove spruce lumber and sits on four creosoted railroad ties. The tongue-and-groove lumber was utility grade, purchased because we got a good price on it. On hindsight we should have been less miserly because the imperfections in the wood made it difficult to pull the box tightly together, consequently, leakage occurs. The ties were set on the ground, spaced evenly along the length of the proposed box and were leveled.

At another area, where it was easier to work, the long sides were each assembled and held in place with large bar clamps. Two lines were drawn 2½″ apart near either end of the sides, then a channel was cut ¾″ deep along those lines and the piece between the cuts was chiseled out to provide a snug notch for the shorter sides to seat in (plate 1).

Once the chiseling of the channels was completed the walls were taken apart and were lugged up to the site. The nine floor boards were laid across the ties and were pulled tightly together, using the bar clamps underneath, between the ties, so they wouldn't interfere with work. (plate 2). The sides were constructed in courses, 2 long pieces set in place and the shorter pieces tapped into the channels. The courses were raised in this manner without the use of nails until all the sideboards were raised.

12- 4 x 4 supports were cut into 2 lengths; six pieces being 53½″ and 6 being 56″. Holes were drilled as close to the sides as possible into the shorter supports which horizontally span the sides, top and bottom, on either end and at the center. These holes accommodate the ½″ threaded bar stock rods which hold the opposing supports together. Nuts and washers were fastened finger tight on all the ends of the rods to keep them in place. The longer upright supports were then positioned and dealt with in the same manner and each nut was slowly tightened evenly and in succession with the others, going around the box as many times as necessary for a snug fit, stopping just prior to the walls deflecting (plates 3 and 6).

The interior of the box was divided into two chambers by a removable wall of 1 x 10's fitted into grooves created by four upright 2 x 3's that were nailed into the sides. The wall is neither nailed together nor

TAP END
BOARDS INTO
SLOTTED
SIDE WALLS

REBAR THRU
UPRIGHT 4"x 4's
DEFINES SHAPE

TIGHTEN
BOLTS

LARGE CLEAN
OUT HOLE
AND BUNG

FINISHED
WALLS ARE
PRESSED DOWN
BY 3 HORIZONTAL
BEAMS HELD
TOGETHER WITH
THREADED ROD

③

④

⑤

to the box for easy removal during cleaning. It could be made from any size lumber or waterproof plywood. When making any measurement for a water box, remember that wood swells when it is wet. This works to your advantage when you want a tight fit to prevent leakage, but against you when you want to remove any portion after the box has been filled. The smaller chamber is 2' wide, designed as a space for depositing the incoming sediment which passes through the intake screen instead of going on into the main chamber via the high 2" x 18" screened opening located at water level on the divider wall. (See plate 8).

There are three screens for filtration inside this box, all made from heavy-guage stainless steel screening acquired from a juvenile detention home. The primary screen, 24" x 24" is tacked to a frame of 2 x

78

⑥

3s and placed at the point of entry into the box from the dam. The secondary screen is in the divider wall (plate 7) and the tertiary screen is shaped into a 10" square box and fitted over the outlet pipe (see plate 8).

So the progression of water then is: from the dam it goes through 2" plastic pipe to the intake screen and into the smaller chamber. There it gets filtered (not entirely, unfortunately) and progresses out of the secondary screen into the main chamber. We installed a V-shaped notch into the top board of a long side of the box to allow the overflow to spill out at that point and go down a wood trough into a natural gully instead of spilling out randomly and eroding the surrounding plateau. The water that remained in the box went through the outlet and down the pipe to irrigate the garden, fields, and dwellings. The outlet now consists of a 2" hole in the floor of the box with a galvanized fitting screwed into that hole. This fitting has a male end that accommodates 2" plastic pipe (plate 8).

⑦

The first winter glaringly exposed four mistakes in our design. Luckily, they were easily rectified the following spring. First, the water froze at the overflow trough because it was directly exposed to the weather. We substituted a 2″ plastic pipe long enough to carry the water to the gully.

The friction caused by the steady flow of water in the pipe kept it from freezing (plate 9 and 10).

Second, we laid the plywood cover on the 4 x 4 supports which protrudes 3½″ above the box. This allowed the wind to whip under the plywood, leaving behind a skating

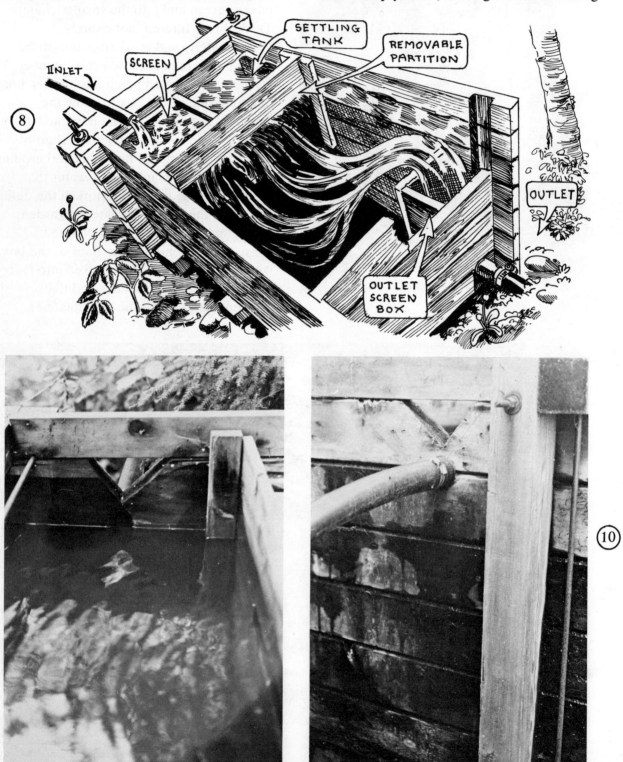

rink on the surface of our water supply. Since we nailed 2 x 4's around the top perimeter of the box, between the crossing supports, this problem has not reoccurred (plate 11).

Our third mistake was to place the outlet hole on the side of the box, above ground, forcing the pipe to be exposed until it could be gradually bent down into the 18″ deep trench where it is buried the rest of the distance to the houses. Even when we packed it with sawdust it still froze at this point, almost leaving us without water for the remainder of the long cold winter. Once the snow melted, we emptied the box and cut a hole out of the bottom for the outlet pipe, then put dirt around the small portion of the pipe which goes above ground before entering the box. This alleviated our problem.

Fourth, we used a wooden V trough of 1 x 8s supported on crossing 2 x 4 braces to carry the water from the dam to the box. The water froze in it as well. We have since substituted a 2″ pipe which was laid in the trough and covered over in winter with 1x boards for added protection (plates 12 and 13).

(11)

(12)

(13)

(14)

CONCRETE DAM

CEMENT FORMS
SPRING
OUTLET PIPE SET INTO FORMS
TEMPORARY DRAIN PIPE
HOLE DUG 18" BELOW WATER LINE
OVERFLOW
COVERED SPRING
FLUME CARRIES PIPE TO BOX
PLYWOOD COVER
INWOOD 75

⑮

When the box was completed we built the dam. The natural pool of the spring was excavated a bit to make it deeper and larger. At first we tried using the scrap pieces of tongue-and-groove lumber from the box to make the dam wall but there was too much leakage under it, consequently, we decided to reconstruct it, using cement when we had more time to deal with it. A wooden wall is adequate if you are in a hurry and have enough of a flow so you don't have to be worried about every little drop when the usual late summer dry spell hits.

To make the cement dam we dug a trench across the ravine where the water flows which was 18″ deeper than the water level. Forms were built for the 7″ thick wall and a pipe was laid under the forms to drain the accumulating water while the forms were being secured and while the cement was setting up. Since the pipe could not be pulled out when the cement hardened (it became

encased) it was threaded so it could be capped. To accommodate the outlet pipe which will take the water to the box, a hole was drilled in each form and the pipe was pushed through the holes prior to the pour. We also placed a small block of wood into the wet cement at the top of wall to form a channel for the overflow during heavy spring runoff (plate 12). This pool was then entirely sheltered with an A-frame roof to keep out the debris and a sheet of plastic was put over the exposed front to prevent freezing (plate 13). With this protection there is no need to screen off the intake end of the pipe at the dam.

Now that the corrections have been made, this water system has been working great, supplying our domestic and homestead needs from a tiny spring that would otherwise just seep back into the ground unnoticed.

Chapter Four

A Recycled Hot Water System

Even though I choose to live deep within the forest, far from the madness of civilization, I still enjoy some of its conveniences and have given a few of its castaways new purpose in my primitive creations. I've gathered the elements of the hot water system and shower while shopping through society's greatest bargain centers—its trash dumps. I entered these establishments with little preconception of specific merchandise, and remained quite flexible in my design. I picked up an old radiator here, a discarded water heater there, and fittings and faucets and lengths of pipe wherever I could find them, then trucked the whole mess home to figure out what would come of it all.

With a few basic principles of hydraulic engineering surfacing in my consciousness as I pondered over my latest acquisitions of useful junk, a design began developing. Then came the hard part—making all the pieces fit together to become what I intended. I'm sure most of the pieces would have rather remained where I found them, continuing their return to the earth. Most every fitting gave an unwilling struggle, voicing its disgruntled objection with each twist from

my wrench. Finally, after what would have netted a paid plumber a goodly wage the system was completed. The time spent on it was well enjoyed, unhurried, and thoroughly involving. For I had no other commitments—no bills to pay and no places to be except staying right here amongst my peaceful surroundings doing what I want to be doing.

The hot water system consists of a wall-type radiator, a 30-gallon hot water tank, a lot of piping, fittings, valves, and a shower head. The radiator is located well outside the structure so a fire could be built on it. It was set on its side and tilted slightly upward so the front outlet would be raised a bit higher than the rear one (plates 1 and 2). This facilitates the convection process. The radiator then acts as the convection generator. When it is heated up by the fire above, it initiates the circulating movement of the water by warming up the cold water that enters through the low inlet. The water fills the radiator, gets hot, and flows upwards through the outlet pipe, returning to the 30 gallon collection tank as hot water. This cycle keeps happening until all the water in the tank and pipes is as hot as the fire will allow.

The collection tank is an old electric water heater tank stripped of its fancy enameled jacket. That jacket was replaced by protective layers of fiberglass, gunny sacks,and galvanized roofing which act as insulation to keep the heat in (plate 3). It came complete with fittings in the proper places to facilitate the convection process. The water comes down the mountain from the source via plastic pipe to the galvanized tee at the bottom of the tank where it goes to the radiator and fills up the tank. Just prior to this union is another tee that goes off to the vertical cold water inlet to the left of the tank. At the top of that cold water inlet is a shut-off valve to control the flow of cold water to the sink. This valve makes it possible to mix hot and cold water in the

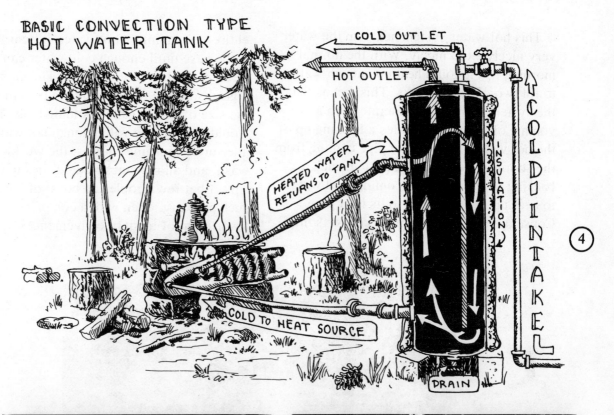

BASIC CONVECTION TYPE HOT WATER TANK

COLD OUTLET

HOT OUTLET

HEATED WATER RETURNS TO TANK

INSULATION

COLD INTAKE

COLD TO HEAT SOURCE

DRAIN

④

⑤

⑥

lines to get the desired water temperature for sink use (see plates 3 and 5).

6″ below the top of the hot water tank is the inlet from the radiator. At least 6″ of space is required at the top of the tank to allow the hot water a chance to rise and create a convection area with that enclosure. The outlet comes out the top of the tank and elbows to the left to the shower and sink. Before it reaches the vertical cold water inlet it is interrupted by a control valve that regulates the flow from it. From that valve it either goes to the shower head or the sink faucet which ever is in use (plates 4-6).

This hot water system heats up the water very nicely—too nicely. With the normal morning fire it could heat up enough water to fill two 45 gallon tanks. This means that the system's ability to generate such a volume of hot water creates a backing up of the hot water in the intake pipe coming from the source. In the present system such a backing up causes the incoming cold water to heat up before it gets to its inlet pipe. Consequently, it temporarily converts the entire system into a hot-water system. This is the case until enough cold water can run through the line to cool it off. The most logical solution to this problem is to increase the size of the 30 gallon holding tank. This would provide me with enough hot water for a leisurely morning shower, the weekly wash, and all the stacked up dishes in the sink. I bet few people can boast of having such a luxury, even with a complete assortment of modern conveniences.

SECTION III

Some Animal Shelters And
A Little About Care

You wouldn't believe the miles we've traveled to gather first hand information about efficient and practical animal shelters that have most of the ingredients necessary to house and maintain common homestead animals in the Northern four seasonal climate zone. The specifications and the measurements of the shelters are as subjective and unique as are the homesteaders themselves, although each dwelling had a few basic ingredients in common. And amazingly enough, no matter how radical the design, most of the well-constructed shelters without obvious building mistakes were suitable within their own variables. Even though most of the builders couldn't explain a lot of the reasons for specific sizes, shapes and designs.

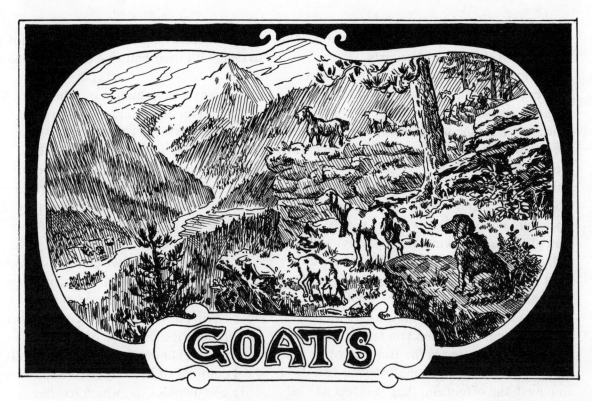

Chapter One
Goat Shelters

Among all the farm animals goats are either the most notorious or the most **complacent**, depending on the circumstances and the management involved. Opinions concerning the animal, from the people I visited range from "never again will I attempt to deal with those stubborn, ungrateful beasts," to "they're the most gentle, loving critters we have". Why such a diversity? Several reasons I'm sure, but the greatest single reason has to do with the shelter. Lack of genuine heart-to-heart contact is second. From our own personal experience with goats I realize that proper shelter and management could have prevented much anguish that we had with these sensitive creatures. Now that we've shared the experiences of many successful and unsuccessful goatspeople we're about ready to try developing new relations with that animal.

We bounce back and forth from a communal cow, which is shared by a few families, to two or three goats. We love the dairy products from the cow—the milk, yogurt, cheese, butter, ice cream, etc., but we are overburdened by the cost of maintenance. One cow eats about the same amount as 16 goats and doesn't give as much in return. If you are on a small piece of land without much cleared acreage and have to depend on bought or traded hay and grain, a cow would be rather expensive, even more so than a small herd of goats. Though goat's milk is harder to deal with for butter and other cream products since it is naturally homogenized meaning that the cream doesn't easily separate) it is much easier to digest because it consists of smaller fat globules and is more in tune to the needs of the human body. Goat milk is very versatile for cheese making and other byproducts.

Just ask a few people who know about goats for some of their special recipes.

The main problem with goats in so far as shelter goes is that they are second only to Houdini as escape artists. They get out of places that are inconceivable to the inexperienced goatkeeper. This is especially true of the kids. They have the ability to spring high up or squeeze through small holes. If they find a weak spot in their enclosure goats will gnaw, bang against, or butt at that section until it gives way. They will get out and head straight for tender little fruit trees, colorful flowers, and tasty garden vegetables with no conscience whatever. They'll eat and eat until they are as wide as they are long. And when you return from that trip to town to see the fruits of your labors laying in ruin, no matter what you do to punish the offenders, they will feel no remorse and the first chance they get they'll do it again. So now that you are a bit familiar with the "nature of the beast" you

can plan accordingly, and hopefully not have to deal with their bad side or expose them to yours.

Like any being, human or otherwise, the more contact and interaction you have with the goats, the more rapport and understanding will be developed. Be prepared and do your homework before starting out with any animals. Exercise your advantage of being able to obtain textbook knowledge about them even prior to beginning the relationship.

Since in our travels we could not locate any ideal goat shelters which incorporate more than a small percentage of the labor-saving devices in their construction, we will describe one type of shelter, critically explaining the good points and short comings of its features. Then, we will share our own design, which has been checked over and approved by local experts.

The goat setup that most appealed to us, but was far from being error free was this

90

system involving two base shelters and a light-weight portable pen and tethers for controlled grazing. The main shelter was built to house 4 kids and 3 adults in small communal type pens. Communal pens such as this, especially with a larger herd, are much more in tune with the animal's gregarious nature. Such a space offers interaction, choice of area, excercise, liberty, and social amenity, as opposed to stall-type housing. Stalls isolate the animals and do not provide them with enough area to exercise in. Generally, the only time it is really dangerous to put goats in such a communal environment is if some of them are horned and others aren't. The dehorned or unhorned ones do not stand a chance against their opponent's weapons. Even in the most gentle goats there is a lot of the old pecking order, but in my experience the competition never gets too serious because the order is soon established and usually all the members of the group accept their status.

The 20′ x 16′ main enclosure is separated into four sections. Two of the sections are covered with a shed roof for protection against the weather and the other two are open exercise yards. All are complete with feeders and water bowls (plate 1 and 2).

The covered sections consist of three areas. The two 5′ x 8′ areas within the sheathing are indoor quarters for the kids and does. The area on the right is partitioned from the area on the left and is open to the front section. It is for the milking does. The upright pole and heavy-guage 2″ mesh poultry netting partition prevents the kids from getting to the does, yet allows them some restrained contact (plate 3). Most breeders recommend taking the kids from the does immediately after birth, not even letting them get their first natural meal. This protects the does udders, which is said to extend her productive years. It also makes the transition of separating the parent and offspring much easier, especially if restrained contact can still be made.

The does' quarters is nothing more than a loose shelter. In the colder months it is closed off by the door that separates it from the excercise yard (plate 4). Beside the door, on the outside wall, is a feeder box that is used in winter to feed the confined does.

The hay is placed in the box from the outside. The does go to the wall from the inside and eat through small holes within the wall which ration the hay but deter the trashing of it by only allowing a small amount to come out at a time. Certainly this wouldn't prevent the goats from slowly working it all into the shelter and using the spoiled hay for bedding, but it does make it more difficult than if they were using an open feeding system. The best control against food wastage is the American feeder which I will describe later (see plate 33).

LOAD HAYBOX
FROM
OUTDOORS

DIVIDER
WALL

The same type of controlled feeder is used on the wall that divides the kids' shelter from their small outside excercising yard. This feeder box can be used at either side; from slots through the inside wall or through openings on the front of the covered box (plates 5 and 6).

A larger feeder for does is located on the inside of the lattice-fence enclosure. This supplies them their food in the warmer months when they do not need to be enclosed (plate 7). Though goats should be separated while being fed grain, there appears to be no advantage to isolating them at other times except when particular problems such as kidding and disease control occur.

The flooring both inside and out follows the principle of underfloor heating which goats themselves originated. Goat's natural bedding is of accumulated droppings mixed with whatever grass and other roughage they could find. This provides a warm and comfortable bed which absorbs and evaporates the urine, making its odors inoffensive. It is the most economical in labor and materials and seldom needs to be changed. In fact it should be left to accumulate all winter to provide sufficient heat and prevent floor drafts. It can later be put on the garden. As any experienced homesteader will attest, goat manure is one of the best nitrogen rich manures for the garden and is also the easiest to deal with. I personally prefer wood shavings that are free from turpentine, such as cottonwood, birch, or poplar, for bedding and flooring. Wood shavings or sawdust are easier to lift off the floor when ready to be changed because these materials consist of small particles that don't intertwine and blanket together as does hay or straw. They are also cheaper and readily available wherever there is a sawmill near by. The fences around the enclosure are of latticework designed for beauty and not so much for efficiency though they have proven to work well for containing the adults (plates 8 and 9). They did not work so well for kids, on the other

hand, because these nimble little creatures could easily squeeze and push through most of the few-inch spaces between the cross members, and once they did so they proudly pranced over to the nearest goodies. When using a wooden fence of any type to contain kids, the rails or members should have no more than 3″ of space between them. Anymore than this and the kids would either get their heads stuck when attempting to escape or make good their attempt. The designer constructed a removable upright

10

12

11

MILKING DOE PEN

STORAGE

BRRAAAA

MAKE A SERIES OF PERPENDICULAR CUTS — RASP OUT WITH SAW

⑬

HORSE SHED

MILKING STAND

MORTICE ~AND~ TENON JOINT
á la CHAINSAW

partition similar to the one he built between the kids and does in the shed to separate their excercise yards but failed to use poultry netting of sufficient gauge to reinforce it. This resulted in an eventual breakout, as can be witnessed in the photograph. Diagonal slots were sawed out of the supporting uprights for the cross members of the partition to fit down into for easy removal of the partition when the kids are old enough to run with the adults (plate 10).

Since the main criteria for this structure was to provide a small, comfortable, lightweight and portable shelter that could be easily moved when the occasion arose, its most definite shortcoming is that it is not adequate for protection against the cold winter. Barn weather should be regulated at around 55 degrees F. If does are not provided with proper shelter from the extreme weather they will utilize their energy to keep warm instead of to produce milk. This problem could be easily remedied

with the addition of insulation and the closing off of all openings, but that would make the structure less portable; unless of course all the walls and fences were built as separate units which could easily be taken apart when the landlord's will deemed it necessary.

The secondary shelter is a combination milking doe quarters, storage shed, stanchion area and open-horse stall which incorporates some very intricate and interesting notchwork and other unique construction designs. The enclosed area consists of two stalls and one outside area. The stall to the rear is a smaller shelter for a couple of the heavy-producing milking does. It has a feeder attached to the front outside wall that allows them controlled hay through two slots in that wall. It is conveniently placed near the raised milking stanchion in front of it and the feed shed beside it. In the feed shed the grains and other perishables are stored in large galvanized trash cans to prevent rodents or other pests from eating and spoiling them (plates 11-14).

The milking stanchion is raised high enough for the milker to stand during this operation. This particular milker prefers this position. The platform is held up from the underside with diagonal braces. The neck-locking device is attached to the front outer wall. It consists of a frame of two uprights straddled at top and bottom by 1x cross pieces. Another center upright is held at the bottom by a dowel that loosely fits through a hole in it. It is free to swing from side to side at this point. At the top it is sandwiched by the upper cross pieces and

positioned by a peg which goes through those supports. When the movable upright is on the outside of the peg the goat can be led up the steps and put into position, her head going in between the far uprights. When she is in position the milker removes the peg and swings the top of the upright toward the goat, locking her neck in place, then he replaces the peg. Here the goat stands patiently until milked out (plates 15-17).

A milking doe will usually happily go straight to the milking stanchion without any trouble since her udder is full and getting quite uncomfortable. Such a stanchion is useful for several reasons. It should contain a platform that raises the udder to a level that is comfortable to the milker whether they prefer a standing or sitting position (plate 18). It should also have a neck-locking device to prevent her from squirming around or backing up while being milked, and perhaps upsetting the bucket after she has finished her grain. Grain is usually fed while the doe is being milked to distract her and keep her content throughout the operation.

(14)

(16)

(15)

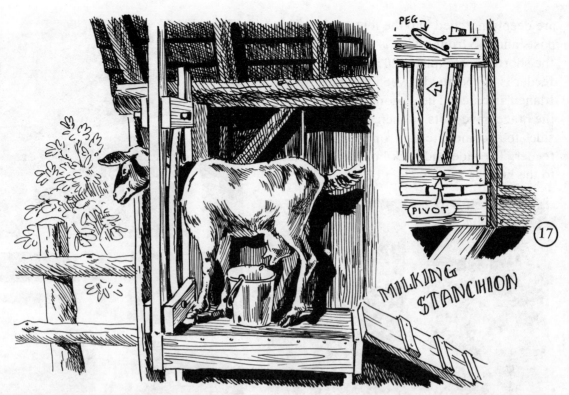

MILKING STANCHION

17

But there are some goatspeople who prefer not to feed the does when they milk, but instead, keep their heads in a controlled locking mechanism so they can contentedly chew their cud and peacefully meditate while being milked. This method discourages the nervous gulping down of grain that is usually the habit of a goat that is fed while being milked. She races through her portion, seemingly competing with the milker, seeing who can finish first. If she finishes first she usually fidgets, cries for more feed, and sometimes holds her milk back because of the distraction.

The milking stanchion should be away from the main pens or stalls and removed from possible sources of contamination. It should be kept spotlessly clean because milk is quick to pick up surrounding odors and bacteria.

The outside horsestall is worth mentioning here because of its interesting notch work and construction. It is a large area providing the horse plenty of exercise room even when it is confined within this area. It is of simple shed roof, post and beam construction with a shoulder height rail around it that keeps the horse in. The roof

consists of pole rafters, sheathing and asphalt paper. The upper side cross members are mortised and tenoned through the opposing uprights to create a strong joint (plate 19) (also see plate 13). The side rails

18

are deeply notched into the long upright posts and the front railing is notched over the shorter posts (plates 20 and 21). The feeder is supported between two rails by a triangular brace. The diagonal members of the brace have slots on their inward facing sides to accomodate the front boards of the feeder. The side and back boards are nailed to the bracing (plates 22 and 23).

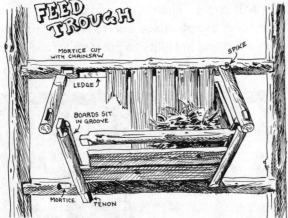

FEED TROUGH

MORTICE CUT WITH CHAINSAW
SPIKE
LEDGE
BOARDS SIT IN GROOVE
MORTICE
TENON

One of the most laborious methods of controlling animals and one which is definitely against the inherent nature of goats is tethering. Its only saving grace is that it allows them the controlled grazing of various portions of a pasture or a forage area without letting them get near gardens, fruit trees or other ''no-no'' areas. The disadvantages of this system are that the tethers have to be frequently changed; they only allow a circular area to be foraged; and they are difficult to maintain and easily broken away from if they are poorly designed. The proper post tether should consist of a rod that is at least 24″ long that can be pounded deeply into the ground until only its top ring is exposed above surface. Attached to this ring should be a swivel ring and a strong lead chain. The chain should be no longer than the radius of a daily portion of forage, 10′ at the most, and should have a swivel ring attachment where it connects to the goat's collar to help prevent the goat from getting tangled on the lead. Even with all these precautions the animal usually finds some way to make this method inefficient by either getting tangled up or pulling out the post.

An alternative to this primitive method is the running tether which allows the goat to cover more lateral ground thus more efficiently foraging a given area. It is also less demanding of maintenance. Since it covers a larger area it only has to be changed every few days, and even then only one post

has to be moved. Using the other post as a stationary point, the one you are moving could be positioned at various points and eventually encircle it or each post could be moved forward every other time until the running tether is staggered along the forage area. The running tether consists of a short length of chain or rope no longer than 3′. It is attached at one end to a swivel collar and at the other to a swivel ring which runs on a wire or rope that is stretched taut along the ground between two posts. The posts are pounded into the ground so all that is exposed is their top loops. These posts could be placed to an excess of 100′ apart if terrain allowed (plate 24).

One goat alone on the tether, out of the sight of the others is an unhappy animal. A number of goats tethered within sight of each other will be much more contented and

USE SWIVELS

3 FT.

30 FEET

RUNNING TETHER

2 WAYS TO MOVE STAKE

STAGGER

CONCENTRIC

24

25

㉖

㉗

quiet. Their productivity and general attitudes will also be considerably better.

Another alternative to the tether is the movable pen, of which this eight-sided enclosure is a good example. It is made up of eight equal 10′ sides that are 4½′ in height. Each side is comprised of two 2 x 4 end posts with four 1 x 4 horizontal boards approximately 1′ on center apart. The spaces between the boards are filled to a height of 30″ with heavy duty 2″ mesh poultry netting which is stapled to the boards and stretched from the top with a spiralling rope. The sides are held together with two heavy duty hook and eyes on either end. Each piece can be easily moved by one person. And the structure can be added to or sides can be taken away, depending on the shape and size you want the enclosure to be. This enclosure is excellent for adult goats but is not recommended for kids. The older a goat gets, the less spring it has. Young kids have plenty of spring—too much. The only problem with this enclosure is a simple one to remedy. The hooks are just not long enough to clear the bottom of the eyes by more than ½″. This makes it quite easy for an energetic, rambunctious goat to buck at the side highest on a slope until the hooks come out of the eyes on one end. The remedy would be to have longer hooks that at least extend 2″ beyond the bottoms of the eyes (plates 25-28).

A large number of variables determine the design best suited for a goat shelter. These

KICK

PIN IS NOT LONG ENOUGH

㉘

CORRECT BY USING LONGER PIN

are found around the immediate exterior of that shelter. Is there plenty of surrounding browse and forage? Is there water near? Is there shelter from direct sunlight? Is there room for an outdoor exercising pen? Are there a lot of immediate temptations such as a garden, fruit trees, and flowers? Each question has to be considered before locating the optimum site for the goat's main living quarters. It should be close to forage, browse and water so the goats don't have to be led across long distances in order to be taken to the desired areas. It should be in a place that has some shelter from direct sun so they can go out to a good sized exercise yard and still get shelter from the heat when they need it. It should be out of the way of unprotected fruit trees, flowers, and gardens. Actually, it would be beneficial to have the garden nearby if it were properly fenced to facilitate the transferring of manure from barn to garden.

The building itself should be well insulated and draft-free, containing a large enough loft above the living quarters to hold all the hay and bedding the animals will need for the long winter. Our goat living quarters design is taking into consideration the housing of 4 to 6 milking or dry does, 4 to 6 kids, and 1 or 2 functioning billies. Included in the design is as much pole construction as possible to give the place a warm, natural feeling.

One enters the gambreled roof, 24′ square (outside diameter) barn from the west dutch door entryway. To the immediate right of that entrance is a supply cabinet containing milk pails, rags, medicines, detergents, tools such as nail clippers, knives, etc., and disinfectant for the milking stanchion. The cabinet has a double door and a latch to

prevent it from being opened by a curious goat who has managed to escape its confines. To the right of the cabinet is the 3′ x 5′ hay drop chute which is directly under the lidded hole entrance to the loft. Beside the chute is a stairway and a pulley rope for easy opening of the lid. On the far side of the ladder is a deep bowl galvanized sink for washing (plate 29).

As you continue facing the aisleway down the center of the barn, there is a doe's pen and milking stanchion to the south, and kid, billy, and isolation pen to the north. The 9 x 6′ milking stanchion has a 4½′ high horizontal pole partition separating it from the entrance area and another separating it from the adjacent doe pen to the east. It is located to the far south, facing west, away from the doe pen so the doe that is being milked will not be distracted by the pen. There is a long double window of salvaged, shatterproof windshield glass above it to allow in the southern light. The milker goes into the stanchion area, through the gate at the east and readies the area for milking. Then she goes into the doe pen through the gate within the stanchion area and gets her usually willing doe. The doe climbs up on

TRAP DOOR TO HAYLOFT

29

SUPPLY CABINET

SINK

FRONT ENTRANCE

INWOOD 75

(30)

WATERER

(31)

DRAIN PIPES

DRAINS OUTDOORS IN SUMMER

FRESH WATER

DRAINS UNDERGROUND FOR WINTER USE

the 3′ x 5′ stanchion platform which is about 1′ off the floor. This height makes the udders easily accessible to the seated milker. The doe puts her head inside the neck locking unit and busily nibbles at her grain while the milker milks. The feeder unit for the milking stanchion consists of two 36″ uprights spaced 4″ apart. These uprights were held together at the top with a crossing 1 x 4 and were braced to the front end of the platform. Below the crossing 1 x 4, a 12″ long by 1½″ wide piece was cut from the

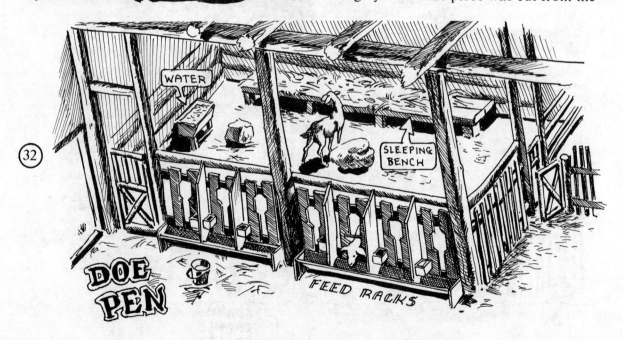

(32)

WATER

SLEEPING BENCH

DOE PEN

FEED RACKS

insides of the uprights to allow the goat's head to freely enter and slip down the narrower 4″ channel to the raised 8″ x 8″ x 6″ deep feeder box. After her head goes down the channel the applewood bolt is drawn across the branch intersection latches. Her head is then locked in the narrow opening until after the milking (plate 30).

The 10 x 14′ doe pen is plenty sufficient for the growing herd. At least 12 to 15 square feet of floor space should be provided for every adult goat. This area is well lighted for solar heat in winter by three windshield glass double windows along the south wall and one on the east wall, making the pen a cheery environment instead of a dark, depressing one. The floor is dirt, covered with a thick layer of fine poplar, birch, or cottonwood woodchips which are the quickest species to decompose and are the best for garden compost. The droppings and urine mix and soak up well in this porous material, and it is all easily transported into the garden once it is the proper consistency. There are two 3 x 6′ portable raised platforms, approximately 1′ off the floor along the south wall for the goats to sleep on. They are set 1′ in from that wall to avoid wall drafts. Don't use slats for this platform because goats do not

like them. Two rather large stones were brought into the pen for winter excercising. Goats naturally crave some contact with hard, abrasive surfaces such as stones. This contact helps keep the hooves trimmed and cuts down on unsightly surplus growth in which foot rot develops. This growth will not accumulate if the goat is regularly excercised on hard ground for even a short period each day.

Contrary to popular belief, goats are quite fussy about what they take into their bodies. They won't drink soiled or contaminated water and they won't eat food that has been even nosed over by other members of the pen. But they do need plenty of water to produce milk. For this reason I prefer a self regulating, running water system with a steadily trickling intake and a high outlet to control the overflow. This system consists of a five-gallon can raised on a 1′ platform. It is located just inside the east wall. The intake pipe tees up from the underground water line and elbows into the bottom of the can. The outlet nipple is also brazed to the bottom of the can. It has a fitting for a length of plastic pipe which extends to about 2″ from the top. The water fills up in the can and the overflow spills down this pipe to the runoff pipe below (plate 31) (see chapter 4, plate 10). This runoff is buried under

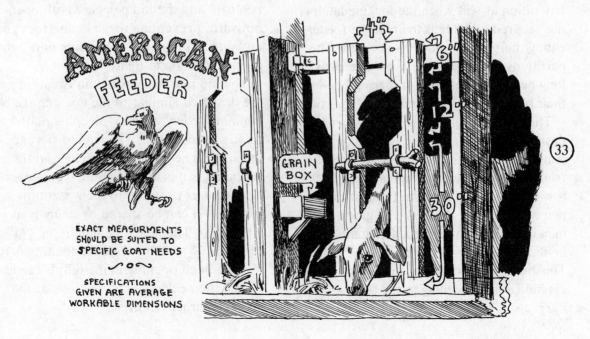

AMERICAN FEEDER

EXACT MEASURMENTS SHOULD BE SUITED TO SPECIFIC GOAT NEEDS

SPECIFICATIONS GIVEN ARE AVERAGE WORKABLE DIMENSIONS

GRAIN BOX

4″
6″
12″
14″
30″

33

woodchips and sufficiently protected against freezing in the winter. It empties into a subterranean boulder pit. In the summer it feeds the outside waterer.

The water is kept warm through the winter by a tube heater which is suspended near the waterlevel by a float attachment. Half the can top is covered by a lid to lessen the chance of the water being contaminated. The salt lick is placed beside the waterer to encourage the goats to drink.

Goats are wasteful feeders. If their food is dropped on the bedding they refuse to eat it, yet if allowed to they will pull out large quantities at a time, spreading it out over the floor and eventually spoiling it. Therefore a well-designed feeding system is a major consideration for an economical, efficient goat operation. It should be a system that enables you to feed them without having to enter the pen.

Along the center aisle, opposite the kid and billy feeders is a row of partitioned American feeder type racks which act as a center enclosure for the doe pen and separate it from the outside feed trough. This system has proven to work extremely well because it prevents the goats from pulling the hay back into the pen and wasting it. It also allows the does to eat their hay ration at will when the locking latch is not secured and keeps them at the feeder eating their grain when it is secured. The partitions discourage the more aggressive, long necked ladies from slithering beyond their own areas to their neighbor's portions.

The feeder racks of the various pens are designed around the basic dimensions of the American type goat feeder but they deviate from the original design in many ways. The row of uprights across the front of the doe pen which end at the east wall gate are 48″ in height with crossing 1 x 4s on either side holding them all in place at top and bottom. This rack is supported by upright poles that extend from the ceiling to the floor at 30″ intervals. The feed trough partitions are attached to the rack uprights with metal brackets, separating the feeders. They can be readily removed for easy cleaning of the long feeder trough.

The 14— 1 x 4″ feeder rack uprights are spaced in such a way so there is 18″ of distance between the centers of each neck slot and 4″ of space allowed for each neck slot. They are 48″ long from top to bottom. 6″ down from the top a 1½″ wide by 12″ long strip was cut from the insides fo the uprights, making a 7″ head opening between the boards. The doe's head goes into the opening and her neck comes down into the neck slot as she feeds. This allows her to feed comfortably and not spill her hay into the pen. When grain rations are served the handy applewood bolt is drawn across the latch below the head opening to prevent the more aggressive goats from gulping down their portion, pulling out and bullying the weaker goats into giving up theirs (plates 32 and 33).

The gate at the east end of the feeder rack opens the doe pen to the sliding back door. This door acts as a dual entranceway to the two outside areas. If the door is slid halfway to the north it opens the pen to the forage grounds. If it is opened halfway to the south it leads to the small excercise yard. The doe pen gate and the kid pen gate both open outward, preventing the animals from going any direction but out the sliding door when it is opened to them (plate 34).

The kid pen, billy pen, and isolation pen are designed similiar to the doe pen. Each contain feeder, waterer, sleeping platform, rock, and salt licks. The main difference is the sizes. The kid pen is 8 x 10′ and the billy servicing pen is 6 x 10′ including feeders. The waterer is built into their partition railing so it can be shared by animals in either pen. The head opening in the kid's feeder is 6″ and the neckslot opening is only 3″. The head opening in the billy's feeder is 9″ and the neckslot is 6″ because of the animal's larger features.

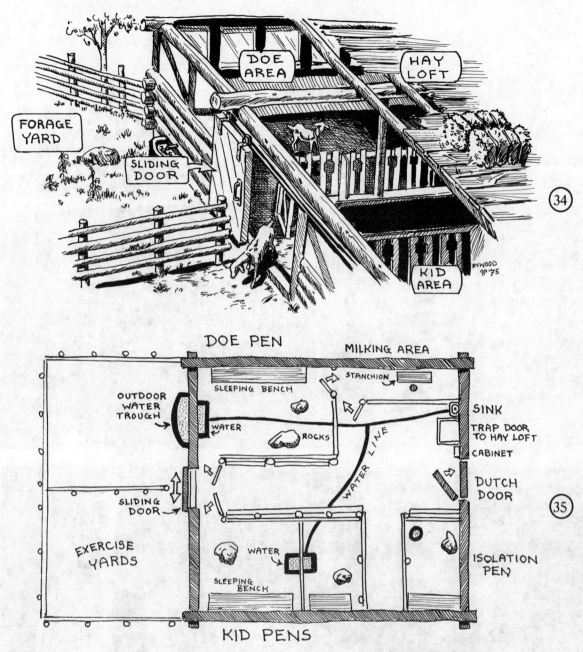

DOE AREA

HAY LOFT

FORAGE YARD

SLIDING DOOR

KID AREA

INWOOD JP '75

(34)

DOE PEN

MILKING AREA

STANCHION

SLEEPING BENCH

OUTDOOR WATER TROUGH

WATER

ROCKS

WATER LINE

SINK

TRAP DOOR TO HAY LOFT

CABINET

DUTCH DOOR

(35)

SLIDING DOOR

EXERCISE YARDS

WATER

SLEEPING BENCH

ISOLATION PEN

KID PENS

BARN PLAN

The isolation pen at the northwest corner is 5 x 10′ including feeder. It is reserved for does who are preparing for labor, sick animals, and new born kids. The enclosure is reinforced with heavy gauged, 2″ square poultry netting to hold the kids in. This stall only has a bowl for water since it is not in use throughout the year (plate 35).

Well here is my design. I don't expect anybody to copy it but I do hope that it inspires some thought and creativity in designing your own goatherd shelter. And take into consideration that the oversize dimensions of this shelter are designed for a growing herd. Goats do not need as much room as I have allowed them.

A Cluck Cluck Here

Chickens—no homestead or farm is complete without these multipurpose little noise makers who welcome us to each new morning with vibrant glee, usually way before we're ready to start the day. From my travels I've noticed that the potential of this necessary and versatile beast is grossly underestimated. They are usually confined in areas that are too small and are not allowed to forage for their own food, but instead are fed with expensive mixtures of grain and mash. The nutrients they get from these purchased products could be easily supplied from garden trimmings and wild greens. Some people forget that all our presently domesticated animals, in the not so distant past, made it on their own, gathering their own food, finding thier own shelter and producing their own offspring. Sure, I grant that egg production of the wilder birds isn't as efficient in the first 2 seasons as are the chickens' production in the larger poultry farms, but compare the egg production after that initial chemically stimulated period . . . and the quality of eggs throughout the laying period. If the worn out, bedraggled commercial birds were still laying after their bout with the conditions they suffered during their first two seasons it would be a miracle. The wilder birds I'm sure would just be reaching their prime, still healthy and proud, laying thick shelled eggs with bright orange-yellow yolks and firm whites. That is what we've witnessed anyway with our own birds and others who are allowed to roam around large open areas to find their own nourishment. And come to think of it, when ours returned to the coop in the evening, full of natural greene, plump little bugs and sandy grit for digestion, they took their place on the roost and the next morning when I came to collect the eggs each nest was full, meaning that most of the birds were laying

the bright orange-yellow yolked eggs daily. What more could we ask for? But of course our system had to be worked out with the variables we had to deal with. We have to supplement their natural forage with some grain and we still use laying mash in small quantities. In fact, the laying hens barely touch the commercial mix when the weather is good enough for them to go out (and when I don't forget to open the gate for them).

The main problem with our system is that

③

someone has to make sure to let the hens out in the late morning after they had a chance to lay their eggs in the familiar nests and close them in after dusk when they return to the roost on their own. If they are allowed to go out in the early morning before they lay their eggs they will search out hidden nesting places, making it difficult to collect the eggs. Also, be sure to fence in your garden well when using this explorer method because thats the first place they'll head for. And protect the new flower bulbs and seeds too. Some friends of ours actually go as far as setting up chicken paths through compost heaps, outhouse holes and areas for future garden additions so the omniverous birds can peck through the heaps, helping break down the decaying compost while they supplement it and the future garden spot with their own nitrogen rich droppings. Other people we talk to don't use commercial laying mash at all. Instead, they just purchase the individual grains and mix their own feed—by far the cheaper way to go. This way you know what your animals are eating instead of having to trust vague labels that never really explain how all the ingredients are proportioned. A good home mixture would be 18 percent corn or other whole grains for scratch, plus a goodly amount of cracked oyster shells to replenish the calcium lost in egg shell making. We save up all the old egg shells, bake them until they are crisp and dry, then crush them and return them to the hens. The protein supplement is necessary unless the chickens have a large area to forage in.

Here are examples of two efficient poultry coops which we found in our travels. Both are complete for care of adult hens; the later explains some necessary hints in introducing new hens to a coop of seasoned layers:

In my opinion the design of this barn is by far the most practical multi-animal structure I've come across. It is made up of three sheltered areas covered by a huge 18' x 50' modified gambreled hayloft with long, steep sides that extend 18" beyond the walls of the 12' x 50' lower structure for optimum hay storage. A spacious 15' x 50' chicken yard is located behind the barn to provide the birds with plenty of foraging space, yet it keeps them enclosed and protected from the wild beasts that prowl the area. This building is constructed mostly of log post and beam with slab sheathing for the walls and lower sections of the loft roof. The upper sections are cedar shakes to prevent leakage through that low-pitched area. The loft has space for much more loose hay than could possibly be needed for the farm's own use. Such a large space comes in handy though when the hay has to be brought in early to dry before it gets rained on. It is just spread out on the crossing pole floor so the air could circulate through it and dry it out.

The 15' square front section of the lower area is the quarters for the cows when they

④

HAY SHOOT

108

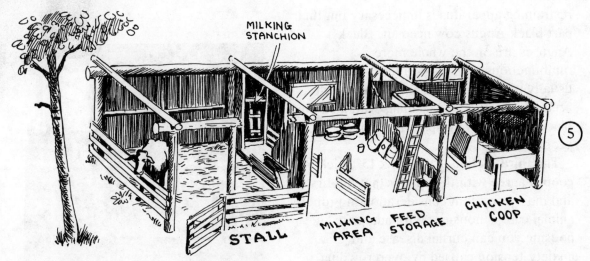

MILKING
STANCHION

⑤

STALL   MILKING
AREA   FEED
STORAGE   CHICKEN
COOP

need to come in out of the weather or when a calf has to be separated from the milking mother. Its simply a comfortable open area that protects them from direct precipitation and chilling winter winds. That's all the shelter cows really need. It is complete with a slatted feed trough that is fed from a convenient hole in the loft floor directly above it (plates 1-5).

The center section is split into two areas, a narrow 5' wide milking area just inside the doorway and a larger storage area for feed, grain,and other supplies. The milking area is a long corridor which leads to the milking stanchion in the rear. It is fine when you have a cow with a good reverse gear but would be a difficult space when dealing with one who insists on turning around to head out when finished milking. The stanchion is supported at top and bottom by horizontal 2 x 4s braced by three uprights. It is comprised of 6 boards nailed and bolted together and is suspended on a chain to make it mobile instead of rigid. Two 18" long horizontal pieces sandwich in the 4' uprights at the bottom. The upright to the left is stationary to these cross pieces, the one on the right is loosely bolted between them. Two 24" long horizontal pieces are also on either side of the uprights at the top. A loose bolt with double nuts holds the movable upper crossing boards to the left upright. This is the pivot point when the crossing boards are raised and lowered over the right

upright. This right upright then can be adjusted to either side of a bolt near the center of the crossing boards. When it is on the inside of the bolt there is a parallel space of 7" between the two uprights. This is just wide enough to hold the cow's neck and keep her from fidgeting and possibly kicking over the bucket during those movements (plates 6 and 7). For many cows such a

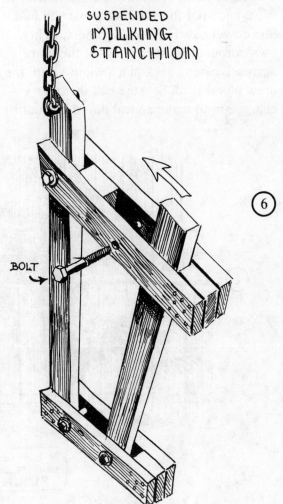

SUSPENDED
MILKING
STANCHION

⑥

BOLT

109

restraining apparatus is unnecesary but their part black Angus cow needs it. Black Anguses are on the whole more rambunctious than most breeds (they are usually raised as meat); and require such precautions. I've had dealings with a milking black Angus and sympathize with the problem.

⑦

The third section is the 15' x 15' chicken coop. I agree with the builder that the first and most important consideration in proper animal care is housing. With adequate housing you can curtail disease and anxiety-tension caused by overcrowding. Sufficient space for the birds is very important since there are so many of them sharing the same dwelling. Allow at least 4 square feet per bird, less than this amount causes havoc (remember what it was like back in the city?) It promotes cannibalism and pushes the weaker birds off the roosts. The so-called pecking order can be easily witnessed in an overcrowded hen house. It is easy to spot the weakest, most shy hen. She cowers away from the others, in her own corner. I've seen a few of the more aggressive hens peck at a "wimp" until they drew blood from her, then all the others charged in to make a meal out of her until I

pulled them off and gave her a separate cage so she could strengthen up.

This chicken coop is more than adequate size for as many chickens as the average smallholder would care to deal with. It is laid out very efficiently and care has been taken in the design of all the essentials. The builder feels that a chicken coop should be as spacious as one can afford to construct and be properly insulated from the cold. Chickens like a lot of room and they crave a lot of light. He put in a high watt unfrosted bulb to compensate for the short days of winter. The south wall has several large

⑧

BUK! BUK!

4 INCH DEEP
SAWDUST ON
FLOOR

110

 ⑨

 ⑩

windows of opaque plastic, screened with poultry netting so the birds won't peck through the plastic. Chickens should have adequate lighting so they can see their food because they identify their food by sight. They do best in a well-lit coop with good ventilation. A dull, gloomy coop makes the birds lethargic and nonproductive, but too much artificial lighting can cause a false molt which would result in the premature ending of that season's egg production. About 12 to 13 hours of light a day seems to give the best results.

Chickens thrive on a warm, dry environment where they have plenty of indoor scratching room and sufficient roost for the meditative evening hours. Their floor should be covered with some type of absorbant litter that can be kept as dry as possible. A 4″ layer of sawdust is used on this floor. It is turned quite frequently to mix the droppings in and provide a clean, dry surface. The hens even help in keeping their floor dry by scratching through layers of sawdust. This material is one of the best for litters because it is so absorbant and can be thrown on the garden after it has soaked all it can take. Only hemlock, birch, poplar, and cottonwood were used on this floor because these species break down the fastest and do not contain turpentine which could

be harmful to gardens in large quantities.

The two roosts go the length of the coop between the north and south walls. They are 18″ off the ground, both of equal height. Roosts should be on the same level when there are a lot of chickens in the coop to prevent excessive bickering over who gets the highest roosts . . . the old pecking order again (plate 8).

Controlled feeding and watering with minimal maintenance are other highlights of this chicken coop. The waterer provides an endless supply of the vital liquid without any maintenance. In fact it fills and regulates itself without demanding time and energy as one of the multitude of daily chores. There's so much routine that has to be contended with when dealing with animals that you want to get a break from it whenever possible. The watering system consists of a 5 gallon can with a ¾″ galvanized elbow intake that is soldered to the bottom center of the can and a length of 1″ plastic pipe which extends from a soldered nipple at bottom to about 1″ from the top of the can as a drain. It is capped with a perforated metal plate to prevent the birds from pecking at it. The upper edge of the can is lined with a split heater hose to keep the "dumb" chickens from cutting their necks when watering (plates 9 and 10). The water slowly

111

trickles up from an insulated pipe under the coop, entering the can through the elbow. The water then fills the can to the top of the plastic pipe and the unused water drains down the pipe, running out below the coop. This simple system works fine, doesn't freeze in the winter, and provides a constant, dependable flow of water year-round (plate 11).

The feeder consists of a lidded bin and a feed trough. The bin is 12" wide and 42" long with a sloped roof that is 38" tall at the highpoint. It is large enough to hold 200 pounds of feed and has a lifting lid to prevent the birds from entering it from above. It is enclosed with 1x boards except for the 4" at the bottom along the length. An 8" high feed trough rim, extending 3" out beyound the open bottom, surrounds the bin, providing a lip to keep the feed from uncontrollably spilling out. At first we had the trough enclosure only 4" high but soon doubled that height because the chickens could get in and peck out all the corn, leaving the oats and laying pellets. With the addition of another 4" board it is impossible for them to get down far enough to choose their favorite food, leaving the rest. Chickens should have a continuous food supply which should never run out. This is a

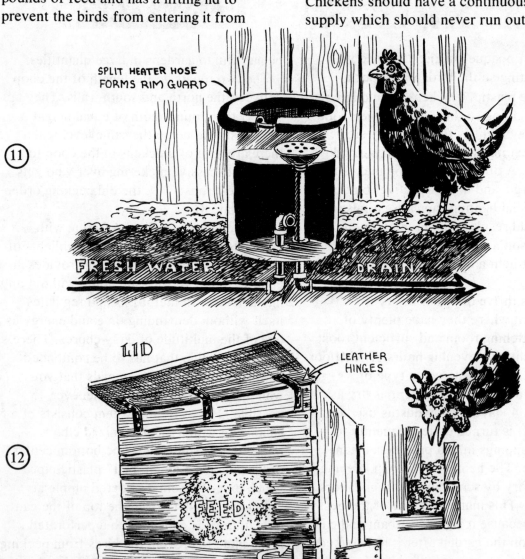

SPLIT HEATER HOSE FORMS RIM GUARD

⑪

FRESH WATER   DRAIN

LID

LEATHER HINGES

⑫

FEED

112

dandy feeder for the job, which requires filling only once every several days (plates 12 and 13).

Another interesting and efficient feature of this coop is the covered group-laying box, complete with large hinged door, ramp, and small entranceway. The hinged door is kept shut and is opened only when the eggs are being collected or when the box is being cleaned out. This keeps the laying hens in the dark, preventing them from eating their eggs or pecking at the others. All the eggs that are collected are whole and unbroken, proving that this method works well (plates 14 and 15).

An improvement to this design would be to include an outside collection setup so the eggs can be gathered without disturbing the temperature of the coop in the cold of winter (plate 16).

And of course, the chicken yard. At the south wall there is a small doorway (see plate 11) that leads out to the enormous chicken run. The larger the run the better it is for exercise and the greater the variety of food the birds will forage for themselves (saving you the expense of being sole provider). This southern-exposed yard is shaded by a forest of surrounding trees, keeping the direct midday sun off the area. Chickens become dull and inactive in the heat. The run is fenced with 7'-high stakes split from large cedars. They not only keep the chickens in but deter the prowling wildcats, bears, and coyotes which still claim their rights to this land that was once their domain.

Give chickens as much room as possible to grub up worms and scratch the dirt for goodies and you'll save plenty on the food bill and get the richest yellow-orange yolks you ever seen. And throw in your weeds,

13

14

15

16

garden trimmings, and compost . . . They'll love you for it all (plate 17).

Another quite interesting chicken set up is this double yard hen house and post-brooder quarters combination. The baby chicks are transfered to the post-brooder quarters when they can withstand the natural temperatures and do not have to be warmed by artificial heat. This length of time varies with different breeds and existing weather conditions. The chicks are housed in a small, tight, well built dwelling that insulates them from the cold and protects them from extreme weather conditions. It is small and cozy and is adequate for them during this growing stage when they want to spend a great deal of time outside curiously venturing around, exploring their exciting new world. This yard is a good size for them to get the excercise and exposure they need (plates 18 and 19).

The pullet yard is adjacent to the hen house, allowing the developing hens to become familiar with their future environment and also giving the existing hens a chance to have some preliminary contact before they share their coop with them. Just prior to the amalgamation both doors to the yards are left open so the hens can share a common foraging ground (plate 20). This cushions the shock of the move and acquaints them with each other. If the newcomers were just thrown in with the established residents there might be quite a battle. Its usually easier to share one's belongings with someone somewhat familiar rather than a complete stranger, especially when it is a home one is sharing.

The existing hen coop is rather small but adequate for up to 15 layers. It is a shed-roof dwelling with approximately 8' x 8' interior dimensions. The two large southern windows and the diamond-shaped west window allow in all the light that the coop needs and provides it with enough source will be required. The roosts are two crossing lengths of slab on upright braces. Behind them on the west wall is an entrance

(17)

(18)

to the yard. Just in front of the entrance is a small portable feeder (plate 21).

The nest area is divided into 4 partitioned laying boxes, 1' wide by about 14" deep, sufficient for abut 4 chickens each, one at a time. The high partitions prevent the neighboring layers from looking over and pecking at a nearby egg while they are laying their own (plate 22).

Such a chicken set up would be fine as a temporary shelter in the warmer months but the buildings should be more insulated to be warm and cozy during the long northern months. If the dwellings are not properly insulated to retain the birds' own body heat and the heat of their droppings, the egg production will go down considerably and the hen's will be lifeless and disgruntled. Keep them warm and dry and they'll return the favor by laying efficiently all winter long, greeting you with healthy activity instead of with droopy frowns.

(19)

(20)

116

Chapter Three

The All-Weather Stock Waterer

After one has been sufficiently exposed to the time-consuming chores which are omnipresent on the homestead, one begins developing the ingenuity it takes to design labor-saving devices such as this handy tool. "Let them water themselves", the homesteader stated as he explained his creation. He needed a stock waterer that was maintenance free, which supplied water to his cattle throughout the year, even in winter without freezing. He designed just that, consisting mostly of old items that were salvaged instead of discarded after their initial use. Never throw anything away if there is a remote possibility that it could ever be used again for something.

The stock waterer consists of an insulated tub with an intake and outlet system and a floating electric heater. The intake is a ¾″ galvanized pipe that tees up from the existing water line to just above an old drain hole in junk washing machine tub. The intake pipe was cemented in to the center of this hole to prevent leakage. The pipe is reduced in diameter shortly after it enters the tub. An elbow is connected to the top of this nipple to accommodate a float valve.

The float valve regulates the amount of water that enters the tub. As the cow drinks, the float valve opens, allowing water in until it automatically shuts off the intake (plate 1). In case the float valve system fails or a large amount of rain enters the tub, the excess water can escape through the 1½″ plastic pipe outlet tube that extends to just above the regulated water level. This outlet tube prevents the water from overflowing and possibly causing the whole system to freeze. It is fastened over a plastic fitting which is screwed into a larger galvanized hex reducer. The galvanized reducer is brazed into the center of the tub bottom where the agitator mechanism used to come through

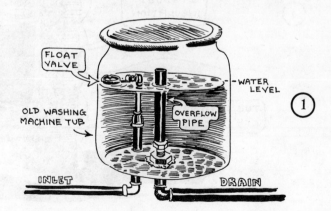

(plate 2). Fastened to the 2″ male end of the reducer, on the underside of the tub bottom, is a coupling which takes the male end of a plastic pipe fitting for the drain pipe. The drain pipe extends to well beyond the waterer so the overflow won't collect around it. The tub is mounted about 12″ above the ground on two 2 x 4s which are notched into the slab sides of a surrounding box. This is a convenient height for the animals. The 32″ x 32″ outer box protects the system from direct contact of the animals and shelters it from the elements. The inner system is also protected by sawdust insulation to prevent it from freezing. A plywood lid keeps the whole box covered. Only an 8½″ diameter hole is allowed in this lid for the cows to extract the water. This is sufficient for them (plates 3-5).

②

③

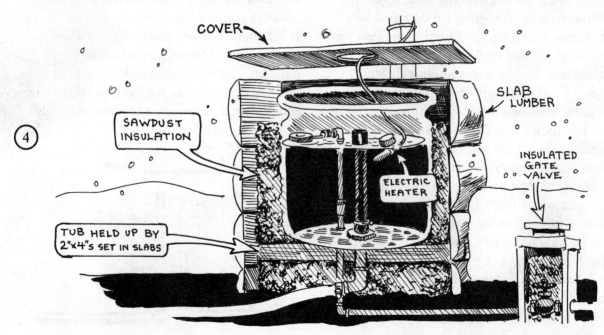

④

COVER

SLAB LUMBER

SAWDUST INSULATION

ELECTRIC HEATER

INSULATED GATE VALVE

TUB HELD UP BY 2″x4″s SET IN SLABS

The water inside the tub is heated with a small electric tube heater that is attached to a floater. This electric heater is submerged just below the water level, heating it up to the temperature cows like most, between 60 to 70 degrees. It maintains this water temperature, helping keep the whole system from freezing, even in below zero weather (plate 6).

The cows love the waterer. They go to it and just slurp until they get their fill, anytime they want instead of having to wait for someone to haul it. The average milking cow requries at least 15 gallons a day . . . thats a lot of water to be hauling for them in the middle of winter when most outdoor water systems are frozen solid (if they haven't been drained).

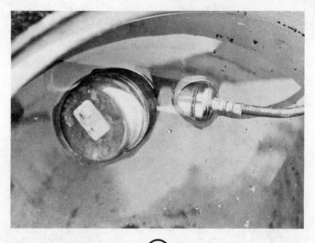

Chapter Four

Gates and Fences

A word about gates and fences. Gates and fences, like shelters, dwellings, and other homestead buildings, can exemplify the uniqueness and creativeness of the builder. There are no other rigid design rules except becoming familiar with "the nature of the animals" you are enclosing or keeping out. Wisdom of their individual capabilities, habits, and personalities will prevent hostile actions which usually result after an offender has butted, gnawed through, banged against and finally collapsed or otherwise negated the exhausting efforts of the designer.

Here are a few gates and fences which are outstanding examples of how detailed some builders are in creating an efficient and aesthetically pleasing environment, expressing their sensativity to the surrounding elements. Working with care and beauty inspires one to remain careful and beautiful.

Hand Hewn Gate

INWOOD '73

AUGER 3 HOLES IN POSTS

NAILESS FENCING

PUT IN RUNGS

INWOODP '75

STACKED

INWOOD '75

HEWN FLAT WITH A BROADHATCHET

DRILLED AND CHISELED

WHITTLED DOWN

LARGE DIAMETER AUGER HOLE

125

EASY CHAIR
FROM AN
UNUSUAL TREE

RIP IN
HALF WITH
SAW

CURVE OF SEAT
MADE WITH STRAIGHT WOOD PIECES

SECTION IV

Chapter One

Stoned

It isn't necessary to waste thousands of dollars on a shelter when most of the materials are right out in the open if people took the time to look for them. Utilizing timber and local stones, one could bypass the enormous expense of lumber and concrete in mass. After working with logs for awhile I couldn't even consider dimensional lumber as a main material for a shelter. It is too limiting and expensive, and is a huge drain on several natural resources. There have to be fallers to fell the trees, skidders to take them to the trucks, the trucks in turn drive them to the mill where the timbers are sawed into right-angled boards, wasting much of what remains. This process involves hundreds of thousands of people, huge machinery, and an enormous expenditure of the energies which we are quickly running out of. An alternative to this would be to find a piece of wooded land, thin out a few of the crowded trees and build with what you have. Sure, there is a lot of labor involved but at least you'd be working for yourself with materials that don't tend to suppress creativity as does dimensional lumber. I am against working with this material because of its rigidity. With it you are dealing with straight lines and right angles, you are not allowed to flow with the incredible array of shapes and contours that you can with natural timber.

And rock . . . so few people even notice the beauty and potential of this extraordinary and omnipresent material. And few realize how permanent and maintenance-free a stone foundation or wall can be if done right. But then again, stonework isn't for everyone, the same as finding a wooded lot and working with logs and natural timber isn't for everyone. It requires a dedication. One must really get into working with it and not worry about how long it takes to accomplish one's goal. But we should enjoy the act of creating beauty. People should be able to sit back and appreciate their efforts and not worry about spending too much time on a project. I helped a friend build his stone foundation for his home. It took us two years of working on it when we felt like it, and we never regret the time spent (plate 1).

I apprenticed with limestone, but give me the strength and finish of granite any day. It is the least affected by the weather, while limestone and sandstone are the most affected because they are so porous. Granite is not at all porous; in fact it has irregular seams and grains and is very difficult to split properly. So when working with it take this into consideration and always try to find the most square and angular rocks you can.

The durability of any stone wall will be determined by the quality of the joints between the stones. Incas, Egyptians, Greeks, and people of other ancient civilizations used dry-fit mason work of incredible precision. Many of their structures still stand. Depending on the climate, a variety of elements can attack stone. In colder climates water can seep between the joints or into cracks, freeze,

then expand and cause even huge rocks to shift or break. This is the most important factor to be conscious of in stone wall building. If you do not prevent this your wall will not last the first winter. Wind can also erode stone, or though it is a much slower process than is running or dripping water.

Before we got into figuring out the design and materials needed for my friend's house we chose a building site. Actually, the first site chosen was in a small clearing of usable soil. We soon decided against it since there was so little cleared area on his land. Why waste the part that has some topsoil when there was a huge hunk of bed rock nearby which couldn't be used. Besides, with bedrock we are guaranteed against shifting and erosion. What more natural complement to the bedrock could we offer but a foundation of granite stone? Our decision was simple. We trucked in several loads of beautiful, multicolored, granite rocks of all sizes and shapes. As we began working with them we soon realized the solidness of this material. We attempted shaping and splitting possible beauties with a two-pound mason's hammer. First we chipped a line across the

section we wanted to cut and went back over that line several times, patiently with the sharp end of the hammer, then trying to knock off the unwanted piece with the blunt end. The more you chip at the line the better chance your rock will split at that point. This is a process that works well with softer stone but was just too unpredictable with granite. We ended up breaking several pretty rocks into small chunks which were later used only to fill in behind the facing. But we did have a few rocks with small protruding knobs which were usually quite easy to knock off in this manner (plate 2 and 3).

There are other tools that would be useful in cutting stone. The stone chisel is excellent for scoring and cracking. With it one should have a sledge hammer light enough so it could be swung often without getting the builder overly tired.

Needless to say, we became more selective, gathering rocks that we did not have to shape. We searched for large rocks with at least two flat sides, preferably with a long flat face and a flat seat that was no more than 9″ in depth to fit our design specifications. We needed good sized rocks

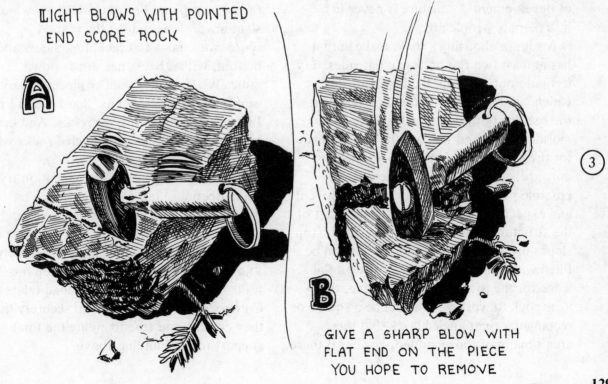

LIGHT BLOWS WITH POINTED END SCORE ROCK

A

B

③

GIVE A SHARP BLOW WITH FLAT END ON THE PIECE YOU HOPE TO REMOVE

but none heavier than what the two of us could lift. It was important to maintain a personal thing between us and the rocks without the interference of machines and tools to lift.

We found many rocks from a nearby construction site where they were blasting in a new road. Most of these rocks were exceptionally angular and proved to be ideal for the foundation walls, in fact they enabled us to build incredibly smooth, flat-faced walls that we could never have made without such material. We got into precision straightness because we were finding rocks that expressed that style. I'd never suggest this design unless there is optimum material at the builder's disposal . . . and plenty of time. This project took about 150 six-hour days to complete. Six hours is a full day of masonry work.

There is one basic preconstruction hint to keep in mind. Learn to select rocks as you go on trips to town, outings, or on visits to friends' homesteads. Be constantly on the lookout for possible rocks. Sometimes a simple trip up the road would take us hours but would reward us with several usable pieces. This is all part of the organic process of development . . . nature is never in a hurry—only people are.

Again, in choosing a rock, make sure it has at least two flat or nearly flat sides. Try to figure out the face, the broad surface which will be seen after the rock is set in; the seat, or bottom that will adhere to the mortar below; and the top, the resting place for the seat above. If the top slopes outward, forget it, because there is no possible way you can secure a rock above it and expect it to hold the immense weight of the structure it will be supporting. If the top slopes inward—fine—the space left can be filled with smaller pieces to provide a flat ledge for the rock above. Of course, the ideal rock to work with would be a square or rectangular right angled brick, but there aren't many of those around, besides if there

were you would become limited in the design. The next best rock would be one whose top slopes slightly back with sides angling into the backing (plate 4).

Gathering took us about 50 percent of the actual working time. We used 50 tons of material that was handled at least three times. Some rocks went through the whole history of the building without being used. So be wise and select the proper rocks in the beginning. It will make your job so much easier.

These are some of our names for several fo the usable rock shapes: (one can devise one's own nomenclature). A *piece of cheese* is a wedge shaped rock slice with a broad face, flat top and bottom, and sides which slant inward, meeting at the rear. A *wedgeback* has a flat face, top, sides, and bottom, with a back that slopes down radically. *Bulas* are smaller pieces of any usable shape (bula means ''hard bread'' in Jamaican). Brutus' are big rocks. And bricks are the very square, right angled rocks which are a dream to work with (plate 5).

When planning a wall or foundation try to avoid openings and corners as much as possible. Corners take five times as much attention because cornerstones are special brick-like shapes which should alternately ''tie back'' into both walls and keep the walls from falling out under a load (plate 6). Corners should be planned so securely that they could stand free to create the total support fo the building above.

ROCK TYPES

PIECE of CHEESE

WEDGEBACK

BULA

BRUTUS

BRICK

⑤

To the layperson the hardest part of working with rocks is interlocking the pieces. If you are not good at putting together jigsaw puzzles don't attempt rock masonry. Here is a test for those interested in checking their skill of visualizing in three dimensions. If you can figure out this problem you are ready to work with stone. If not, then you should take the time to familiarize yourself more with this media before attempting to build any supporting structure out of it.

You have up to three cuts to shape a 1″ round rod of any length so that it will pass through a 1″ square, a circle with a 1″ diameter and an isosceled triangle with a 1″ base and a height of 1″. The rod has to pass through each of these flat geometric designs perfectly, leaving no excess spaces and without destroying the shapes and designs in any way. You can practice on doweling or other material (plate 7).

Before beginning to set up the walls get to know the individual rocks as you would pieces of a jigsaw puzzle. Lay them flat on the ground, attempt to create designs with them . . . mix larger ones with smaller ones, triangular with square . . . visualize what

⑥

they would look like on the wall . . . see which ones complement others. Once you mortar them in place they are permanent . . . there is no changing them around. After

131

GIVEN AN INFINITE LENGTH OF **1** INCH DIAMETER ROD...

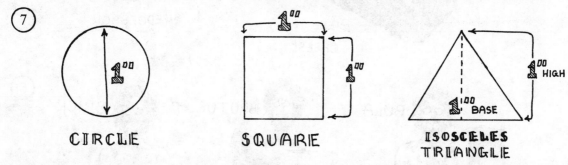

1"—{

YOU ARE ALLOWED UP TO **3** STRAIGHT CUTS TO CREATE A KEY SHAPE THAT WILL HAVE WITHIN IT THE FOLLOWING SHAPES...

⑦

1°° ↕

CIRCLE

1" ←→
1" ↕

SQUARE

1" HIGH
1°° BASE

ISOSCELES TRIANGLE

you are satisfied with a section, try setting it up as a dry wall to see how it stands. Which you are pleased with how each rock sets and balances among the others take that section down, making certain not to disturb the positioning and mortar them together. Remember, never hurry—be extremely patient. Sometimes it takes a long time for the ancient wisdom of these rocks to communicate, for they have been silent since long before any of us have been

around. But in time, they will express their own design that most complements them (plate 8).

At this time, before actually setting up much of the first wall, be sure to figure out all the openings, vents, electrical holes, drains, waterpipe positions, etc. It would be a near impossible task to install these necessities as an afterthought when the walls are set up. I'm sure I wouldn't want to attempt it.

A — LAY OUT PORTIONS OF WALL JIGSAW FASHION ON THE GROUND

⑧

B — TEST BY LAYING PATTERN IN UPRIGHT DRYWALL

C — MORTAR IN ROCKS

If you are not using a small cement mixer it is wise to make a mixing pad of some sort before you begin setting up the walls. Ours is a 2" to 3"-thick pad of hardened Portland cement, made from a 1.5 mixture. It is 6' in diameter, poured right on the ground. On this we mixed the mortar. The mortar is a mixture of 1 part manonry cement to 4 parts sand. The sand should consist of ⅔ fine river sand and ⅓ coarser sand. Since the adhesion of mortar to sand is critical a test should be made to make sure the sand is clean enough to use. Fill a quart jar ⅔ full with sand then add water to fill the jar. Shake it up and leave it for a few hours. If more than ⅛ inch of silt settles atop the sand, then it is too dirty to use without first washing; an arduous job requiring a large flow of water and hand turning of the dirty sand.

We first mixed the mortar and sand dry in the center of the pad, making certain that it all had a consistent mortar grey color. Then it was spread out over the pad, drilled with a fine spray of water, and was all brought back to the center and worked, gradually adding more water, until it had the desirable sticky, clinging (*cloy*) consistency (plate 9). Do not put in any more lime to achieve this stickiness. Masonry cement has enough lime already mixed in with it—anymore will weaken the strength of the mortar. Also, be sure that the mortar is never richer than the 1.4 mixture. The more excessively rich the mixture is the larger the coefficient of expansion, thus the greater will be the chance that it will crack and shrink.

Starting anywhere along the wall with the first course of stone, we worked toward the corners. This is because the cornerstones are usually the hardest to stand up freely. Having the wall next to the corner already complete aids in supporting the cornerstones. However it is often necessary to "juggle" (curse and coax) the penultimate rock that fits next to the cornerstone as the corner is a fixed point and can only go in one position (see plate 6).

The outer dimensions of the foundation are 20' x 26'. To figure out the rectangle we

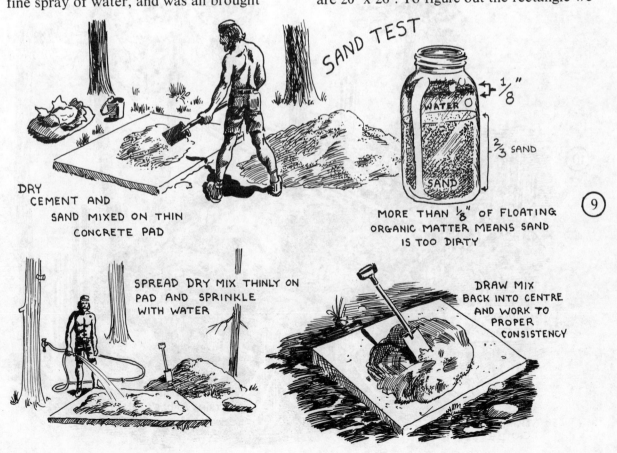

SAND TEST

DRY CEMENT AND SAND MIXED ON THIN CONCRETE PAD

1/8"

WATER

2/3 SAND

SAND

MORE THAN ⅛" OF FLOATING ORGANIC MATTER MEANS SAND IS TOO DIRTY

⑨

SPREAD DRY MIX THINLY ON PAD AND SPRINKLE WITH WATER

DRAW MIX BACK INTO CENTRE AND WORK TO PROPER CONSISTENCY

simply made a scale drawing and found the length of the diagonals from opposing corners. That length was converted to actual size. The exact center was marked and the crossing diagonal was also staked. A 20′ side was measured and the stakes were adjusted accordingly. A right angling 26′ side was then checked and a string was placed around the perimeter. The corners could be confirmed by running a 6′ line along one side and an 8′ line along the intersecting side. If the diagonal of those two lines is 10′ then the corner is a right-angled square corner.

Once we found the perimeter of the rectangle we set up the vertical templates or upright guides to make certain our walls would be plumb and straight. We used two template frames at each corner, which consisted of 2 parallel vertical boards spaced the width of the wall (18″) apart and were put in a couple feet directly beyond the end of each wallface to allow us enough space to maneuver the heavy stone without colliding into them. They were rested on the ground

and braced securely to stakes, stumps or trees in such a way that they would remain exactly in place in case we bumped or fell into them. We even left some trees around to brace these posts. After they were secured in place, two horizontal strings, about 2′ apart vertically were extended from template to opposing template. The strings were both plumb above the face of the wall they guided and could be moved up as the courses were laid. The templates and lines were a headache to work with because we were always becoming entangled with them as we were struggling with the heavier stones. But never attempt a structural support such as this foundation without such guides because you can't do it (plate 10 and 11).

The walls are 18″ thick all around, consisting of an outer face of no more than 9″, a Portland cement and "bula" backing, a vapor barrier of ½″ styrofoam, an inner wall backing, and an inside wallface. The two faces were set up first. The styrofoam was

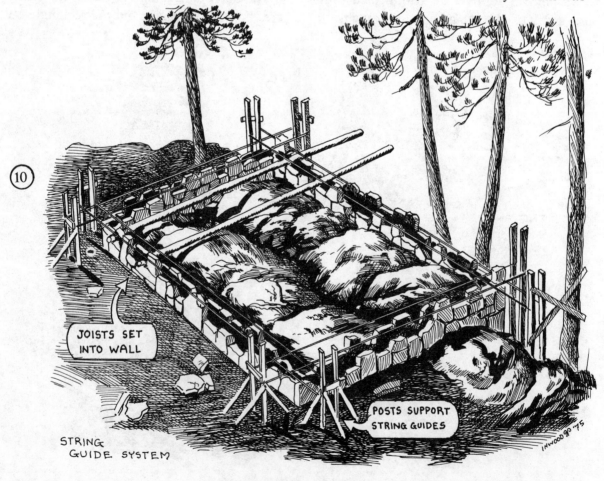

⑩

JOISTS SET INTO WALL

POSTS SUPPORT STRING GUIDES

STRING GUIDE SYSTEM

INWOOD 90 '75

then placed in the trench created by the opposing faces and pieces of heavy gauge wire were poked through the styrofoam on approximately a 2′ grid. Each bent end was sunk into the fresh cement backing between the inside and outside face creating a tie for

DETAIL OF STRING LEVEL

(11)

TOP AND BOTTOM LINES ARE PLUMB

the two walls. The backing mixture was poured on either side of the lapped styrofoam sheets before the surrounding masonry had a chance to completely set up, allowing it all to "monolithically" tie together, usually about one hour after doing the faces (plate 12).

NOTE: On rainy or very humid, damp days it takes as much as three times as long for mortar to set up, depending on the moisture content in the air. Be extremely careful when attempting to lay stone during a light rain because the heavy moisture content will cause the mortar to sag and droop under the weight of the stone.

Styrofoam insulation or "styroshit," as we began calling it, is brittle and cracks quite easily but has proven to be an excellent thermal and vapor barrier. This vapor barrier prevents the movement of warmth and humidity from inside to outside. If this was

OUTSIDE WALL

BENT REINFORCING WIRE PENETRATES STYROFOAM TO TIE THE 2 RUBBLE AND CEMENT FILLED SECTIONS TOGETHER

LARGE STYROFOAM SHEETS ARE LAPPED WHERE THEY MEET

(12)

STYROFOAM VAPOR BARRIER

RUBBLE AND CONCRETE FILL

INSIDE WALL

not prevented the warmth would meet the snow, ice, or frost on the outer wall which would then seep back into the wall, possibly refreezing and causing the wall to crack.

If moisture were allowed to penetrate through the walls, splitting and cracking of the mortar would also eventually occur. We installed the styrofoam mainly as a thermal insulation because stone has a very low *R factor* (18″ of rock provides less insulation then 3½″ of fiberglass). But even with the thermal barrier some cold still manages to come through the walls during the winter. So ½″ of styrofoam didn't prove to adequately solve this problem. If we used 1″ of styrofoam I think this chill factor would have been greatly reduced. Besides being thicker, that size is much easier to handle and it wouldn't have cracked so readily as we worked with it. We are not advocating the use of "Styroshit". You can use anything that proves to be a good vapor barrier with insulative value. You can even fill garbage bags with old cardboard or waxed cartons for this purpose.

Before going on to the next course of stone be sure to clean off with a steel brush the rocks which were just set in place. If you wait much longer than within 2 or 4 hours afterwards the mortar will have set up on the faces, thus making it necessary to employ an acid chemical (muriatic acid) to remove the dry mortar. This chemical is a costly, odorous, and unpleasant alternative to taking time as you go to clean off your stone. Besides, the cleaning process will give you a little time between courses to sit back and appreciate your work. Many such breaks are imperative when indulging in any creative endeavor, especially one that will be so permanent. Also, the best time to do the pointing or cutting back is just before the mortar completely sets up. Pointing is the process of trimming the excess mortar that sticks out between the joints of stone (*snots*). There are several styles of pointing. Some masons prefer a deeper look. This provides rich, full shadowed joints and is

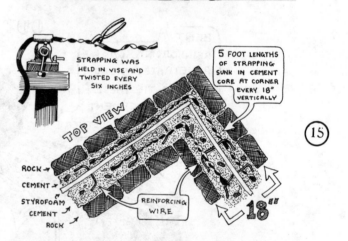

best for contrasting the dimensions of the rocks. It also weatherproofs the mortar by cutting it back, sheilding it with overhanging stone (plate 13).

There is a noticeable difference between the lower portion of the north wall where we started and the upper area of that wall. It looks much more raggedy and rough than the others. We got progressively better with experience, concentrating more on the finish as we felt more comfortable with the mortaring (plate 14).

Before taking the corners up again we reinforced them with twisted strapping bands. These bands were 5′ in length, extending at right angles 2½′ in either side from the corner, one on each side of the styrofoam. They were laid in at vertical intervals of about 18″. The twisting provided them with much more bonding strength, making them immovable within the concrete (plate 15). We searched through several building supply and hardware stores to find a material for this purpose but everything was so outrageously expensive it was prohibitive to use. Outside of one store we found a pile of strap-metal shipping bands. We were told we could have them. We searched for more in other places, including the local mill and soon brought home all we needed for free.

The walls went up to about the 3½″ level where we inserted the floor joists, cellar vent openings, and door frames. This height was chosen because the high point of the bedrock extended 3′ higher then the low point (plates 16 and 17) and we wanted to allow another 6″ to bring the joists above the ground. The joists were spaced at 24″ intervals, extending from a short distance out past the front wall to 8′ beyond the rear wall as supports for an outside porch area (plate 18 and 19). These longer ends will be sheltered from the direct weather by the porch, but the short stubs in the front, east wall have no protection, they were left exposed (plate 20). If we were to put them in

again we would just extend the front ends to meet the styrofoam, this way they would have a vapor barrier protection and still have plenty of support from the 9″ inner wall section.

There is no creosote or other preservative around the joists where they come in contact with the mortar and concrete. We didn't feel it necessary since they are of durable cedar and we don't have to worry about getting capillary action from the soil beneath because we have a floor of bedrock. But even if the joist ends rot in time, which they are bound to do anyway, our children or grand children or whoever will be around then can just pound them out and insert replacements, trimming them where they meet the walls for proper fit.

Below the floor level we put in a 6″ vent on the east and west walls to allow the warm air to escape from below the floor. These vents were formed with 6″ stovepipe pieces which were left in. Earlier we put in

BEDROCK   INWOOD '75

openings at the bottom of these walls to allow the cold air to come in and circulate through the basement. This air flow provides proper ventilation and prevents mildew and vapor build up (see plate 21). This will probably be a great root cellar once we complete the house.

The door jambs were also put in at this level. We used uncreosoted railroad ties for this purpose because they were durable and available. They have spikes driven and bolts drilled into their sides to tie into the masonary and join them to the wall logs. These frames were made plumb and they acted as a guide for the new inside corners of the rock work (plates 21 and 22).

After the frames came the waterpipe opening. This was put in above the floor, in the west wall. For this we just sank a piece of ½″ galvanized pipe which we could later deal with (plate 23). Be sure to plan all openings before you begin construction because there is no way to accommodate them once the walls have set up.

We slowly raised the walls a bit higher, carefully considering the design of each as we went. By now we got emotionally envolved with some of the rocks, we handled them so much. But many of them just didn't sem to fit anywhere. Up to this point we could use whatever size rock we could lift into place, the larger the better, but now we had to prepare for the sill logs, which meant narrowing down our supply to the special shapes needed, without disturbing our design.

The long sill logs which rested above the east and west walls were set in place on the center of the wall and held there with braced uprights. The shorter side logs were round-notched onto them. This meant that

the two long walls had to be raised to one height and the side walls had to extend a few inches higher to accommodate the sills above them (plate 24).

It was a difficult, painstaking operation to fit the last courses under the logs. But at least we had a permanent horizontal line to work up to instead of an estimated line that could not duplicate the exact contour of the log. The styrofoam barriers were set in so they touched the bottom center of the sills, then we experimented with several rocks until we could find the right combination for the first outer wall. We set up the outer walls first, then filled in the backing from inside. This was a tricky manuever which I'll explain in turn. After we figured roughly out the last course of an outer wall, spikes were driven into the bottom of the sill that rested over it. We were careful to position the spikes so they would not interfere with the last course of rocks, but would extend out into the mortar and cement instead (plate 25). The outer wall rocks were then mortared into place. Now the tricky part. The styrofoam was bent back, which sometimes broke it, and the rubble and concrete for the outer wall facing was shoveled in and tamped hard around the sill log to provide a solid seat for it (plates 26 and 27).

The styrofoam was then bent into vertical position, and the last courses of the inner face were carefully dry fitted. The spikes were driven in and a few of the top course

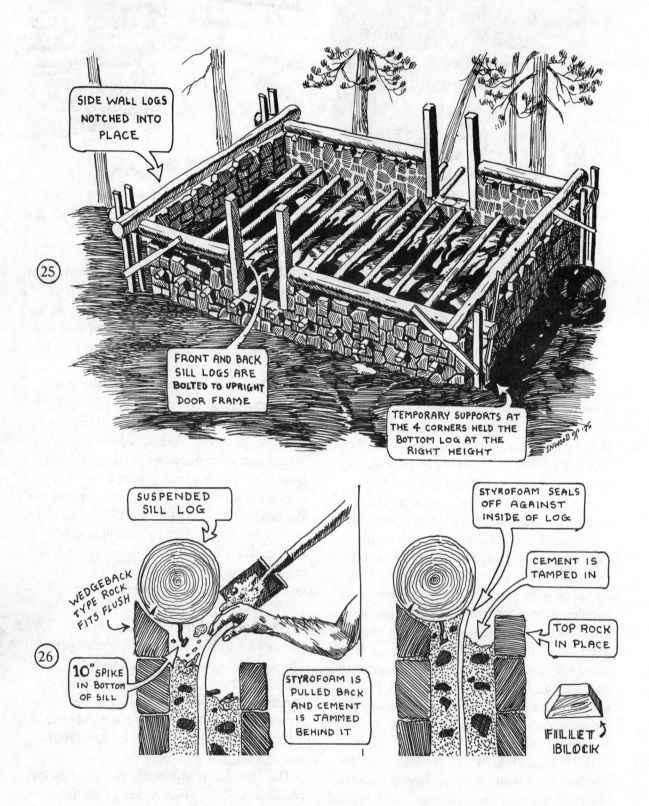

140

(27)

SCREWS COUNTERSUNK THRU LEDGE BOARD AND DOWN INTO FILLET BLOCK

FILLET

CROSS SECTION

(28)

WHERE WOOD AND STONE ARE TOGETHER HAVE AN OVER-HANG SO THAT SHADOW CREATES ILLUSION OF A CLEAN EDGE

rocks were mortared. The rubble and cement backing was then tamped in behind the face and a few more rocks were set in. This process continued until the last rock was placed in. Then on to the next wall.

Before finishing the ledges above the inner walls, we sunk "fillets" or small wedge-shaped pieces of wood, into the mortar to provide nailing blocks for the wood pieces which will cover them (plates 28 and 29). These wooden ledge covers will be useful caps, providing needed shelf space. They will also shadow the very top of the inner stone wall and give it a contrast of timber with stone.

As you can see, our careful, meditative approach proved to be not in vain. We have succeeded in constructing not only a useful, strong, foundation, but an aesthetically beautiful monument that should still be standing long after we are all dead and gone. I wish you could see the richness and array of colors in these rocks. They are so pleasing to look at that I can sit and trip on

them for hours, and I do just that sometimes. This is the feeling I want everytime I complete a project, how about you?

ANSWER TO PROBLEM:

First cut is angled from dead center of circle, 1″ long until it meets either side. Second cut begins at same dead center spot and angles out to other side, also being 1″ long. Third cut severs angled end from remaining rod (plate 30).

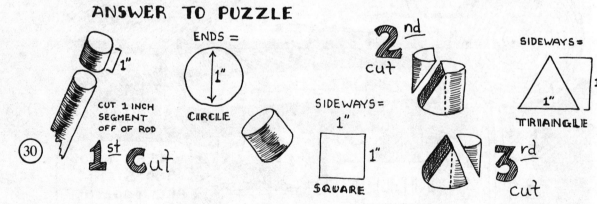

142

Chapter Two

Starchy Arches

Along the tiny unpaved roads that surround our little bakery where there are many dwellings and homesteads which have been carefully constructed out of the available materials that we are so lucky to be endowed with in this area. Some make good use of the forest, some make good use of the stone, some combine the two materials to put a bit of beauty around them. So I wanted to contriubte to this beauty by adding a little of my own heritage into the bakery. And what more Scottish building material is there than stone.

I had a design in my head for a dream house in the round, built out of stone. I made a little model of that round house and put in a few round windows. I still haven't made it a reality and probably won't for a while so I decided to give the bakery touch of my dreams by making the kitchen front out of rock with arched windows (plate 1).

I constructed the building, using a post-and-beam style, leaving the front kitchen wall open between the 6' spanning posts. I wanted to give a contrast to the logs and stuccoed exposed beams which comprise the rest of the face, and I wanted this contrast to be stone. Though I hadn't really worked much before with stone I

knew enough principles to get me started. First, I made sure the bottom course was the thickest and wide enough to support the weight that was to be put on it. Second, I made certain that the outside face was very straight and plumb. I knew my upright posts were plumb so I nailed 1 x 6 boards across the posts, all the way up the front. This was my outside form. I then collected as many of the straight, flat face rocks as I thought I needed. This was quite easy since the nearby lake shore is full of such angular and extremely colorful rocks.

I piled the rocks jigsaw puzzle style on top of each other, making sure the flattest side faced the front and the bigger rocks were at the bottom. I tried the rock that fitted in best, then mortared it in, giving each course a chance to set a bit by going along the whole wall before beginning another course. For this purpose I made my own mixture of Portland cement and lime. Pre-mixed cement is like cake mixes—if you want to buy it premixed you have to pay for it. I mixed two parts lime to one part Portland cement and added nine parts of sand. This made a good workable mortar. Be careful when you use the lime because it burns your fingers. I worked with rubber gloves to prevent the lime from burning me.

The stone wall was built in this manner for about 30″ in height. At that point I wanted to put in my windows. To prepare a sill for them, the mortar was formed and flattened above the rocks. This way bolts to hold the sill boards in place could be sunk into the mortar instead of into the rocks. It is much easier to sink bolts into wet mortar than into granite rocks (plate 2).

The trouble with using forms that cannot be easily removed before the mortar has a chance to set is that mortar, no matter how careful your are, builds up around the rock. This leaves ugly clumps in the joints that cannot be cleaned off because the mortar has already hardened by the time the form is taken off. If a person were to use removable forms here this problem could be remedied (plate 3).

Because the building is post and beam, none of the structural wieght is on the rock wall, it is all on the outlining posts. This gave me freedom to experiment with the windows. My fondness for round and oval architecture inspired me to devise a way to put arched windows into the front wall. This method actually worked quite well. First I took a sheet of 4 x 8′, ½″ plywood and laid it on the floor. I found the exact center along the length and drove a nail in at that

② UPRIGHT STRUCTURAL POSTS

FORM BOARDS NAILED TO INSIDE OF POLES

CONCRETE SILL

6 FEET LONG
6 INCHES WIDE 4 INCHES HIGH

BOLTS SUNK INTO CEMENT

point. Then I attached one end of a 4' piece of string to that nail and the other end to a pencil. I drew an arch, starting from one corner to the middle of the side opposite the nail, and down to the other corner. I didn't like that shape because it was too wide at the ends, but the height was just fine. The nail was moved 1' closer to the apex of the arch and the string was shortened to 3'. I drew that arch and left the bottom foot beyond the nail on either side straight to make an elliptical arch instead of a half round (plate 4).

After the shape was figured out I cut it out with a skilsaw and finished the edges with a hand plane. I then took a thin strip of 3"-wide veneer and tacked it along the edge of the half-oval form, off-centering it to one side to affix the window framing to it. I felt

it wise to make the framing now and attach it to the form and casing. This would give the form, casing, and frame additional strength, tying it all together as one interlocking unit to hold it all in place (plate 5).

1 x 1" strips were used for the window

③

CUT FROM 4 FOOT × 8 FOOT ½" PLYWOOD SHEET

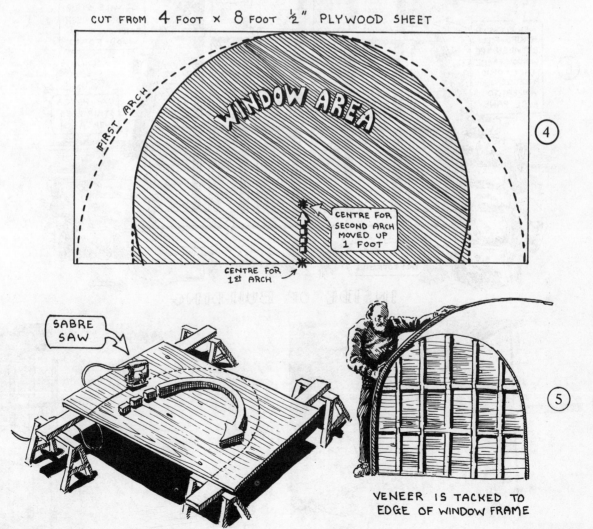

④

FIRST ARCH

WINDOW AREA

CENTRE FOR SECOND ARCH MOVED UP 1 FOOT

CENTRE FOR 1ˢᵗ ARCH

SABRE SAW

⑤

VENEER IS TACKED TO EDGE OF WINDOW FRAME

frames. This framework is comprised of five upright pieces of varying lengths following the arch. The outside edges of these uprights were dadoed ¼″ on either side to provide laps for the 12″ x 16″ window panes, leaving about a ½″ tongue in the center to hold the panes in place. They were also grooved strips that interlocked with them to frame the panes. These 12″ horizontal strips were rabbeted on the outside edge and a sill strip was nailed in place across the bottoms of the upright pieces. Holes were drilled 1′ apart around the veneer border for stove bolts which would be sunk into the setting mortar to hold the strips in place around the window frame. The spring tension of the bent strips would aid to keep it in place after the form was removed because the constant compression against the rocks would prevent it from coming out. Each of these 3 window forms were made ready before going any further (plates 6 and 7).

The 2 x 6 sills were bolted over the formed mortar seats below the window

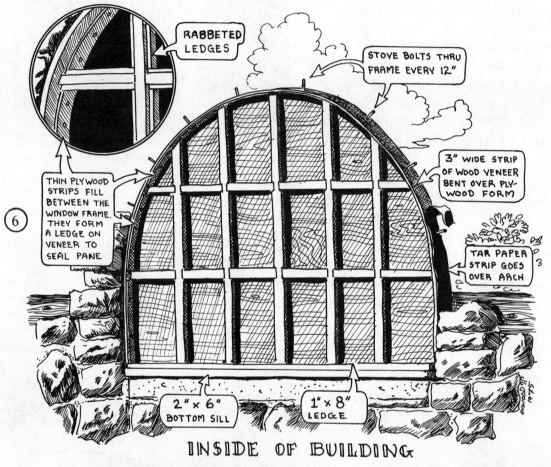

INSIDE OF BUILDING

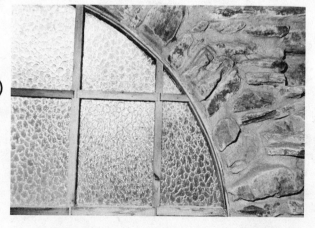

⑨

⑩

opening and the completed window forms were placed above them, with the plywood facing the inside. A few temporary nails were then attached to the outside form to keep them in place and the rockwork was mortared around the arches all the way up to the 2 x 6 wall plate above. The only tricky part of this whole operation was slanting the rocks above the arches and still making the design blend in with the other stones. It all worked to my satisfaction. After the mortar set for awhile the plywood window forms were removed. Care was taken not to disturb the veneer and 1 x 1 window frames. The outside forms were also taken off at this point and I got to see the mortar-clumped rocks. Oh well, at least I don't have to look at that face all day. I was very careful to trim the mortar between the inside rocks and clean them off, leaving a nice finish on the rocks. After all, I will be looking at them several hours each day as I prepare the baked goods for the upstairs bakery (plates 8-10).

I used opague, corrugated plastic instead of glass for the windows to keep out the glare and because I didn't want to go through the trouble of cutting rounded glass. It is hard enough to cut straight glass, let alone getting fancy with it. These windows were held on the inside with curved slats that follow the arch. They were nailed along the veneer strip, which covered the bolts and holes (see plate 7). The windows were puttied on the outside. Putty did not work so well because it did not properly adhere to the plastic (plate 11).

A question might come up about the insulative value of this rock wall in a cold area such as this. I realize that stone is not a good insulator but I haven't been uncomfortably chilly at all. Once the ovens are going the ktichen remains quite warm and what little heat that might escape through the stone is welcome to do so.

I am quite pleased with the way the rock wall came out. It has even temporarily satisfied my desire for a round stone house with round windows.

⑪

Chapter Three

Slip Form Cellar and Sauna

Since the surrounding hillsides, lakes, and streams are so richly endowed with beautiful mulitcolored stones with stripes, and other designs, I thought it only natural to use this available material in the foundation walls of our house. In searching around the lake shore I found hundreds of flat-faced stones that were smoothed to a polish and washed clean by the flowing water. I gathered several loads and trucked them to the building site. Then I spent some time figuring out just how I was going to create walls that had inside surfaces of the clean, flat-faced rocks. (plate 1). I knew that I had to either attempt building a wall without a form or figure out some type of sectioned form which I could periodically remove to clean the concrete off the rock faces before it dried and covered the rocks with permanent ugly stains. Well, because of my

①

lack of experience with stone masonry, building a foundation without forms was out ot the question. I soon figured out a slip-form system that solved the dilemna. It is a simple design, consisting of a long continuous 1x form, 22″ high, braced by upright 2 x 4s every 24″. This is about the maximum height the forms should be for

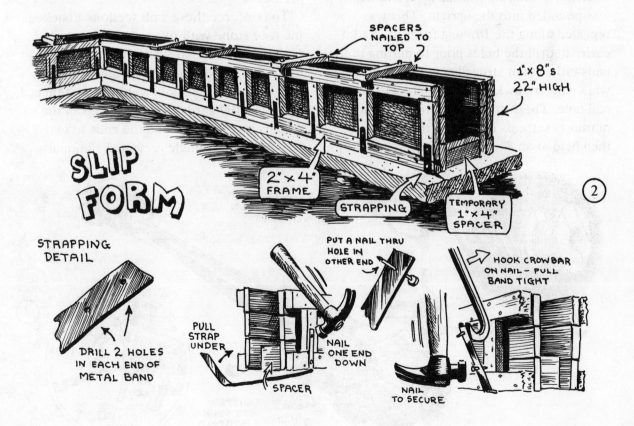

SPACERS NAILED TO TOP

1"x 8"s 22" HIGH

SLIP FORM

2"x 4" FRAME

STRAPPING

TEMPORARY 1"x 4" SPACER

②

STRAPPING DETAIL

DRILL 2 HOLES IN EACH END OF METAL BAND

PULL STRAP UNDER

SPACER

PUT A NAIL THRU HOLE IN OTHER END

NAIL ONE END DOWN

NAIL TO SECURE

HOOK CROWBAR ON NAIL — PULL BAND TIGHT

each pour, to allow easy tamping of the mortar around the rocks.

The 16″ wide by 4″-high footings were poured first, and after they dried, we set up the first course of forms, one on either side of the proposed 8″ wall. We were attempting to have only an inside stone face. The outside face would be of the rubble-concrete filler that backs the stone face and cements it in place. Straps of banding steel were cut long enough to extend beyond the sides of the form uprights, holding both sides in place around the 8″ long, 1 x 4 spacer blocks. These blocks kept the forms the right distance apart and would later be knocked out. Two holes, 1″ apart were drilled through an end of the straps; one for the nail that will be stretched by the crow bar and one for the nail that will secure the forms together. Two holes were also drilled in the other end of the strap, and that end was nailed to the outside form. The strap was then brought underneath to the far side of the inside form. A nail was put in the first hole for the crowbar to grip against and stretch the strap tight while a second nail was pounded into the upright. This was repeated along the 16′-long form. It is a lot easier to drill the holes prior to putting in the nails rather than struggling with the crowbar while you are awkwardly attempting to start a nail hole. These straps are removed while mortar is setting. The top of the form was then held at an 8″ width with another set of spacers that were nailed in above. Be certain that the forms are absolutely plumbed before the pour because you don't have to be out much in 22″ to throw the whole wall off. When you feel that the forms are plumb, secure them with diagonal braces so they do not move during the tamping. It would be wise to set up some kind of plumb vertical brace the length of the wall to provide a guide for the stacked forms. I wish I had taken precautions, it would have saved a lot of time, rather than having to plumb each set of forms individually (plate 2).

When the bottom forms are set up securely on your footings, put about 2″ of pretty soupy concrete into the bottom of the formed space and begin setting in a line of wall stones. Be sure to jamb them tight against the inside form with pieces of rubble rock to prevent the soupy concrete from getting in front of the face of the wallstone. This well create a flat stone face wall and make your cleaning task much easier. Then just set in some more wall stones and pour in the concrete-rubble mixture until the forms are filled.

To reinforce these wall sections I backed the face stone with two runs of wire *rebar* per pour. This rebar was homemade, utilizing a roll of 8-guage spooled wire. The wire came off the spool 8 strands at a time. I unwound 100 yards, trying to keep all the strands together as I tied the ends to two vehicles. One vehicle remained stationary

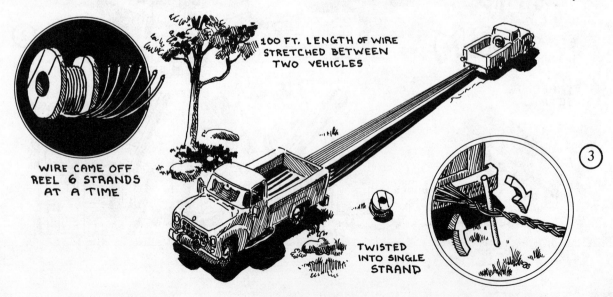

WIRE CAME OFF REEL 6 STRANDS AT A TIME

100 FT. LENGTH OF WIRE STRETCHED BETWEEN TWO VEHICLES

③

TWISTED INTO SINGLE STRAND

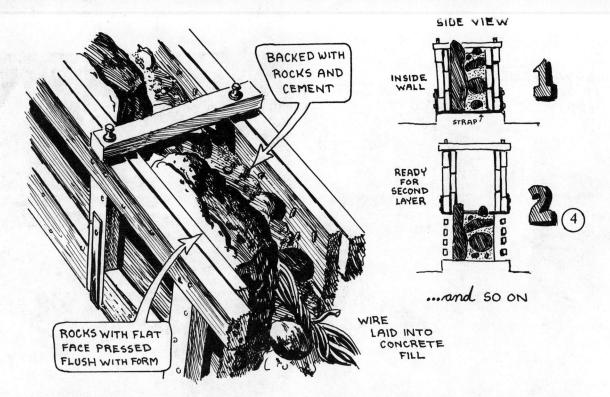

BACKED WITH ROCKS AND CEMENT

ROCKS WITH FLAT FACE PRESSED FLUSH WITH FORM

SIDE VIEW

INSIDE WALL

STRAP

1

READY FOR SECOND LAYER

2 ④

...and SO ON

WIRE LAID INTO CONCRETE FILL

while the other moved forward, putting tension on the strands. Then I stuck a piece of wood through 4 of the strands and twisted it all together. It stayed tightly entwined and didn't even unravel when I cut it. The rebar went completely around each pour and the ends were spliced together with smaller pieces so they all remained securely in place.

Be sure to leave a few wall stones sticking up along the length of the top of the forms so the next course of forms have something to grip on. And be very careful that they don't go out past the face or they will throw the wall out of plumb.

Tamp rigorously throughout each pour so the soupy mixture can work its way between all the face stones, otherwise there will be a lot of "beehive" holes in the face. I just keep poking the mortar with a stick, pushing it into every crevice. Wherever necessary I also tuck it into narrow openings with my fingers or with a pointing trowel, making sure no spaces are left unfilled. I recommend wearing a pair of rubber gloves for this operation because the wet mortar is very abrasive (plates 3 and 4).

The mixture I used was two parts Portland cement to five parts sand. Even without the lime the mortar adhered well to the clean

rock, and was less expensive. The strength of concrete is not in the amount of cement but in the amount of water used. The soupier it is the better it all mixes. But you don't want it too soupy or it will leak out of the forms. Coarse sand and gravel is ideal for the rubble-concrete behind the face, but for a smooth facewall finish you need a finer mixture. I put in at least one shovel full of blue clay with every mix for a finer consistency.

After the walls were left to dry for about 12 hours the inside form was carefully removed while the mortar was still green but firm enough to not slump. This is the best time to clean the cement stains off the rocks. I scrubbed them thoroughly with a wire brush, then hosed them off really well. This method is a lot easier than having to later treat them with muriatic acid, a highly toxic and dangerous chemical that eats through the cement. Just think what it could do to your hands.

We waited 48 hours between pours to give the lower section a chance to set up a bit. Don't wait much longer than this or you will not get a good bond between the courses. The following courses of forms were held together in the same manner as the first,

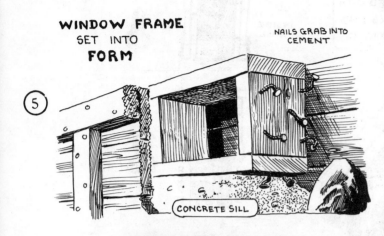

WINDOW FRAME
SET INTO
FORM

NAILS GRAB INTO CEMENT

CONCRETE SILL

⑤

⑥

⑦

⑧

using the protruding wall rocks from the section below to give them something to grip to. The courses went to the top of the side and rear walls and to the window openings in the front wall. Four 18″ x 28″ windows were placed along that wall to bring in the morning light. To ensure a good bond between the 8″ window frames and the mortar, 4″ *ardox* nails were pounded into the frames. The frames were then set into the forms, and the surrounding stones and masonry was set in (plates 5 and 6).

⑨

152

SAUNA

Though a wall like this is very beautiful it is very difficult to make it entirely water tight. I used a thick coat of block foundation coating, but it still leaks periodically. Actually, the only time it does leak is when someone leaves the hose running alongside the wall. This problem could have possibly been remedied if drain tile were used just outside of the footing to catch the excess runoff. Instead, I used only loose gravel, hoping that would be enough.

Though 8″ of stone and mortar or 8″ of concrete have an insulation factor equal to only ¾″ of wood, the basement remains very toasty throughout the winter because the furnace is located in that area. The only place it loses heat is through the windows and the upper 2′ of the front wall that sticks up above gound level.

The stones below ground level actually help to keep the basement warm for several hours after the furnace fire goes out since they retain the heat so well. Because of this factor I decided to construct a Sauna at the

153

southeast corner of the basement. The sauna area gets lots of light from two front wall windows and remains warm for a long time after the cook stove fire dies out. The only problem is it takes a long time for the fire to get the rocks warm. But when it does, you can just throw some water on them and really get the place steaming. But part of the hassle of getting the sauna warm enough is the flat-surfaced, small fireboxed cookstove we use (plate 7). We are going to take that out soon, sacrificing its flat surface which we use to put rocks on for additional steam, for a more efficient air tight heater that would throw off a lot more heat.

The sauna compartment is about 6′ x 8′, consisting of two 1 x 4 tongue-and-grove cedar slat bathing benches. The lower one is 18″ above the concrete floor and the other is 18″ above it. Both are held up by 2 x 4″ horizontal braces at the inner cedar wall and 2 x 4 uprights at the outer wall. The ceiling is of 1 x 4 cedar with a raised section above the windows to provide indirect lighting (plates 8-10).

The sauna works well, except that it takes so long to heat. It is really convenient to have such a relaxing, meditative, healing and bathing place right in the house, with a nearby shower area to cool off in (plate 11). And the entire basement, though it is an enclosed secondary cellar space with minimal direct lighting, is rather comfortable and private. It is an excellent space for a guest or for just getting away from the mainstream of the house activity. The colorful exposed stones tone down that dingy, cold feeling of most cellar spaces (plates 12-14).

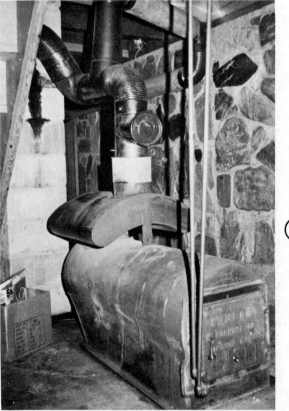

HEAT EXCHANGER

HOT WATER   COLD WATER

CONVERTED COAL FURNACE WITH HOT WATER COIL

(14)

COPPER PIPE HOT WATER COIL

BED OF SAND

Chapter Four

Putting Metal Through Changes

The basic function of a forge is to heat up iron so it can be formed and shaped. It should be able to contain a fire that is hot enough to get steel or iron to the workable temperature, using coal, coke, or some such fuel. It is best to use a soft or bituminous coal that is relatively free from impurities. The impurities when heated up to malleable form will combine together to make clinkers which eventually clog up the air intake and have to be removed. A commercial blacksmith coal is preferred to regular hard coal.

Coal alone is not enough to heat the metal to the proper workable temperature. You need an oxygen source to supplement the fuel. I use a hand blower to regulate the air. The hand blower is attached to the right of the top edge of the 20″ split rim wheel drum which I use for the bowl or hearth of the forge (plate 1). The air from the blower is directed down and then over to the center of the forge, below the bowl, then blows up through a *tuyer*, into the drum. The tuyer is the perforated steel plate at the bottom center of the drum which allows a controlled amount of air into the bowl or drum.

The drum is raised to 32″ or table height and is supported by an 8″ core pipe that extends up from the base. This height is comfortable to work with and is great for tool placement. The rock work was mortared together with a mixture of gravel screened through a ¼″ mesh screen, portland cement, and a small amount of fireclay. The fireclay makes the mix muddier and stickier, thus enabling it to adhere well to the rocks. I soaked the rocks for at least 10 minutes so they would take on moisture. The moisture also helps the mortar stick better. I cleaned off the rocks with a trowel and sponge as I finished each mix. This rockwork extended behind the drum, high enough to support the above hood (plates 2 and 3).

A 3″ air intake pipe made from an old drive shaft comes down from the bottom of the hand blower. It supplies plenty of air through its wide diameter. It is 12″ in length, long enough to extend to below the bottom of the drum. At this point it is welded to an elbow pipe that brings the air to the center of the forge. Another through pipe comes down to meet the air intake and to drop the clinkers and slag down to the clean out at the bottom. I built a little catch shovel below this intersection to direct the air into the drum when the blower is working. This tool prevents air from being lost down the clean

out. When the forge is not in use I just pull this shovel back a couple inches and let the slag and crap that went through the tuyer drop down into the cleanout hole (plates 4-6).

This drum bowl is wider and deeper then the hearths of most portable forges. To concentrate the fire more within an 8″ diameter and protect the metal drum I lined it with a river clay refractor. The clay comes in flat for 2″ from the edge of the drum and slopes down toward the bottom of the drum for another 3 or 4″ acting as a reservoir for the coal. This provides the fire with more depth than the usual set up. A short pipe extension comes up from the bottom of the

(1)

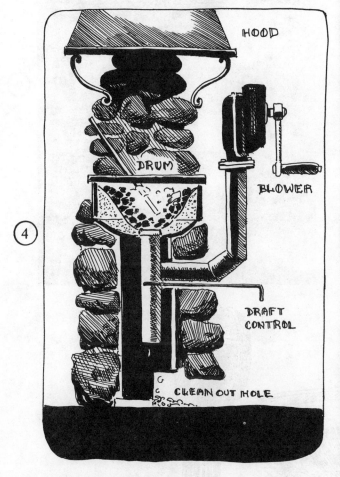

(2)

(3)

(4)

HOOD

DRUM

BLOWER

DRAFT
CONTROL

CLEAN OUT HOLE

drum to the top edge easy clean out (plate 7). Once the clay gets hot it vitrifies and becomes a great refractor to protect the drum. This inner barrier doesn't have to be clay. It could be any material that serves as a refractor, is resistant to heat, and provides insulation for the drum.

The hood is made of plate steel and is 3′ long by 2′ wide at bottom, tapering in 20″ to a narrow 8″ x 10″ opening at the top to accommodate the stack. It is 30″ above the drum to provide proper draw without being too much in the way. This hood also picks up the fumes if I'm welding nearby. The flue stack should be at least this 8″ x 10″ size for sufficient draft. Anything smaller wouldn't

⑤

⑥

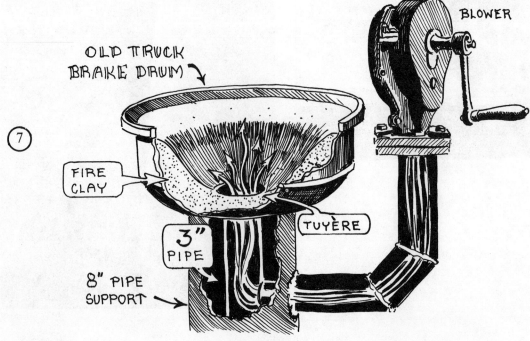

⑦

OLD TRUCK BRAKE DRUM

BLOWER

FIRE CLAY

TUYÈRE

3″ PIPE

8″ PIPE SUPPORT

effectively do the job. The hood is attached to two bolts that stick out from the rear concrete support. It will also be braced at the stack. This stack will be welded to the top of the hood and will extend straight up through the peak of the roof (plate 8).

I use the forge for making hand tools and manipulating and forming steel. It is cheaper and easier than welding in certain operations. With welding you can change the shape of a piece of metal but can not alter the cross section. If you have a 1″ square stock you can cut it. If you heat that 1″ bar stock in a forge you can actually make it fatter by dropping it (beating it) on the anvil. You can also draw it out and make it thinner.

There just aren't that many fine blacksmiths around anymore. So much has been lost that the books on the subject haven't been able to recapture. But its actual experience that counts . . . and I just love to see metal go through changes.

Here is a simple project involving a few of the basic forging techniques. This will give you an idea of how easy it is to make your own useful tools.

Start out by purchasing some blacksmith's coal from a local hardware store. This product is best for the job because it contains fewer impurities than regular hard coal, thus it leaves fewer deposits known as clinkers. Clinkers are globs of crystalized matter which weld together as the coal burns. They gather at the tuyer or air nozzle and block the flow of air coming in from the hand blower. They should be cleaned out often so the air can properly be fed to the fire.

To activate the forge, make a well in the center of the bowl and clear the tuyer of any foreign particles. Wad up paper in the well and build up the coal pieces around and over it. When the fire is lit push the coals in from the sides to supply the well with new fuel. Turn the crank of the blower and supply as much air as needed to really get the coals hot. When the fire spreads throughout the bowl, dampen the periphery of the well to confine the fire to the center. At first you'll get a lot of harsh smoke, but it will soon clear as the residue burns off and the coals reach the hotter temperatures. Watch where you set up. It has been the demonstrator's experience to set up too close to a neighbor's clothes line, consequently the soot from the forge got all over the neighbor's laundry. It is also advisable to protect your eyes with some kind of shield to prevent sparks from burning your eyeballs.

Once the coals are red and the actual fire has subsided you are ready to put in the metal (plate 1). For this project a length of ½″ round stock was used. A 12″ bolt or most other salvagable iron of this thickness could be used. The bar was heated up to a very hot white heat so it could be easily cut to length on the anvil. When heating metal, create an oven with the coals by enclosing the metal with the coals. Enclosing the metal in this manner also slows down oxidation. Oxidation causes pits which show up on the surfaces. These pits are unsightly and are hard to grind out. They leave an uneven finish, especially in finer projects like knives. Leave a little corridor so you can watch the metal turn from red to yellow and finally to white. Work the coals with a stoker, bringing the new coals into the well. Take out clinkers as you go and clean out the trap below the forge to maintain a proper flow of air to the fire. Keep the fire steady. Do not put too much of a blast of air on the metal but slowly crank the blower to supply a continuous supply of air. Be careful not to get the metal so hot that it begins to melt. Check it when you feel it is hot enough. If tiny sparks come off of it when it is lifted out of the well it is beginning to melt.

Since the round stock was too long for the hook it had to be cut on the anvil. The anvil should be solidly mounted on a heavy stump or round of hardwood. It should be raised to the height of the blacksmith's knuckles so he or she could work continuously and comfortably for several hours in a straight, standing position and not have to bend over while working. Cutting is usually done on the hardy attachment which fits into the hardy hole at the butt of the anvil surface. If this attachment is not readily available cutting can be done on the shoulder behind the horn. Cutting should never be done on

the surface plate face because that section of the anvil is of harder steel than the shoulder. This hard surface will dull a tool if it hits it. The shoulder is of a softer temper and will give when hit . . . even so, when you are cutting try not to let your tool go entirely through the metal you are working on. Cut almost through it then bend it back and forth at the cut until it breaks (plate 2 and 3).

⑧

Chapter Five

Making a Hook

The first step of the actual hook is punching the ring or eye. This employs the technique of *upsetting*. Upsetting is bringing more metal to a given area by beating down on it. In this case we want to gain material for flattening. Upsetting requires a very hot heat, close to the melting point. To upset, bring the metal to the anvil with hot end down. Beat on top until the opposite end begins to flare. Don't let it bend (plate 4). Once it begins to bend keep turning the bar and beat on the bottom. Bevel the ends as you work to constrict the flow of metal. Bring the flow into the center instead of making the sides mushroom out. Use several lighter taps with the ball peen instead of smashing it hard. The pounding effect rarely reaches the core of the bar anyway so save your energy.

Some blacksmiths use the ledge of the shoulder as a guide while they beat on the rod, twisting in a circular motion as they hit (plate 5). This gives the rod a shelf to be pounded against.

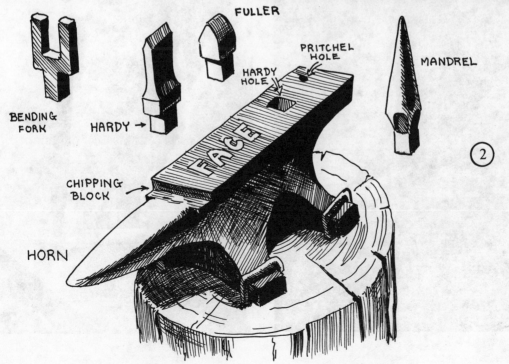

BENDING FORK

HARDY →

FULLER

HARDY HOLE

PRITCHEL HOLE

MANDREL

FACE

CHIPPING BLOCK

HORN

If the tip starts spreading quicker than the area where the ring will be, quench the tip immediately to cool it off so the area behind it will spread instead of the tip. When you quench, move the metal around instead of keeping it still to make it cool off more slowly and evenly. The faster metal cools the quicker its molecules freeze and become brittle. This might cause your project to crack at the most brittle part.

Other causes of cracking are letting the piece burn when heating thus making it lose

its temper and become too brittle; working it until it gets too thin; or working the piece too cold.

Once the tip of the rod is upset enough, it is ready to be flattened with a large ball peen hammer. The flattened tip of the rod is then placed over the *hardy hole* of the anvil and a hot punch is centered on the peened area. The punch is hit several times with a hammer until it makes a dent into the peened area (plate 6). Be careful not to drive the punch through the rod or else flaring may result. Instead, turn the flat side over and find the nub from the punch, then go through the piece from this opposite side. Again be cautious not to work the metal too cold especially when it becomes this thin.

Now widen the hole, using the front tip of the horn. Put the horn tip through the eye while holding the unworked end of the hook with tongs. Hammer toward anvil face first with downward pounding motions, then work around horn, turning the eye as you hammer around the tip and sides (plates 7 and 8). The tip should have the greatest concentration of heat.

Since the horn tip makes a tapered hole because of its shape instead of an even one, the eye should be worked around a *drift* to make it the same size on both sides (plate 9). Be sure to work the sides flat as you widen the hole to prevent them from getting too

⑦

⑨

⑧

thin. This can be done by intermittently flattening the sides on the anvil face with a heavy hammer. After this process, the outer rim of the sides should also be beveled in for additional strength with the drift pin reinserted in the eye so it is kept round. Repeat until even and proper size. After the eye has been worked to the desired diameter, the sides and tip can be shaped in the same manner. Then the project should be hammered over the horn to true up the base of the ring. To finish the eye and sides, round off any points with a small hammer (plate 10).

The next process involved is *drawing out*. This process makes the cross section of a given area of material thinner while it lengthens the whole piece. Drawing out should be accomplished over the horn, pulling the rod toward you with tongs while pounding the top of it with a heavy hammer. This enables the metal rod to be worked over the convexed high point of the horn,

10

11

stretching it out as it passes over the contour. The project should be turned as you work it to get an even stretch on all sides (plate 11).

After it has been drawn out a bit take the rod to the anvil plate and true it up to keep it straight. Repeat the drawing out process until the rod is the desired length. Then bring the tip to a point and taper it from the shank by beating around it on the anvil plate until it becomes the proper shape.

Now comes the bending. Bending doesn't require as much heat. Heat up the tapered tip until it is just beyond cherry red. Position it on the anvil horn and beat the tip until it bends slightly with the contour of the horn (plate 12). Heat the whole shank to the same cherry red color. Be careful not to heat and weaken the eye. Then turn the rod over and shape the shank around the horn in the same manner (plate 13).

From this point the finished design is up to the individual. If you want a hook that hangs straight, you have to create a curve in the hook shank that will evenly distribute

gravity. Gravity seeks the lowest and highest points of a hanging object, thus you want the gravity line to bisect the eye and the curve of the hook shank. After the project has been worked to the desired shape, flatten it out and bevel it for strength. If necessary, tap it again to realign it and always be careful to maintain the balance. Then dress it up with light taps with a ball peen hammer for a rustic finish. Finally, heat it up one last time all over and quench it completely to provide an even temper (plate 14).

Chapter One

If You Heat With Wood, This Is The Heater

Where I live, wood for heating is abundant and costs only the labor of hauling it. There are many roads being built nearby and much of the removed timber is pushed into piles to be later burned. There are also several second-growth forest areas surrounding us which are filled with dry, easy burning deadfall and standing snags—ours for the taking. It would indeed be wise to use the cheapest, most available resource to heat my

①

house, but I didn't want to deal with the hardships of cutting and splitting small rounds for a conventional wood heater. Also, I can appreciate that my wife has no desire to be constantly sweeping up wood debris and washing down soot-covered walls. She has enough thankless tasks.

When visiting friends who heat with wood I usually notice a premature drowsiness which comes over the group until someone takes the initiative to open a window or two. The fatigue is caused by the lack of oxygen in the room. As wood burns it uses up the same oxygen we breathe. But opening the windows of course allows cold air in. The stove then has to be adjusted to put out more heat, thus using up a greater amount of fuel.

After much thought, solutions to each of these problems came to me. To prevent pollution of debris and soot, the ideal wood burning stove should have an outdoor loading chute and must be air tight, having no leaks to the interior. To prevent oxygen depletion, this stove must draw its oxygen from other areas instead of the area which is being heated. To save physical energy, the stove should be able to take large pieces of

wood so one does not have to split short rounds. I soon developed a workable design for the ideal wood-burning heater.

Since there is a basement in my house, I decided to locate the damper there instead of exposing it to the variables of the sometimes severe weather. The oxygen comes up from this area to feed the fire. For convenience I knew that I would have to also devise some method of working the damper from the living area so whoever was enjoying the comfort of the warm living area did not have to leave it to adjust the air intake (plate 1).

I began figuring out the workable dimensions for the wood heater. Since the only real constant was the size of the open 45-gallon drum heat exchanger unit, I had to first do the necessary welding on it. This consisted of cutting through from end to end and opening it up to a half oval shape. After achieving that shape, I set the open drum on the floor and estimated the outer dimensions of the brick enclosure that would house it. The size of the hole would be the area of the drum plus 2″ air space around the drum plus the width of the surrounding brick enclosure. The 39″ x 39″ opening was then cut out (plate 2). This facilitated the

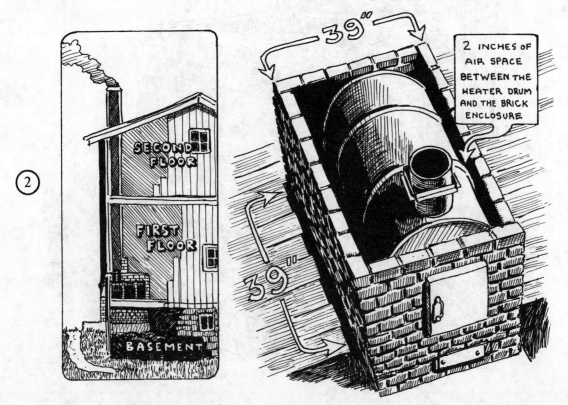

2

SECOND FLOOR

FIRST FLOOR

BASEMENT

39″

39″

2 INCHES OF AIR SPACE BETWEEN THE HEATER DRUM AND THE BRICK ENCLOSURE

following operation of constructing the concrete pad which is located less than 2′ below the floor. Cutting the hole first allowed me plenty of room to stand as I built the forms and poured the slab. Its thickness is irrelevant as long as it can support the weight above it; 6″ to 8″ is adequate. The pad is made up of an inexpensive mixture of sand, portland cement, and a large quantity of rock for volume. The perimeter of the pad is the same as the perimeter of the hole in the floor because the pad will be supporting the base and the brick enclosure.

After the pad set up, a few courses of brick were mortared inside its perimeter. An inner lining of fire brick was then stacked along the inside surface of the red brick and was cemented together with a commercial fire clay. Mortared rock could substitute for the outer brick but because rocks have a greater tendency then red brick to crack by expansion and contraction, they should not be used in direct contact with fire.

Below the floor, low enough so the entire fire box will be in the basement area, I installed a four holed manifold type damper system. I tried to locate an old truck manifold for the job but could not find one the proper size so I had one made up. This manifold had to be mortared into the brick base in such a way that instead of any structural weight being on it, all the weight was carried on the bricks between the four tubes.

Bolted onto the damper and sealed with an asbestos gasket, is a commercial air intake vent. This vent has a tongue which protrudes above a pivot pin. When the tongue is depressed by the vent rod, the vent opens and allows oxygen in. When pressure is removed, gravity atuomatically shuts the vent. I prefer utilizing gravity in closing the damper to prevent the damper from being left open by accident.

BRICK FIRE CHAMBER

FIRE BRICK

RED BRICK

SAND

CLEAN OUT HOLE

CONCRETE PAD

BEDROCK

20 DO

8″

③

On the outside of the basement, below the loading door space, I installed a clean out slot to collect the accumulating ashes. This slot can be any size as long as it can be easily covered. It should be located just under the level of the damper to prevent clogging. This clean out hole has a removable cover which is held on by two wing nuts and sealed with an asbestos gasket (plates 3,4, and 5).

After the manifold damper was installed, the red bricks and fire bricks were set up to floor level. At this point the fire brick was completed and two ¾" angle iron ledges were welded on the bottom ends of the drum so it would fit directly over the firebox. Care was taken to make certain the inside diameter of the fire brick agreed with the inside diameter of the drum ledges. The outer red bricks were then extended up into the livingroom area. Having the firebox below the floor gives the house a warm basement and a warm floor area.

④

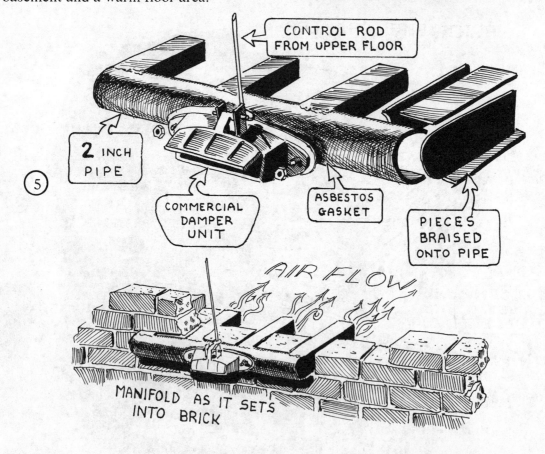

⑤

CONTROL ROD FROM UPPER FLOOR

2 INCH PIPE

COMMERCIAL DAMPER UNIT

ASBESTOS GASKET

PIECES BRAISED ONTO PIPE

AIR FLOW

MANIFOLD AS IT SETS INTO BRICK

CUT WITH WELDING TORCH

45 GALLON FUEL DRUM

ANGLE IRON

END PIECES

HEAT EXCHANGER DRUM

10"

COMMERCIAL 8" FLUE DAMPER

⑥

ANGLE IRONS WELDED TO BOTTOM SIT ON TOP OF FIRE BRICK

The heat exchanger drum was at this point made ready for installation. After the ledges were welded on, an 8″ hole was taken out of the top front of the drum. A thick-walled length of pipe, 8″ in diameter by 10″ long was welded above the hole. A commercial 8″ damper was then set into the flue support pipe, and square base of 1″ angles iron was welded to the top of it. This angle-iron base allowed the flue liner to temporarily be supported by the heat exchanger until the bricks were mortared around it.

A heavy ¼″ iron frame was then welded on to the front of the drum to support the salvaged boiler loading door and a 14″ by 16″ hole was cut out for it. A lip was added around the 14″ by 16″ opening to enclose the

door and two rod supports were attached above the opening for it to hang from (plate 6).

Because the door is held tightly shut by its own weight working with gravity, it keeps the wood burner airtight and free from draft (plates 7 and 8).

The gravity closing feature is also a safety factor. When loading dry branches into the fire box, the existing fire sometimes explodes and leaps out. If I had to take time to stop and think about shutting the door when such an explosion occurs, there's be a good chance I might be singed before being able to do this. With gravity, the door shuts when I let go of it.

My original thought was to make the heat

exchanger out of brick instead of a 45-gallon drum, but I later realized that brick takes much longer to heat up than the drum. When you come in from the cold you want to be able to open the damper and get immediate warmth instead of waiting a ½ hour before the bricks get hot. True, bricks would last almost indefinately but so will the drum, if it is not allowed to get red hot. Since the drum is only a heat circulator it does not come in contact with the actual charcoals, thus it will not burn out from contact with fire.

The ornamental brick enclosure around the heat exchanger and the chimney were then continued up from the base. I wanted adequate air circulation around the heat exchanger so I allowed 2″ of air space between the drum and the bricks. This air circulation factor allows for maximum heat circulation throughout the living area. Before raising the brick enclosure, I made sure to allow several openings between the bottom bricks to draw in cold air from the floor, which would prevent draft problems. Without this precaution the cold air would

creep up to the top and get heated without properly circulating.

The brick enclosure and chimney were then raised and a tapered (for aesthetic purposes) chimney front was built above it. This front rests on a heavy 3″ angle-iron support that extends from outside enclosure brick on the opposite side. When completed the enclosure was high enough to easily sit on. Directly above the drum, a heavy-gauge mesh screen was fitted in. It is a safety screen and sometimes seconds as a drying

DOOR PLACEMENT ON
FRONT OF DRUM

⑦

BRICKS ARE
STEPPED IN
TO EQUAL
SLANT OF
LOADING
DOOR

172

8" SQUARE OF ANGLE IRON WELDED TO 1st FLUE SECTION FORMS LEDGE FOR FLUE LINER

3" ANGLE IRONS MORTORED INTO THE BRICK SUPPORT THE WEIGHT OF CHIMNEY

DAMPER

AIR VENTS

⑨

rack for clothing and other items . . . but by no means should the air circulation space around the heat exchanger be interfered with for obvious fire reasons.

This brick enclosure is the favorite spot in winter for my friends. First thing they do is come in and sit their cold bums on the bricks . . . then after everybody thaws out a bit, the conversations begin (plates 9 and 10).

The flue lining was then stacked above the support and the chimney bricks were mortared in the usual alternating tier method. The chimney was raised to a height of 10" above the peak of the roof for safety (plate 11 and 12).

A word of caution to those who do not want to foot the price of a commerical flue liner. If you build your own flue, make sure it is smooth inside and out and it is an equal diameter top and bottom fro proper draw and easy clean out. Creosote sticks in crevices and can be very difficult to remove from a rough surface. Also, if you don't use a ceramic or stacked oil can flue liner there is danger of the liquified creosote seeping into the mortar and discoloring your bricks or rock work. Creosote is made up of a very

⑩

small molecules and can seep into the tiniest cracks. Because of this characteristic it is an excellent wood preservative. This is one place to definitely not chance a short cut.

173

3" FIBREGLASS
INSULATION
BETWEEN THE
BRICK AND WALL

CERAMIC
FLUE
LINER

3" ANGLE
IRON

⑪

Nyean '75

⑫

In my opinion, the safest and easiest chimney to deal with is one that is straight up and down. A straight chimney allows creosote to drop into the fire box instead of collecting in angled areas. To check for creosote build up, I simply open the door, stick my head into the furnace and look up. If I can see the sky I don't clean the chimney.

I have had little success with burning creosote out of chimneys. It is a waste of fuel and it is bad for the heat exchanger to get the furnace hot enough to liquify the residue. Even if you do get the furnace hot enough, you never get all of the creosote. The residue that remains crystalizes and becomes part of the flue. This build up eventually disturbs the draw and must be removed. For clean out I use a 20′ long 1″ x 1″ stick with a flat scraper on the end (plate 13).

Even though this heater is designed to burn wood slowly, I have to clean out the flue

CREOSOTE FALLS DOWN CHIMNEY AND IT IS RE-BURNED IN FIRE BOX

LOADING DOOR

ASH DOOR

FLUE SCRAPING TOOL

20 ft.

1" x 1"

SHEET METAL

(14)

(15)

only every six weeks because the chimney is well insulated. There is 3″ of insulation between it and the outside wall to slow down the condensation of smoke. Creosote is condensed smoke. If the chimney is kept warm your creosote problem is cut in half.

The width and length of a chimney are not critical with this heater design as long as the opening is uniform top and bottom for draw. A friend of mine has a similar setup with a 3′ x 6′ chimney in which he built a smoke chute. He put in a large air-tight door enabling him to walk into the stack and he installed grates for hanging bacon and sausages for smoking. This proved to be an excellent smokehouse because creosote smoke is cool and does not cook the meat. The draw is not interfered with either.

Smoke curls out of the heat exchanger drum and curls through the huge opening.

As a final touch to protect the loading door from the weather and to ensure that it is air tight, an outer door was added. This painted plywood door encloses the loading door and its inside is lined with aluminum foil to reflect any escaping heat back into the heat exchanger (plate 14 and 15).

The heater was then ready for the big test. Before lighting the first fire, I protected the bottom cement pad with a 4" layer of sand for the charcoals to rest on. With the sand there is no need for a grate. I used any type of wood that was available, cedar, fir, birch, larch, etc. Cedar burns fastest but not hottest and birch is excellent when you prefer a warmer house . . . but I usually do not have time to pick through the pile, so I use the wood as it comes.

I began the fire with very dry wood and once a solid bed of coals was established I used slower-burning green wood. The initial test proved successful. The unit heated the entire house and absolutely no oxygen was taken out of the living areas. The fire stayed in the fire box and the heat exchanger then circulated heat out into the house. There was no pollution in the house and I could put in logs up to 30" in length, which saved tremendously on wood cutting energy. In fact I only put in one full wheel barrow every evening and the fire kept slowly burning. Where it gets its oxygen I do not know because I keep the damper shut most of the time. I only open it to get a sudden burst of heat after coming in from the cold.

The stove's efficiency amazes me. When I put the logs in the burner in the evening they turn into charcoal during the night and that charcoal gives off heat practically throughout the entire next day without giving off much smoke. When I open the damper, cold air gets in and takes all the heat up the chimney, so I made sure to keep it closed down as much as possible to save fuel.

It takes approximately two months of constant everyday use before the fire box needs to be cleaned out. When the ashes reach the clean out slot I move the hot embers to the rear and take out the cold ash. These ashes are then taken to the garden because they are an excellent source of lime and should never be wasted. Because the clean out slot is located a bit lower than the manifold damper, the ashes never interfere with the damper. I also found that creosote collects in the heat exchanger and never interferes with the damper.

Another amazing discovery I made was that even after I left the fire for a couple of days it did not go out. Very little heat rises because the damper is shut, thus the heater is constantly giving off combustion heat.

Sometimes I went off on short trips, came back after the weekend, stoked the fire with dry wood and waited . . . it always eventually started smoking again. It never failed. I lit the first fire in September and it burned through to April, non-stop.

Chapter Two

The Fireplace

My wife and I were already fimiliar with the warm, earthy presence of an aesthetically beautiful fireplace and its natural attraction to people like ourselves who enjoy intimate get togethers with

friends. Such a fireplace is a must in our home and became the major consideration in the design. We wanted a fireplace with which we could participate while eating, while conversing with friends and also while

A DOMINANT ATTRACTION

working in the kitchen. It is important for us to have as much exposure to its warmth and nourishment as possible.

Upon designing the house we figured out size and location of the fireplace but had no idea of what the finished product would look like until after gathering the materials. I began working with the materials—and let it flow. Soon it started to communicate and began to determine its own form.

My accumulation of stone consisted of several shallow, flat-faced pieces and a whole lot of rough, square ones. I knew a plain straight fireplace would not be the natural outcome, so I experimented with the stones. I laid them out on a flat surface and played with them as one would a jigsaw puzzle. The flat stones seemed to want to gather together in the center section, leaving the square stones at the ends. I stacked the center stones flatways so only their edges were revealed. This produced a horizontal feeling in the center which protruded out beyond the receding sides. It emphasized contrast and a third dimension. Then I put in a few niches here and a little shelf there where the bears and plants are. I did what kinda felt right as I worked with my materials (plate 1).

There is a popular material that can be purchased for the fireplace. It is a rough, rustic looking rock that is quite sharp around the edges and is precut to produce a clean effect without exposing much mortar or

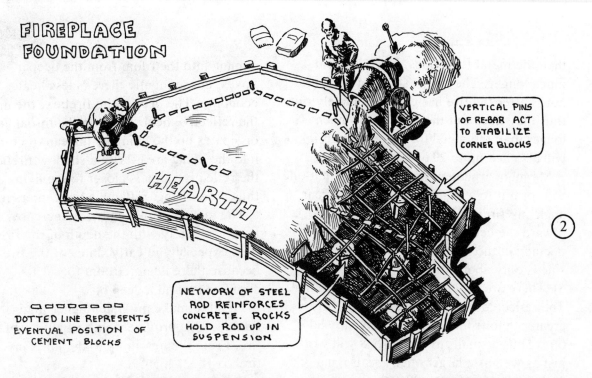

FIREPLACE FOUNDATION

HEARTH

VERTICAL PINS OF RE-BAR ACT TO STABILIZE CORNER BLOCKS

②

DOTTED LINE REPRESENTS EVENTUAL POSITION OF CEMENT BLOCKS

NETWORK OF STEEL ROD REINFORCES CONCRETE. ROCKS HOLD ROD UP IN SUSPENSION

joints. But this material is pretty expensive while the type of stone I used is just sitting there waiting to be picked up. The purchased product robs you of the chance to be totally creative with your design because it is uniform in thickness and lacks dimension.

I began the actual construction of the fireplace by pouring a very adequate *pad* for the heavy structure. This pad should not be less than 10″ thick and should be reinforced with ½″ reinforcing rod, crisscrossed throughout it, especially on the two sides where most of the structural weight is going to be supported. A vertical anchor of 3/8″ rebar, coming out to meet the corner concrete blocks framing the fire box, should also be included. This pad must extend at least 12″ beyond the perimeter of the fireplace in all directions and could also be the base for the hearth, depending on design.

You want a strong pad so you need to make a mixture one part Portland cement to five parts sand. The adhesive strength should not be broken up with too many *plumbs* (large rocks) or else the whole pad will be weakened. Large rocks do not provide enough tiny surfaces for the concrete to adhere to and cement together (plate 2). Remember, if you are going to go

through the trouble of building anything with masonry—masonry being permanent, expensive, and very difficult to alter—build it with the proper materials. Do not skimp—especially do not skimp on the pad. It is the foundation for a very heavy, permanent structure. If the pad cracks or crumbles, so does the fireplace.

Once the pad has been poured you can begin laying out the fireplace in terms of firebox preference. The two most popular alternatives are the double-jacketed metal *heatalaters* or heatforms and the traditional handmade firebrick box.

Heatalaters or heatforms are supposedly the more efficient route. They allow quick emission of hot air into the living area, whereas it takes firebrick longer to heat up before it radiates. The heatalater is easy to install and comes as a whole unit. Firebricks have to be set up, shaped, and adhered together. This usually becomes a long, involved process, but is a very satisfying and creative one.

I personally prefer to build my firebox out of firebrick. It is cheaper than buying the metal unit; is more aesthetically pleasing, and it can be shaped to optimum efficiency. Though firebrick takes longer to heat up than the metal form does, it retains heat much longer. The bricks stay warm several hours after the fire has gone completely out, thus they keep out the chill factor much longer than the metal form does. Firebrick will also last up to 20 or 30 years.

My main argument for firebrick is that one can form it to a desired shape. At the rear, I angle my firebox side walls deliberately toward the center. Though there is a 40″ opening in the width of the front, the back side is only about 16″ to 17″ in width (plate 3). There are several reasons for this design. The reflected heat from this firebox is far greater than from a deeper, conventional one. Thus a small fire in this box will work just as well as a larger one. This is a major fuel-conserving factor, if nothing else. It takes a larger fire to fit a conventional box or heat-formed box because their backsides are deeper. There is far less reflective heat

coming into the room from the deeper boxes, consequently there is less heat economy. The deeper the firebox, the more the reflective heat rises into the throat and dissipates up the chimney instead of coming into the living area. With a shallow firebox, the reflective area is closer to the living area, thus more rising, reflective heat enters it.

The rate of smoke emission increases proportionately with the depth of the fire box, expecially in early states of the fire because there is more room for air to circulate around a deep box.

I tend to make my lintel higher than normal. This provides more of a view of the fire. From the hearth up to the lintel my firebox is 32″ high.

Before actual construction of the firebox I designed a vent system, enabling oxygen to enter in from the exterior, flow under the firebox, and come out the sides to supply

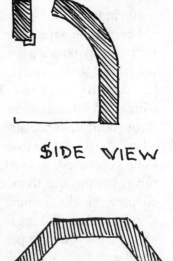

SIDE VIEW

TOP VIEW

FIRE BOX FRONT VIEW

③

the fire. A standard fireplace will utilize a hugh amount of room oxygen, consequently depleting the living area of air. This causes its inhabitants to feel weary and fatigued. Also, without the exterior air supply, chilling foot drafts occur as the fire draws oxygen. A well-known formula explains that a standard fireplace will cause the displacement of over twice the amount of room air requried for optimum ventilation; therefore at least half the amount of oxygen for the fire should be drawn directly from the outside and not be permitted to pass through the room to the fireplace.

The air is brought in from the outside through a 3″ juice can formed opening that goes from the exterior bottom and comes in from directly underneath the firebox, between it and the slab. I allowed an opening for it there the width of the firebox and 2½″ in height. The air intake is located at the lower right of the stonework masonry exterior (plate 4). One outlet comes through near the right front side of the firebox and the other travels beneath it, coming out on the left side opposite the first (plate 5).

④

⑤

⑥

FIRE BRICK

2″ CONCRETE

SHEET METAL

TIN CAN SET IN BLOCK WALL

COLD AIR ENTERS FROM OUTSIDE

AIR FLOWS UNDER FIRE THROUGH BOTTOM CAN, UP THROUGH BRICK CHAMBER, OUT UPPER CAN AND INTO FIRE

The construction of this air intake system was tricky. The first course of brick around the sides and back of the firebox were mortared directly to the slab, leaving a 3″ space near the front of either side as air channels. A piece of sheet metal was placed over this bottom course. It acted as a form for the 2″ secondary pad which the firebrick bottom of the firebox rests on. Rebar was distributed throughout the area above the sheet metal and a second course of brick was mortared in place around it. This second course also acted as the side form for the 2″ of concrete which was then poured over the sheet metal. After the concrete dried, the bottom firebricks were put in over it.

This secondary pad construction created a 2½″ *plenum* over the pad for an airchamber which would allow the passage of air from the exterior air intake through the bottom plenum, out to either side of the firebox. Two 3″ juice cans were used as forms on the lower sides and another course of firebrick was adhered around the firebox. An archway of brick was then mortared around the vent openings to protect them from the later rubble and concrete fill which will be put in between the firebox and the surrounding concrete block (plate 6).

If I were able to redo this vent system I would bring both of the outlet vent 2″ forward, more to the front of the box. As it comes in now, the air hits fire from the sides, blowing it a bit toward the hearth. If the vents were nearer to the front the incoming air would blow the fire to the back where it could more efficiently warm the bricks and radiate its heat.

The sides of the firebox were then laid. The overall dimensions of this area are very crucial but one is free to choose from several designs depending on one's own needs. I used a bell-shaped curve at the back. The mason from whom I learned prefers this design, and so do I. It provides more of a gradual flow in the back of the firebox, allowing the fire to follow a gentle curve. To establish this curve you put a little bit more fire clay between the backs of the firebricks then between the fronts. This tilts the top of the brick face slightly toward the front of the fireplace.

When setting the firebrick a commercial fire clay should be used. You want only a small amount between each brick because it is the firebrick not the clay that radiated the heat. In volume the clay will eventually crumble. It takes only about 25 pounds to do a normal firebox.

Fireclay is mixed with water to a consistency of heavy cream. The firebricks must first be submerged in water for a minute or two until they almost quit bubbling. This enables the clay to stick on

FORK
CHISEL

BEGIN LAYING
WALLS OF FIREBOX

TIN CAN
VENT

TAP
TAP

SHAPING
BRICKS

(7)

SOAK BRICKS UNTIL
THEY ALMOST STOP
BUBBLING

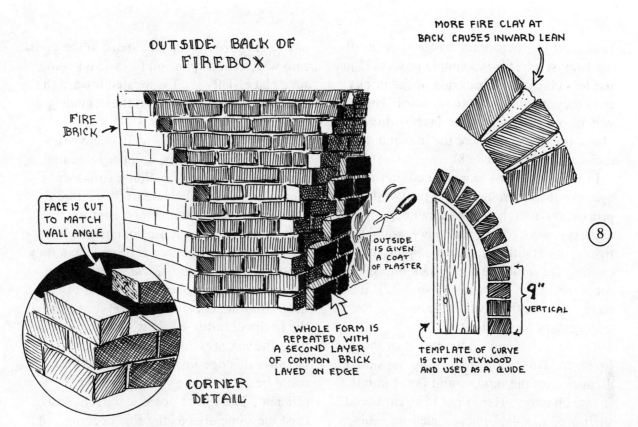

OUTSIDE BACK OF
FIREBOX

MORE FIRE CLAY AT
BACK CAUSES INWARD LEAN

FIRE
BRICK

FACE IS CUT
TO MATCH
WALL ANGLE

OUTSIDE
IS GIVEN
A COAT
OF PLASTER

⑧

WHOLE FORM IS
REPEATED WITH
A SECOND LAYER
OF COMMON BRICK
LAYED ON EDGE

TEMPLATE OF CURVE
IS CUT IN PLYWOOD
AND USED AS A GUIDE

9"
VERTICAL

CORNER
DETAIL

the brick like glue. If the bricks are left in the water too long they have to be dried out a bit before the fire clay will stick. The bricks were then raised straight on the back and sides of the firebox for 9".

Now I made a template form, shaping the end of a piece of ¾" fiberboard to the bell-shaped curve. The bricks were then laid to follow the gradual curve. I periodically used this pattern as one would a level to make sure the curve was true. This curve must be a gradual one to prevent any humps from occurring as the brick courses are raised (plate 7).

To narrow the surface of the back of the firebox as it curved forward, the sides were also splined inward at a good angle. Then the back was soon angled outward again above the center so that the back plane would widen almost to the traditional angle at the throat to prevent smoking. This design improved the radiant efficiency.

In other words, when you decrease the width of the sidewalls by splining or corbelling them, the back wall has to come forward. And since the side walls are angled

outward the back also gradually becomes wider. Corbelling or splining is the process of creating a taper or angle by overlapping each course above it, thus forming an angled or herring bone shaped intersection. There is an added complication in my firebox design of the splined sides also meeting the back at various angles depending on the bell-shaped curve, causing the crossing bricks to overlap. This made it necessary to trim the exposed face of every other brick with a forked-head type chisel, blending it with the others. The backs did not have to be dealt with because they would be covered with the rubble-concrete backing behind the firebox.

To chisel these faces you first mark off the portion you want eliminated, and softly hit the chisel repeatedly on that line until it gouges a groove all around the brick. Keep going around until you make a clean break. Practice this on a few discards before trying it on the actual bricks you will be using. Remember its a gradual process and patience must be exercised to make proper breaks.

To begin the flare I start setting the brick

back a bit just before the half way point of the back side. This is a simple process. I just use less clay on the backside of the bricks until they gradually curve outward. This widens out the back of the firebox directly above the firebox, where the maximum radiation occurs, (plate 8).

I took great pains to make certain the opening at the throat is the proper width in proportion with the smoke chamber and flue area. If it were too narrow there would be tight spots at either end of the lintel, thus causing the smoke to come back into the room instead of going up the throat. If it were too wide there would be an unnecessary loss of heat.

The firebrick ends at the throat of the fireplace. This is the area where the smoke escapes pass the *damper* and flows into the smoke chamber. Here I put in a reinforced shelf of 3½″ x 4½″-thick angle iron. This shelf extends 4′ supported on either side by the concrete block and rock work face. It absorbs the weight of the lintel, mantel, and chimney face, taking any structural weight off the firebox. When iron gets hot it expands far more than the rocks, therefore the expansion must be allowed for. For this purpose a small amount of fiberglass insulation was put in at either end of the iron

shelf. This provides an air space at the ends into which the expansion of the iron could take place. This shelf is located toward the backside of the fireplace at the beginning of the throat (plate 9).

The throat is about 8″ to 10″ above the lintel. This is where the damper is located. You have a choice of building your own damper, having one made to fit the throat area, or buying a commercial damper arrangement. Though the commercial ones are fool proof, they are far deeper than they need to be and fit into a wider throat than the one on my fireplace. Our throat is 4″ deep from the back of the lintel to the top of the firebox, and is 40″ in width. I wanted a wide firebox area for viewing purposes. Because this opening is so wide the throat could be as shallow as 4″ and still be efficient. The throat opening must have at least the same area as the flue opening and it would be if it were even a bit larger. In other words, if a flue were 12 x 12, its opening would be 144 square inches; so the throat area would have to be at least that. The throat on this fireplace has an opening of 40″ x 4″ which equals 160 sq. in.; this is more than sufficient.

I chose to make my own damper. It consists of a long rod with a flat 4″ piece of

FIREPLACE RAISED
UP TO POSITIONING OF LINTEL

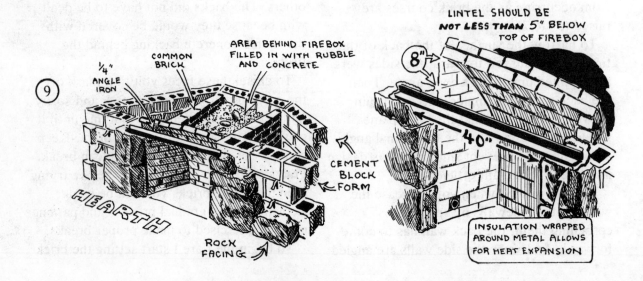

9

¼″ ANGLE IRON

COMMON BRICK

AREA BEHIND FIREBOX FILLED IN WITH RUBBLE AND CONCRETE

HEARTH

CEMENT BLOCK FORM

ROCK FACING

LINTEL SHOULD BE *NOT LESS THAN 5″* BELOW TOP OF FIREBOX

8″

40″

INSULATION WRAPPED AROUND METAL ALLOWS FOR HEAT EXPANSION

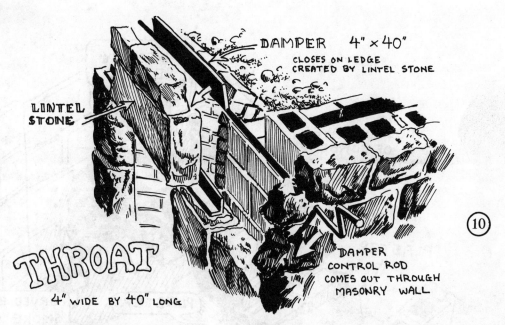

DAMPER 4" x 40"
CLOSES ON LEDGE
CREATED BY LINTEL STONE

LINTEL STONE

⑩

DAMPER
CONTROL ROD
COMES OUT THROUGH
MASONRY WALL

THROAT

4" WIDE BY 40" LONG

iron welded to one side of it and a control rod attachment which is hidden in the stone face of the fireplace. At the end of this control rod there is a kinked or bent handle which manuevers the damper flap. When the damper is flopped down it is closed; when it is flopped up it is open. The damper should be of a size that when it expands from heat it still opens and closes without touching the throat. Also, during construction, be sure to work the damper daily to free it of mud (mortar) which may have fallen from above. I advise installing a damper in, because when you are not using the fireplace you can close it off in cold weather and the room heat will not go up the chimney (plate 10).

Directly above the throat is the smoke chamber. It extends between the long, narrow throat to the 12 x 12 flue opening and is the area in which the size of openings are converted. Because of this conversion a smoke shelf is created. This smoke shelf stops down drafts. When the down draft hits it, it curls back up the chimney. It is located directly above the sloping firebox back, which also helps form it.

The smoke chamber and smoke shelf are built with normal brick because these areas do not get hot enough to warrant the use of fire brick. The sides and front of the smoke chamber are gradually corbelled at about a 60 degree angle until they outline the 12 x 12

flue opening. The backside remains pretty much straight up and down.

Corbelling is a popular method of obtaining a tapered slant. The bricks lay flat instead of gradually sloping to the front as in the bell-shaped curve. Each tier of bricks is stepped up half a brick's width unitl the 60-degree angle reaches the desired height. The courses of brick are alternated, one course consists of a double thickness of brick with the side of the bricks as face, the next with the end of the front brick as face. This chamber should be constructed with this double thickness of brick to prevent smoke seepage in case one layer of brick begins to crack. The building code usually requires this precaution. We're dealing with something that can never be repaired, so it must be done right in the beginning.

I plastered both sides of the smoke chamber to prevent any creosote seepage through the mortar. The inside being corbelled, consequently has a series of rough, stepped up edges. It is a difficult job but this surface has to be made smooth so that the smoke can travel up without any hindrances. The plastering should be done as the smoke chamber is being built. I used a flat trowel and made the plaster good and fat (sticky) so it will adhere well to the joints. Then I plastered the outside, making certain it was sealed thoroughly. You can't be

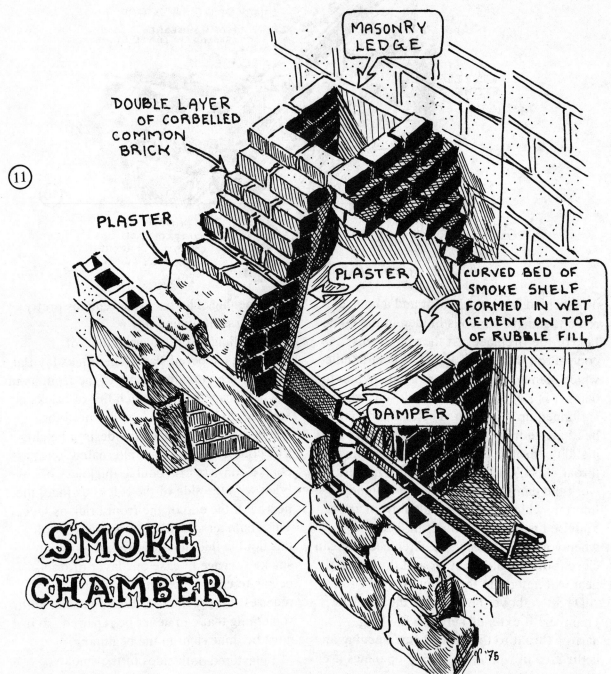

MASONRY LEDGE

DOUBLE LAYER OF CORBELLED COMMON BRICK

⑪

PLASTER

PLASTER

CURVED BED OF SMOKE SHELF FORMED IN WET CEMENT ON TOP OF RUBBLE FILL

DAMPER

SMOKE CHAMBER

overly precautious when it comes to preventing unsightly creosote seepage (plate 11).

The size of the flue is dependent upon the size of the opening of the fire box proper, and the height of the chimney. If the chimney height is 12′ or less you must make the cross-section of the flue at least ⅛ of the total cross-section of the area of the firebox opening. If the chimney is 15′ or thereabouts, the flue opening. If the chimney is 15′ or thereabouts, the flue

opening should be 1/10 of that area, if the chimney is 25′ or over, it can be 1/12th that area. In other words, the higher the chimney, the smaller the flue liner needs to be because the length supplies the necessary area for proper draft pull.

The flue liner can be set on a reinforced shelf of angle iron. This shelf is supported between the stone or block work that surrounds the flue liner. It is located in front, directly above the smoke chamber. It carries a lot of the structural weight of the masonry and brick front of the fireplace.

The flue lining should be raised with the concrete blocks and the outer stone work. To minimize confusion, I'll explain each process separately.

A fireplace should not be built without a flue liner. No building inspector will pass one without it.

I put mortar between each flue lining joint as I stacked them. I was taught to do this and I prefer the results. An architect looked at one of the flues I happened to be constructing and he wanted to know why I was mortaring the joints. He said that within two years after I built it the mortar would crack anyway. I told him I didn't agree; It all depended on how you did it.

Normally your flue is going to have stone work, concrete blocks or brick around it. There should be a space allowed for expansion between the flue liner and this masonry. I always insulate this space with no less than 2″ of fiberglass insulation—sometimes even more. This insulation also cuts down the creosote problem.

I bring the insulation up to within 1″ of the top of the flue liner I am working with. Then I put the mortar on top of the insulation and on top of the joint. The mud is well packed

all the way around it, sealing it in. Above all that I put in more insulation and climb right up with the stack. What I end up with is virtually a well-insulated and mortared flue stack held in place partially by the insulation. It is only tied to the exterior very tenuously by a bit of mud around each joint.

With this method I supply an area for the flue to expand and contract without cracking anything. If it was made solid, sure as mischieve it would expand and crack (plate 12). If you want to bypass the insulation process you should at least put a couple of layers of paper or something equally as porous around the flue liner to create an air space to absorb the expansion.

The flue liner must have at least 12″ of stone, concrete block or brick around it, or a combination of any of these three materials. For economy, aesthetic creativity, and structural soundness I chose to use a combination of multicolored, multitextured stone for the face and an inner structural base of concrete block. The concrete block frames the flue and the firebox. It provides the facing stone with a flat surface for stacking and it is a structural necessity when constructing large, wide fireplaces. Concrete block is far easier and faster to construct than mortared stone and it is an excellent

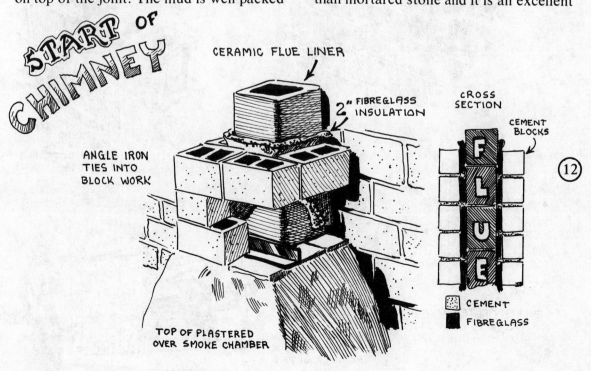

START OF CHIMNEY

CERAMIC FLUE LINER

2″ FIBREGLASS INSULATION

CROSS SECTION

CEMENT BLOCKS

ANGLE IRON TIES INTO BLOCK WORK

F L U E

⑫

TOP OF PLASTERED OVER SMOKE CHAMBER

CEMENT

FIBREGLASS

base for the textured stone.

Since the concrete blocks are uniform in size they can be laid very quickly around the flue and firebox. I suspend a vertical string from an overhanging board at each corner of the area to be covered with the block. A plumb bob hangs from the strings to maintain the true vertical line, then that line is held taut with a bottom brace.

When constructing around a narrow area such as a fireplace or a flue, it is not necessary to have a network of horizontal guides. The blocks can be eyeballed in place horizontally. Care must be taken though to make certain that there is a uniform thickness of ½″ of mud between each layer to make certain the blocks will stack properly. The vertical string guides have to be constantly checked to ensure that the

blocks are true. Also, it is a good idea to tie in every third course of block with a binding wire grid to secure the tall narrow stack in place.

Here are a few hints on using mortar. Make sure the mortar (mud) is of a consistency that when placed on a trowel and flipped a bit, that it spreads across the tool and the excess moisture comes to the surface. Don't have it so wet that it just slops over the edge or so dry that moisture doesn't come to the surface when the mud is worked. If it is of a nice, sticky consistency it will hang onto your trowel as you turn it over onto the block. You then spread a large amount on the top edges of the block already in place and the sides of the block you are setting. Be generous with the mud. You can always clean off the excess later.

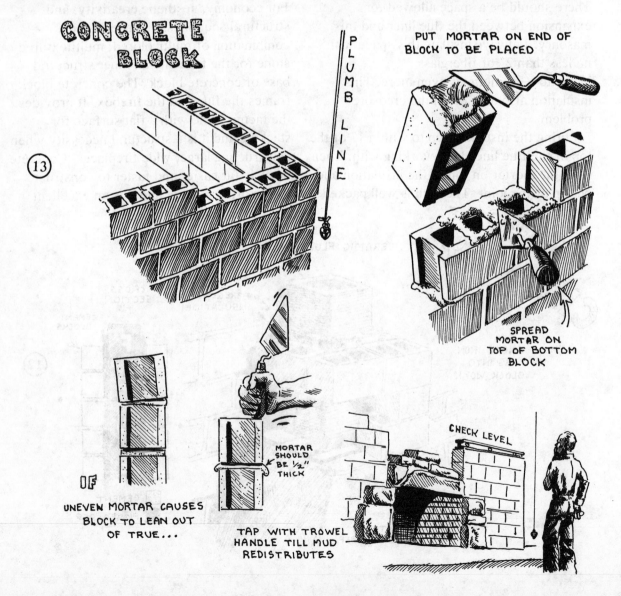

CONCRETE BLOCK

⑬

PLUMB LINE

PUT MORTAR ON END OF BLOCK TO BE PLACED

SPREAD MORTAR ON TOP OF BOTTOM BLOCK

IF

UNEVEN MORTAR CAUSES BLOCK TO LEAN OUT OF TRUE...

MORTAR SHOULD BE ½″ THICK

TAP WITH TROWEL HANDLE TILL MUD REDISTRIBUTES

CHECK LEVEL

188

METAL STRIPS
PLACED IN CEMENT
BETWEEN BLOCKS
GIVES ANCHOR
FOR ROCK FACING

(14)

If the block you have set is lower than the others on that course, lift it and slap on more mud. If it is higher, tap it with the trowel handle until it is the same height as the others. If the back is low, tap the front down to compensate, and vice versa. There are no real secrets to successful block laying, just be patient and remember to use as much mud as possible. It is easier to wipe off the excess mud than to lift the heavy blocks several times (plate 13).

The concrete blocks were raised along with the firebrick in the firebox. Ties must be set into the mortar between the blocks to secure the facing material to them. A commercial flat metal tie can be purchased for this job or strips of rough-surfaced, perforated sheet metal can be used. Also, I filled in the blocks with *zonite* insulation for added thermal protection of flue (plate 14).

When setting up the stone facing you can eyeball it if you want to, but I found that after raising the stones 4′ or 5′, eyeballing becomes too inaccurate so I use string guides.

PLUMB
LINE

PLUMB
LINE
6" AWAY
FROM EDGE
OF WALL

(15)

TIED OFF

STRING GUIDES

(16)

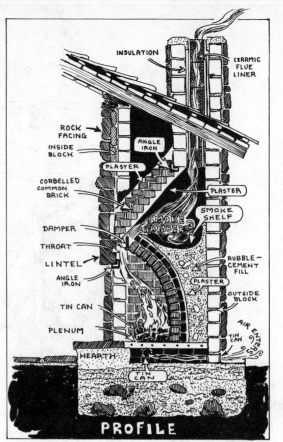

INSULATION CERAMIC FLUE LINER

ROCK FACING

ANGLE IRON

INSIDE BLOCK

PLASTER

CORBELLED COMMON BRICK

PLASTER

SMOKE CHAMBER

SMOKE SHELF

DAMPER

THROAT

LINTEL

ANGLE IRON

RUBBLE~ CEMENT FILL

PLASTER

OUTSIDE BLOCK

TIN CAN

TIN CAN

AIR ENTERS

PLENUM

HEARTH

TIN CAN

PROFILE

(18)

The proper way to build up stone is to begin at one corner and go up 2′ or say 30″, depending on the rocks you are using. If you have two rocks and they fit in real easy—great. Then you move around the whole structure, and by the time you are back at the corner you started at, it is all set up. Sure, its green and you have to be careful not to bang into it, but you shouldn't have any difficulty. I've gone up as much as 4′ at a time. I just started going on a corner and kept right on going. Everything kept falling into place just like a chess game. Every move I made was just beautiful. I always had back up for it. When you get into that kind of mood, well just let her go . . .

flow with it. You have to be extremely careful though if you are attempting to go 4′ at a time. Your rocks can't be too big or too heavy. Its better to stick within 2′.

Before striking the joints—that is, before digging the mortar out, make sure it has set a good 4 to 8 hours, depending on the weather (longer if damper). The striking process gets rid of the excess mortar which squeezes out

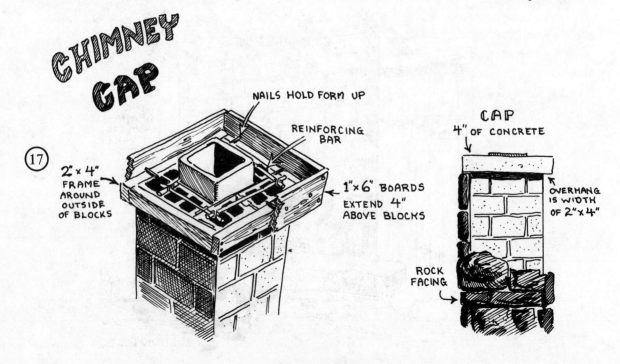

CHIMNEY GAP

NAILS HOLD FORM UP

REINFORCING BAR

(17)

2″ x 4″ FRAME AROUND OUTSIDE OF BLOCKS

1″ x 6″ BOARDS EXTEND 4″ ABOVE BLOCKS

CAP
4″ OF CONCRETE

OVERHANG IS WIDTH OF 2″ x 4″

ROCK FACING

between the stones as they are set in place. Striking helps reveal the rocks and gives them a more rustic, three dimensional feeling. I use a simple screw driver for this operation (plate 16).

The chimney should be capped off with 4″ of concrete. It is best to cap it with concrete instead of mortar because concrete doesn't have as great a tendency to crack in mass as mortar does. But concrete will crack in mass—thats why expansion joints are used in car ports etc., but in a small place above the chimney such a precaution is not necessary.

If the chimney was made of concrete blocks, a form for the cap could be built quite simply. You take 2 x 4s and put them around the top of the chimney. Nail 1 x 6s around the exterior of the top of the 2 x 4s, letting them extend up 4″, then just let the frame hang on nails over the chimney top. This way the cap overlaps the exterior side of the concrete blocks by 1½″, the width of the 2 x 4s. Be sure to leave 4″ of the flue liner exposed as an inside form.

I bring the insulation right up to within a couple inches of the top and lay reinforcing rod around the poured cap.

A similar type form can be used above stone but care must be taken to shape the top of the chimney stack so it will support such a form (plate 17).

The face and firebox were built

simultaneously and everything was taken up at once except the exterior wall. That was constructed later. It took a helper and I 7 or 8 days to do the entire interior area, except for the hearth which was also added later (plate 18).

When laying the slab be sure to take the hearth into consideration, though there is not a great deal of weight on it. I have built hearths on the floor joists and mortared the facing onto a constructed wood box frame. The frame was prepared with paper to absorb expansion and reinforced with a wire for support. This works well if the rocks are not too thick or too big. But with this method you usually get a crack between the hearth masonry and the fireplace proper because the floor joists are bound to shrink and the whole thing is built on them. The hearth of this fireplace is built on the slab foundation.

After I finished the stone face, I cleaned off the joints with a solution of 50 percent muriatic acid, 50 percent water. You can use a steel brush or a stiff bristle brush to take the cement stains off the face of the rock. This is a messy job that should be done with gloves. When all the unsightly cement stains are gone, wash the face down thoroughly to remove the acid residue, then let it dry. Now, I'll let you in on a secret: Take a bottle of coca-cola, put it in a pan, and wet down a sponge with it. Then go over the rocks with the sponge. A mason told me this one. I thought the guy was off his rocker, but it really works. It gives the stones a nice clean feeling. I don't know what that says about coca-cola in one's stomach though (plate 19, 20).

As we finished the interior of the fireplace the weather began to get real nasty so we didn't start the exterior facing until the following spring. I used the same principles as were used in the interior face and it turned out just as beautiful, adding a rustic monument to the entrance of the house (plate 21).

We are indeed happy with our fireplace. It has become the central point where people gather around and communicate, especially in winter. In that season we swing the divan to the middle of the living area to create a semi-circular continuation of the hearth, thus making the area around the warm fireplace snug and cozy.

The fireplace is the structural, aesthetic, and functional axis of the house. It is the center of strength in its dominant form.

Structurally, it is the point where the two roofs join together; aesthetically it is where the design contrasts blend to epitomize the flow of the spaces and relationships within the house; functionally it is the gathering place which provides warmth and nourishment to all who join together around it. It joins everything together just as mortar joins stone, as nails join wood, and as real communication joins people. If care and patient awareness are utilized throughout the development of the fireplace, it will carry on the flow . . . doing its part in bringing it all together.

Chapter Three

The Monolithic Approach

I thought a fireplace would be a bit extravagant but my wife wanted one and I soon succumbed to her wishes. After all, we were building a house that we planned to live in for a long time, so we might as well include all the luxuries we wanted as we constructed it instead of adding them on later as expensive afterthoughts. This is one decision we never regretted. We just love watching the open fire in winter. It keeps the house totally warm and is an excellent social center.

We planned our fireplace to be in the center of the house, dividing the kitchen and livingroom areas. Sure it takes up a lot of space but it is much more efficient being entirely indoors. It is surrounded by its own warmth instead of located on a weather exposed outer wall. It retains its own heat, radiating it back into the house through the rock face and upstairs red brick (plate 1). None of the radiant heat dissipates out of the cold side of an exposed chimney. This also reduces the problem of smoke condensing into creosote because it doesn't get quickly cooled off by the outside weather.

Since we had to build a huge chimney for the fireplace I decided to incorporate as much as possible in the one central stack so we didn't have to deal with several expensive and tedious chimney stacks. I designed this complex so it would include within its 2½' x 6' main base a chimney flue for the basement furnace, a fireplace and flue, a flue for the kitchen cookstove, and as an afterthought a small built-in oven. We didn't really decide on the oven until the basement block foundation was built. There was only a limited space between the

heatform unit and the exterior wall. Consequently, the largest possible oven we could have was 20″ wide (plates 2 and 3).

We used a heatform firebox for several reasons, mainly because it was easy to install and created a nice air circulation flow through its double walls. The cool air enters through two low intake vents and circulates around the fire in the space between the walls. After it heats up it rises by convection, goes out the upper vents and flows through the room as an auxiliary heat source. Heatforms also make it easier to construct the fireplace and chimney because they provide an inner form for the surrounding masonry (plate 4).

Even with all the Heatform's advantages I still sometimes have second thoughts about a firebrick firebox because the thin sheet metal construction of the heatform cools off much faster than firebrick. So when using a heatform the fireplace is warming up rapidly and cooling off rapidly after the fire is out as opposed to 4″ of firebrick taking a while to heat up but retaining heat long enough after you put the last log in at night to keep the house warm until morning. And with a little effort and ingenuity an air circulating unit can be made with firebrick, having both the advantages of retaining heat and giving off extra heat through convection. All you have to do is back the firebrick with an ⅛th″

③

thick double walled sheet metal jacket with air ducts so you can draw the cold air in from below and bring it out through the upper outlet vents. Then back the outer layer of sheet metal with the necessary 4″ of clay brick.

Also if I were to design my fireplace over I'd figure out some way to run a duct or

HOT AIR FLOWS INTO ROOM

④ METAL FIREBOX

VENT FOR COLD AIR

OUTER FORM

INNER FORM

COLD AIR ENTERS

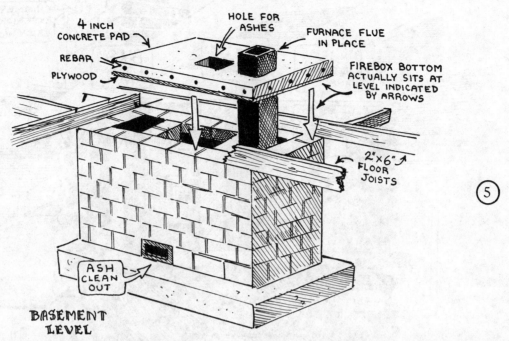

4 INCH
CONCRETE PAD

REBAR

PLYWOOD

HOLE FOR
ASHES

FURNACE FLUE
IN PLACE

FIREBOX BOTTOM
ACTUALLY SITS AT
LEVEL INDICATED
BY ARROWS

2"x 6"
FLOOR
JOISTS

⑤

ASH
CLEAN
OUT

BASEMENT
LEVEL

channel from the firebox to the outside of the house so it would not deplete the oxygen from inside the room (see chapter 2).

We began construction by pouring a 4″ thick pad that extends 6″ beyond the base of the chimney complex on all sides, approximately 5′ x 7′. A mixture of two parts sand, 2 parts gravel and 1 part Portland cement was used. No large rocks were put in for volume. When you want a solid foundation under a structure that is going to be carrying a tremendous amount of weight it would be best to not break up the pad with large rocks but make it of continuous small aggregate. We did not put any rebar in the pad because it was set on bedrock and hard packed gravel. It is usually wise to reinforce the pad with rebar on 12″ square centers, a little below the middle of the pour.

Above the pad we began the block enclousure around the perimeter of the base, allowing for the necessary flue and ash pit openings as the courses were raised. A 8″ x 16″ column was left hollow from the pad to the top of the base (floor joist level) to save on blocks at the right side, then we put in a column of blocks and left another space 2′ long by 16″ wide in the center for an ash pit. This ash pit also extends from pad to floor

level. A clean out slot was allowed in the bottom block at the center of the ash pit at the front wall. On the left, the blocks were stacked solid to a height of approxmately 5½′ where the furnace's thimble pipe intersects it (see plate 3). At that point the 8 x 8 furnace flue stack was started. A hole in the bottom flue tile was cut out to accommodate the intersecting furnace pipe. The flue linings were stacked and mortared together to beyond floor level, creating an inner form for the main floor pad. So at the main floor level, just below the floor joists, two spaces were cut into the plywood bottom form; one for the furnace flue and one for the ash pit. Since the main floor had already been laid and a 4′ x 6′ hole was framed between the floor joists, the surrounding 2 x 6 joists and headers were used as the side forms for the 6″ pad which we then poured. The pad was reinforced with rebar placed on 12″ centers wherever possible (plate 5). The plywood was buried forever.

The blocks for the hearth were placed across the front of the already set up pad, allowing 4″ on the three outer sides for the stone face. The top was then finished with flat sheets of commercial slate (see plate 6).

195

If we were to rebuild the hearth we would make it slightly wider for aesthetic reasons. This would also make it more comfortable for people to sit on. As it is now, its 16″ width is too narrow for a person to sit on and be far enough from the direct fire. Also a wider hearth would help prevent soot and debris from spilling out on the floor. The perimeter of the block structure was laid out with a few courses of block, 4″ in from the

surrounding edge to allow for the rock face.

Next came the heatform unit. On top of the pad, between it and the above heatform a layer of 4″ firebrick was laid. The unit was then set on the firebrick. The heatform is a double jacketed steel unit consisting of firebox, throat, smokeshelf, and damper assembly. Its double-walled construction allows it to take in cool air from the low air inlet vents, circulate it through the space between the walls of the firebox and expell it as warm air out the round air flues in the throat. Once this unit was set in place it was lined with insulation wherever it came in contact with masonry to allow for metal expansion and contraction. Since the firebox and throat area were shaped by the heatform the smoke shelf masonry was an easy chore using rough filler brick between the metal and the outside block work to form the curved shelf. After the insulation and necessary block was put around the heatform a piece of angle iron was set into the blockwork on either side, above the throat. This angle iron supports the 12 x 12″ flue linings and the surrounding chimney masonry.

Meanwhile, the masonry around the furnace flue was also raised and our afterthought oven was allotted for on the other side of the fireplace. Since the heatform took so much space, 46″ overall width in front, 33″ in back, there was little room left for an oven. In fact even to have an oven that had only 16″ x 18″ inside dimensions at the opening we had to steal space from the side of the fireplace, eliminating the bricks that should be between the two structures. There is only 2″ of firebrick and a thickness of fiberglass

⑦

insulation between the oven and the heatform. Actually this does provide the advantage of the oven unit being heated by the fireplace as well as by its own firebox. And there is no problem with the oven burning out since it is constructed out of firebrick.

The 8 x 8″ flue opening for the oven and cookstove was started about 3′ up from the floor, just level with the oven's firebox. This flue opening is located deep into the chimney structure from the kitchen side to allow the oven to have a depth of 24″ before reaching it. This is a dual-purpose flue for the oven and for a cookstove. (plates 6 and 7). Just under this oven there are two smaller compartments, a 10 x 10″ firebox than extends 32″ in depth to the back of the flue opening and a shallower ash pit below. The doors to these three compartments are

⑧

FLUE

OVEN

FIREBOX

ASH BOX

FIRE BRICK WALLS

METAL BARS SIT ON TOP OF WALL BRICKS SUPPORTING OVEN ROOF AND FLOOR

RODS FORM FIRE GRATE

CEMENT BLOCK

HEART TUBES

FIBREGLASS

⑨

STEEL LINTEL BAR

SLATE PLACED ON EDGE FORMS VENTS

HEARTH

old iron furnace doors mounted on steel plates that were embedded in the masonry. The oven and firebox are surrounded by a lining of 4″ of firebrick. The top bricks are held up with a series of 2″ steel straps which go across the top of the oven box. These straps and the ¼″ rebar grate bottom of the firebox are also embedded in the surrounding masonry (plate 8).

The air from the oven fire comes in through the ash pit door air control and goes through the ¼″ rebar grills which the fire fuel sits on. The fire then heats the oven from underneath and from behind as it goes up the flue. It burns terrific. The long chimney pulls the smoke out just beautifully. It heats up great, except it can't be damped down to build up a good, continuous heat in the oven for proper baking. One remedy for this problem would be to put a damper inside the flue above the oven. This would keep the heat close to the oven and cut down flue drafts. One damper would regulate both the cookstove and oven it it were placed above where the cookstove pipe intersects the flue. Right now if we close down all the mechanisms of the cookstove and then open the fire door to the oven, the

cookstove would damp down even more because the draft would be sucked into the fire door opening, reducing the amount coming down from the flue. Also, to circulate the heat around the oven to the utmost efficiency I suggest planning the oven so it would include air channels around the sides. This would provide an even heat around the oven instead of only heating the bottom and back of it.

The inside block and masonry were continued up until the top of the main floor, then the rock face was started. Remember to insert quite a number of corrugated tin ties in between the concrete blocks so the stone face will hold securely to this inner concrete form. We wanted a cobblestone finish on this fireplace, so we searched the nearby creek and river beds for this kind of round rock. You don't have to worry about such rock exploding from heat because none of them will be in direct contact with the fire.

The mortar mixture was the standard mix with one additional part Portland cement. A ¼″ mesh screen was used to screen the sand. I prefer using coarse sand when mortaring rocks together because this material provides more adhesiveness. It has more angles that grip and interlock to each other than does the finer sand. The round stone facing went relatively fast, about 25 sq. ft. or 2' all around the structure in a single day with two of us working steadily. Actually you could go as high as you want with any single course until the mortar and already seated stones can't carry anymore weight without slumping or falling out. We tried to get each stone to fit so it wasn't dependant on mortar to hold it on top of the stone below it. If it was put in a precarious position so we had to hope that the mortar would hold it, it was taken off and altered by either tilting it until it was secure or trimming it with a stone mason's hammer.

The thing about stonework that makes it a good piece of work is how clean you can keep the face of the rocks, rather than leaving them covered with mortar. At the end of a day or half way through the day, depending on how fast the mortar is setting up, I clean off the freshly laid stones with a sponge, making certain to remove all traces of mortar on the faces and pointing where necessary.

The stone face surrounds all the concrete block and the outer edges of the heatform. An iron lintel bar was placed across the front of the firebox, a few inches below the steel frame of the heatform. It overlaps the sides of the firebox opening by 2" on either side so it could be embedded into the mortar face (40" long across 36" opening). Fiberglass was put around the iron lintel where it comes in contact with the masonry to compensate for expansion. This bar was set below the top of the firebox opening to shorten its height because there are doors on either side of the fireplace which bring in drafts that sweep the smoke out into the room. The lower lintel keeps the smoke from rolling out of the firebox. This fireplace burns fuel beautifully even without a grate. When you don't have a grate the coals go into the ashes, radiating their heat longer than if they were suspended over a draft. Being on the firebrick instead of on an open

grate wood burns slowly and more efficiently, thus saving on fuel.

The low intake openings on either side of the firebox were covered with thin layers of slate on end, spaced far enough apart to not interfere with the incoming air. The outlet vent above the box was also dealt with in the same manner with flat stones on edge, allowing an aesthetic contrast between the round cobblestones and the flat materials (plates 9-11).

The concrete blocks were continued above the main floor, around the three flues, but were slightly recessed so the red brick facing would be above the main floor blocks. This portion of the stack was designed this way so the heavy red bricks would not be directly above the lower cobblestone facing, but be raised on the more solid concrete block foundation. These red bricks were stacked almost to the ceiling where they were replaced with a couple of concrete

blocks for contrast and strength (plate 12). The facing was continued out beyond the roof with alternating red and beige bricks. Then the whole chimney structure was capped with an 1½″ of concrete and a lip extending 2″ beyond the stack all the way around it.

If this fireplace were to be reconstructed we would make it 16″ narrower at the base (one block shorter) to have more basement space and save on expensive materials and labor. The basement concrete work could then be corbeled out near the main floor to accommodate the cantilevered hearth instead of supporting it with such a massive foundation. Also as an afterthought I would have put in bolts or hinges for shelving above the cookstove so kitchen implements would be in a handy place above it.

Chapter Four
Cedar Log Root Cellar

(by Kathryn Woodward)

Winter has become our season of plans. As a city child I had never bothered classifying the seasons except as they related to the school year or to the clothes I could con out of my mother, and later to how much I was cooped up with the children. In the country they are definitive.

It was our second winter and we were

GATHERING IN

planning the work for the following building season—the seven months when there is no snow usually referred to as summer. Our land had been bush when we arrived, two couples and two children. We had spent the first hectic summer jointly building our water system, two cabins, an outhouse, a chicken house, a tool shed, a make-shift wood shed, clearing land for a garden, for pasture and orchard and keeping our co-operative running smoothly. By fall, completely exhausted, we gratefully returned to our respective cabins. The first winter was therefore one of minimal plans, mostly for the expansion of what already existed. Our partners were designing themselves a new house to be built in slow stages and we were contemplating a wood and storage shed.

By the second winter our most fundamental needs had been met and it was time to evaluate the accomplishments and weigh them against the dreams. We had had a basic premise when we made the move from city to country: to learn the skills for providing the essentials of human needs with our own hands and minds. The winter nights of talking accumulated as we debated the direction of our future energies, how much of ourselves we wanted to devote to the "place" and where did those non-essentials that have become indispensable fit into our new lifestyle. We were learning that neither of us wanted to live as "Walden Pond," that we both wished to find a satisfactory way to combine the best of urban and rural worlds. We discussed how a homestead grows in stages, each stage being a unit unto itself, dependant for efficiency on total completion of that phase. Keeping a cow creates the need for pasture, a hayfield, fencing, a barn. Truck gardening might involve further clearing, a tractor, sources of fertilizer, good transportation. We were on the last lap of stage one, shelter, water, garden, and winter fuel.

Did anything remain before we chose to tackle another stage? If we were going to the trouble of growing our own food and buying or trading for what we could not produce, were we obligated to provide these fruits of labor with adequate storage? We answered yes. Other people's basements and decrepit root cellars had proven wasteful. Storing jars in the house meant risking total loss by freezing if we happened to spend just a few nights away from home during a cold spell. The freezer, though a miraculous invention, is not useful for all foods and depends upon the benevolence of the power company. And so grew our plans for a root cellar as the building focus for the third summer.

The placement of the root cellar was a foregone conclusion. We had always assumed that one would be built sometime. So during the first summer when we hired a backhoe for the water line trench we had it scoop out a hole into the mountainside. We had little choice about the exact location of the hole. The flat portion of our narrow acreage butts up to the mountain slope and we merely chose a spot that was close to the two cabins, where the hillside is steepest and where there is no spring runoff. The snugger the building fits into the mountainside the less work there is pushing dirt up against the walls for maximum insulation. Proximity to the house is a consideration which can be overlooked only in the summer when snow is a mere memory.

Another consideration is shade and sun. Our main concern is keeping the food from freezing in the winter, since we do not store much during the two to three hot months. Therefore, we picked a site that would be shaded in summer by deciduous trees and shrubs whose leaves drop off exposing the root cellar to whatever bit of sun manages to fight through the snow clouds.

The backhoe dug out a hole whose size ultimately proved to be a lucky guess but it would have been far better to approach construction in the logical order—that is, plan the size of the root cellar first, then get a hole dug to meet the specifications. The hole should be about three feet larger than the outside dimensions of the building so that there is room to work, but should not be made any larger than needed. That will just add to the time or money to have the building backfilled.

Whatever books and pamphlets on food storage we could find were limited to either basement root cellars or outdoor ones, constructed of concrete. We were definitely committed to an outside root cellar. Two families would be using the structure and we felt that it would be better located on neutral ground rather than have one family disturb the other to get its food. We also considered that since fire is always a risk when heating with wood it was advantageious not to have everything under one roof. And of course we had the hole.

Choosing the building material for the root cellar emphasized once again the lesson that country people usually know what resource is most suited for their area. We were all set to build with concrete even though many of the book diagrams were of root cellars so

SIDE SHELVES ARE SUSPENDED FROM 2"x 8"'S BOLTED TO THE CEILING JOISTS

BINS FOR ROOT CROPS

APPLES

MEAT

①

elaborate they resembled bomb shelters and even though neither of us thought concrete a particularly attractive medium. But we had decided to forego aesthetics in favour of practicality—if the books said concrete, then it was concrete. Luckily, Jim found himself talking about root cellars to a long-time resident who warned that concrete was, in his opinion, the worst of all alternatives for this climate where there is so much rain and snow. Concrete retains moisture, doesn't breathe well and therefore presents problems of ventilation. Without proper ventilation mildew develops and food spoils. Seepage of water into the root cellar will also ruin the food there. Our friend suggested three alternative building materials: rock (being more porous than concrete), frame construction packed well with insulation, or log construction. The rock medium was intriguing but is time consuming and we have a fairly short building season. Therefore it was frame or logs.

Up until then all of our buildings had been built with dimension lumber utilizing some poles. We have few large trees on our land due to past logging and to a forest fire; with several mills in this area lumber is relatively cheap. And we had always been building against time. So while we were fast becoming proficient in frame construction we were totally ignorant of log building. But during our first summer we had picked up a bunch of cedar logs for a sauna that wasn't getting built. The length of the logs, strangely enough exactly fitted the hole. They were just lying around soon to decay. We said, "Why not? Let's try it." and our decision was made.

Once we decided to use logs we found the whole building taking on an almost spiritual tone. Providing a space for our own food with materials from the surrounding countryside and designing the whole building to harmonize with its setting became the principal expression of our joy to be living here.

We were now ready to get down to the business of constructing. To fit the size of the hole in the mountain and to accomodate the logs already cut we decided on a two-chamber root cellar whose outside dimensions were 10' x 14'. The inner chamber would be 8' x 9' and be separated from the outside room by an insulated frame wall. Using a frame wall eliminated the difficulty of interlocking logs and provided better insulation than the curved surfaces of logs. Since this wall must insulate independant of backfill dirt, no skimping should occur.

The height of the root cellar, 6' 2", was determined by the heighth of the tallest member of our family and by the number of logs we were able to get. It is best to keep the building as small as the need warrants. Excess space increased building time, but more importantly, proper temperature control is difficult to maintain in a larger structure. The two-room construction is essential because it allows the outside door to be closed before opening the door to the main chamber, thereby keeping the exchange of air and temperature at a minimum. The outside chamber provides an excellent place to hang meat and to store winter apples until the coldest weather (plate 1).

For building logs we used western red cedar, some of which were picked up at a road construction site and the rest came from an abandoned logging operation. Western red cedar is one of the most impervious woods to rot and dampness. When in the ground it is the number one choice for this type of building (plate 2). If cedar is unavailable just ask around for the best wood in your area for underground use and how it should be treated.

When choosing the trees to cut, aim for the straightest logs for uniform thickness. Uniformity of size will make notching much easier. A 6" diameter is the minimum thickness; 8-10" would be better. But for ease of handling, the size of the building and

WESTERN RED CEDAR

INWOOD 9P '75

therefore the length of the logs, should be taken into consideration. Trees which have fallen naturally or have been cut and are lying on the ground must be examined carefully. If an unpeeled log has been on the ground for too long, rot may start to work its way under the bark. If cedar logs are used they should be well dried, because their shrinkage is tremendous. But all logs should be dry and peeled before using.

When our logs were assembled at the site their progression in the building was planned out. Starting with the largest logs we arranged them with an eye toward uniformity in the tiers and toward a steady succession from thickest to thinnest for the courses.

Actual construction was begun by cleaning and leveling the site. An unleveled site produces unlevel walls and therefore a totally wonky building. We went so far as to use a good level on the ground to assess our progress. Once satisfied, we built the forms for the footing, using 2 x 6″ boards. The forms should be strong enough or well enough supported so that they are not pushed out of line when the cement is poured. We braced our forms with outlining stakes which were driven into the ground every few feet and nailed to their outside. To further prevent spreading, holes were drilled and wire braces were put in every 4′.

The footing itself must be solid and strong to avoid settling, to prevent shifting when the site is backfilled, and to ensure that stress is equally distributed throughout the total perimeter of the building. We decided on a concrete footing because it met these standards. Two alternatives are flat or tamped-down gravel. Neither produces the desired stability and in both cases the chances of rot are greater as the necessary vapor barrier is harder to create between a bumpy surface and the log.

The footing is 6″ high and 14″ wide and was poured directly on the leveled ground using a 1:5 mixture of cement to sand and gravel. Immediately following the pour we inserted pieces of 5/8″ reinforcing rods protruding from the center line of the footing, one in each corner and the others at approximately 4′ intervals, which later served as anchors for the first course of logs. The heighth of these rods depended on the thickness of the first log. Steel bar or pipe can also be used as anchors; we happened to have some extra rods left over from another project (plate 3).

After the concrete was poured it was dampened for three days and covered after each watering with feed bags to hold in the moisture. Since cement should cure four to five days before being built upon, we took the opportunity for a break and went camping. Once home, with renewed energy, we recommenced work by removing the forms from the now dry cement and placed a strip of 50-pound roofing paper all along the top of the footing as a vapor barrier. This prevented the first course of logs from sitting directly on the cement which would be constantly wet if in contact with moisture. Logs will rot faster if wet.

Our first course of logs proved our first major mistake. We took the two logs for the long walls and drilled holes to fit them over the rods sticking out of the footing. We then ripped a log in half lengthwise with the chainsaw for the short walls, fitting them over their rods in the same manner. These

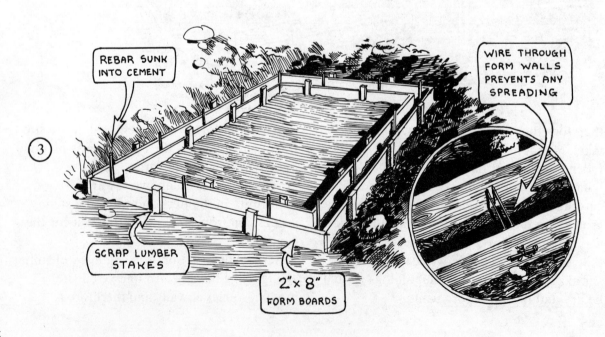

③ REBAR SUNK INTO CEMENT

WIRE THROUGH FORM WALLS PREVENTS ANY SPREADING

SCRAP LUMBER STAKES

2″ x 8″ FORM BOARDS

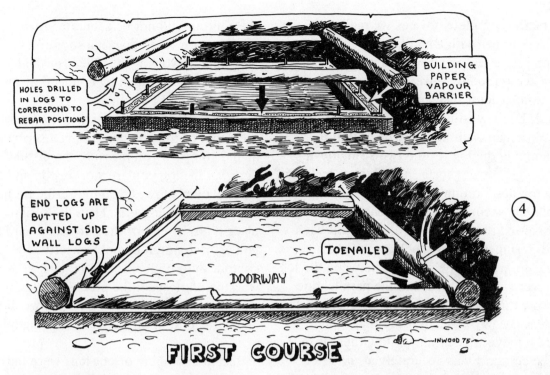

HOLES DRILLED IN LOGS TO CORRESPOND TO REBAR POSITIONS

BUILDING PAPER VAPOUR BARRIER

END LOGS ARE BUTTED UP AGAINST SIDE WALL LOGS

TOENAILED

DOORWAY

INWOOD 75

FIRST COURSE

logs were ripped to compensate for the displacement of height between the long walls and short, perpendicular walls. This half log displacement is necessary for the notching process.

The rectangle of the first course was formed by butting the ends of the short logs against the sides of the long logs at the corners. Much smarter would have been to put down the short half logs first and then notch the long logs to fit over them, thereby creating a more tied-together fit. These first logs are just sitting over the rods, which is sufficient anchorage as only lateral movement is possible. We did not have a drill long enough to go clear through the logs and so were unable to use thinner ¼" rods which would have been bent over the top of the log for a tighter anchor (plate 4).

With the first course down we had reached the point of deciding how to make the door space. The front half log would serve as the door sill. Fitting the outside door tightly and accurately is a necessity for good temperature control and much harder to achieve if the sill is cement, wood being easier to plane. We knew of two methods of making door spaces in log walls: If enough long logs are available a solid wall can be

constructed and a door can be cut out later; or if there are only shorter logs, they can be notched into the structure at one end and later be tied together at the other end by a solid door frame. Since we had few long logs we chose the latter method and stacked the logs at random lengths that were each a bit longer than the beginning of the openings. Using a chalk line as the guide, the logs were later sawed, making straight vertical lines for the door frame (plate 5).

The time has now arrived for our first notch; we could no longer procrastinate. The challenge must be met. Knowing ourselves

BOARD NAILED TO LOGS SERVES AS CHAINSAW GUIDE

CHALK LINE

INWOOD 75

to be the complete novices we really are, we traded dinner with a more experienced friend for a lesson. It proved invaluable and boosted our confidence. If no one is around as an instructor, use an old log to practice on. It beats wasting a good building log.

We began each notching operation by examining the log for the two straightest, flattest, opposite surfaces and these became the top and bottom of the log as it fit into the wall. We secured the log in place for measuring the notch with a log dog at each end. Using a ruler we took an "eyeball" measurement of the distance between the log we were working with and the parallel one below, this would determine the depth of the notch. By "eyeball," I mean that I made sure my eye was parallel with either surface to be certain I was accurately at the low point of the upper log to be placed and the high point of the parallel one below. Once the depth of the notch was determined I followed the contour of the end of the perpendicular log below with the ruler and transcribed a series of dots ⅛″ shallower than the determined depth. I reasoned marking it ⅛″ shallow to allow for miscalculation and overcutting. Be sure that the ruler is always straight up and down or

the contour will not be accurate. Also, use a thick crayon when marking so you'll have a clear line to work with. When finished, a semi-circle was drawn by connecting all the dots as in a child's game.

We later found an easier way to determine the depth of the notches. Using a scribe or an old compass you measure the distance between the log you are working on and the parallel one below. Open the scribe to that width and lock it there. Then the scribe, place it an the end of the perpendicular log you want to notch to and transcribe the contour onto both sides of the end we were working on. Repeat the process on the other end, its as simple as that. Too bad we didn't know this one when we were building (plate 6).

Because so many of our logs were fairly narrow and we did not realize the importance of uniform thickness when they were cut we sometimes came up against a space between the logs that was larger than ½ the diameter of the log at the notch. This means that if we cut the notch large enough so that the log sat directly on the one below we had to cut out much more than ½ the width of the log. This would weaken it. On the other hand, if we cut the notch to a

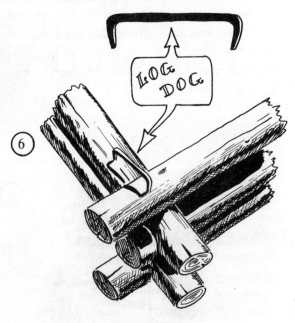

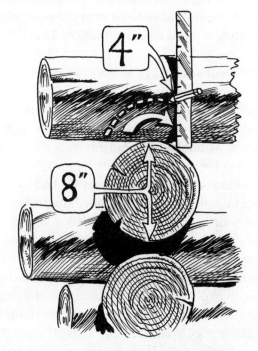

depth that matched the radius measurement, the log did not sit on the one below but hung suspended. To compensate we had to shim in between some of the logs. This also occurs when the logs taper too much so that you are notching a very small top log over a rather large bottom butt. To avoid this, choose logs that are of uniform width or make a progression from widest to narrowest that is steady, and if possible, cut your logs at the same time so they can be compared.

After we individually marked either end of the log, the log dogs were removed and the log was rolled to an upside down position and was redogged for the chainsaw *kerf* cuts. The kerfs were then cut to the lines of the semi-circle. Remember, for safety, when the walls get too high, take your logs off and do the cutting on the ground. Also, until you are an experienced notcher, and maybe even then, always cut out your notches smaller. It is easier to chisel out a little more to fit the

curve than to deal with an oversized notch (plate 7).

Using a hammer we knocked out the pieces of wood between the kerfs and chiseled a flat, accurate border on the edge of the notch as a guideline (plates 8 and 9). With the nose of the chainsaw we smoothed out the interior of the notch (plate 10). It is wise to practise this step. We ruined a few good logs because of our inexperience.

Once or twice we did hit a perfect bulls-eye on the first try when the log was rolled back into place but usually we had to chisel out several times to get a good fit.

Sometimes the notches proved satisfactory but bumps in either the top or bottom log where they met prevented a tight fit. To correct this we wedged up the top log at each end and using the chain saw blade laid flat, leveled the bumps. If done right the logs fell into place when the wedges were removed. When the fit was satisfactory we rolled the log away once more and laid down fiberglass insulation in between the two logs and at the notches. These 2″ wide strips of insulation had been cut with a handsaw when the stuff was still tightly rolled (plate 11).

Fiberglass was chosen as insulating material because it would be permanent. Since the building would be backfilled, rechinking from the outside would be impossible. Once the fiberglass was laid we rolled the log to its final resting place and spiked it down at each notch and at several points along the log to ensure that there would be no movement when backfilling occurred. We used 6″ spikes but the size of

the nails depends on the width of the logs. If you have spikes which are not long enough, a hole can be drilled part way through the top log and the spike-punched down, using a long bolt as the punch (plate 12).

With each succeeding course, the ends of the logs were alternated so that the butt end of the log above sat on the smaller end of the one below, thereby keeping the building level.

When our courses were completed we were left with one tier lower, or two sides lower than the others. To compensate we nailed plates of dimension lumber to even out the final tier. Aesthetically, logs would

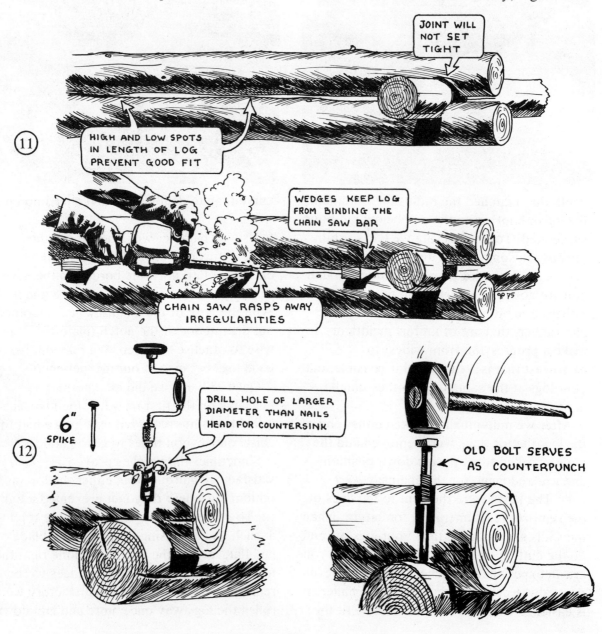

⑪ HIGH AND LOW SPOTS IN LENGTH OF LOG PREVENT GOOD FIT

JOINT WILL NOT SET TIGHT

WEDGES KEEP LOG FROM BINDING THE CHAIN SAW BAR

CHAIN SAW RASPS AWAY IRREGULARITIES

⑫ 6″ SPIKE

DRILL HOLE OF LARGER DIAMETER THAN NAILS HEAD FOR COUNTERSINK

OLD BOLT SERVES AS COUNTERPUNCH

2" x 8" DOOR FRAME

2" x 6" INSIDE FRAME

6" INCHS OF FIBREGLASS WITH PAPER BACKING TO OUTSIDE

1" x 8" CEDAR SHEATHING

2" x 8" BOTTOM PLATE

8" WIDE CEMENT BASE

(13)

have been preferable but our log supply was exhausted.

Once the log walls were up we poured an 8″ wide cement footing to accommodate the interior wall. This is not a bearing wall (one carrying structural weight) so reinforcement was not necessary. This wall was framed with 2 x 6 material. Using a chainsaw and chisel, a channel was notched in each log at the place where the frame wall met the logs. This provided a straight, flat surface for the end studs to be nailed to and created a snug fit for the wall with no air spaces. We stapled 3″ thick fiberglass insulation to both sides of the frame so that the paper backing of the insulation formed a vapor barrier,

then we covered the wall with 1″ cedar boards (plate 13).

Planer shavings that are stuffed down between the walls are also adequate insulation. The shavings must be bone dry and well tamped when first put in, because they settle. If the wall is not properly filled the settled shavings will create a space at the top resulting in heat loss.

By the time we reached the construction of the roof harvest season was approaching and as an expedient we resorted to the use of dimension lumber for ceiling joists and roof rafters. We had been wrestling with the type of roof to build throughout the summer. Originally, we had decided on a flat-log roof covered with 2 or 3′ of dirt. This was cheap, easy, quick, and in our ignorance we believed it to be a good insulator. But the same friend that discouraged our idea of cement walls destroyed this notion to. In our wet climate, he said, this type of roof is sure to leak and as we have rains in the fall often followed by a quick freeze before the snow, we could be left with a frozen mass of dirt covering our precious food. When it did finally fall, the snow would act as an insulator and the big ice cube over the root cellar would remain so until the spring thaw.

Once it was established that we would be building some sort of regular roof design, we had to decide if we wanted to make a functional space under such an exposed roof. Our neighbors had built a log root cellar with a hip roof high enough to allow for a storage area above a well insulated ceiling. Other root cellars in the area have entire second stories built above them for use as workshops. In the end we chose a simple peaked roof with a 45-degree pitch, coming down to the backfilled ground level.

It was fairly economical; we didn't really need the storage or work space, and we were pressed for time. But most important we considered our root cellar to be aesthectically pleasing as is in its surroundings in the woods as a space exclusively for food. This may seem extravagant, a waste of a good foundation, but for us it was appropriate and resulted in a much lovelier building.

For the ceiling we used cedar 2 x 8s as joists and the random left-over 2″ lumber for the ceiling boards. The two boards where the ceiling meets the roof rafters were carefully notched to attain a good fit for better insulation. The roof rafters were also 2 x 8s on 2′ centers (plate 14). The roof had to be strong enough to hold the whole winter's snow load. There would be no interior heat coming up to melt the snow.

In order to determine the pitch of the roof we overlapped the ends of two pieces of lumber, leaving the nail loose so that the boards could move. One of us stood on the ceiling and held the sample rafter while the

(14)

RAFTERS at 2′ CENTRES

212

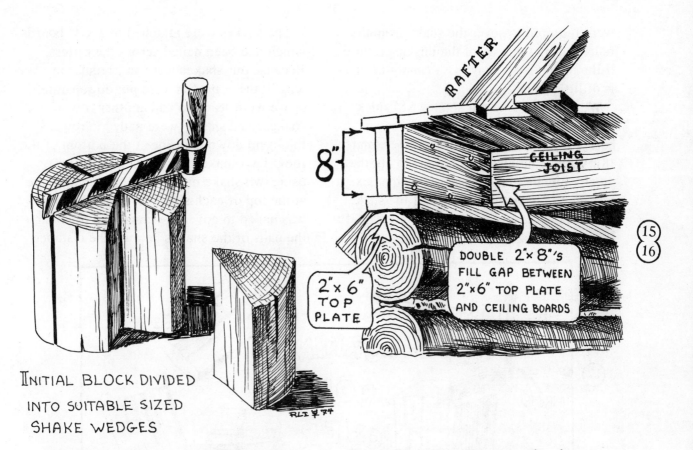

INITIAL BLOCK DIVIDED
INTO SUITABLE SIZED
SHAKE WEDGES

8"

RAFTER

CEILING JOIST

2" x 6" TOP PLATE

DOUBLE 2"x 8"'s FILL GAP BETWEEN 2"x 6" TOP PLATE AND CEILING BOARDS

(15)
(16)

RLI 74

other stood away from the building and studied the effect of different pitches. We were aiming for a roof that blended the building with the slope of the hillside whose pitch was steep enough to shed some of the winter's snow. We finally chose the 45-degree pitch.

The rafters were cut and butted at an angle at top, then supported there with small 2 x 8 horizontal brace. We cut 2 x 8s as blocking for the space between the roof rafters and the ceiling joists and doubled them up to increase the insulative value of the wood (plate 15).

The roof of the root cellar is shaked. The *shakes* (shingles) were split intermittantly during construction as a change of pace. If shake bolts can be picked up in the woods, the shakes would be a very cheap, durable, and beautiful roofing material to use, especially in a building where no fire is to be laid.

Our shakes are far from perfect, but there is no leakage from the roof. We had gathered the bolts before knowing much

about bolt quality. Western red cedar provides the best shake material, but in the west spruces, fir and pine can also be used. We picked up our bolts on a Sunday from a logging operation site. They had been rejected because they came from decadent trees whose centers were beginning to rot out. We were most careless in our selection, lugging home many bolts good only for kindling, but we managed to get enough suitable ones to make the hard chore of gathering them worthwhile. Bolts should be straight grained, dry, clear of knots and if possible from 20″ to 30″ long, though shakes down to 14″ are adequate. The center should not be too rotten so that the shake is of sufficient width, at least 6″. The larger the shakes the faster the roof goes on, the less nails are used, and the fewer cracks there are, minimizing the chance of leakage.

The bolts were sectioned into a few easy to handle chunks and the shakes were split from them with a *froe* (frow) which was pounded with a birch mallet (plates 16 and 17). The heavier the mallet the less whacks were required to sever the shake from the bolt. But by the laws of diminishing returns, if the mallet is so heavy you cannot lift it, it is of little use.

We tried to make our shakes 5/8″ thick and always turned the bolt upside down before the next split for proper taper (plate 18). With cedar shakes it is wise to cut the outer white cambium layer off with an ax. It rots much faster than the rest of the shake and will decrease the life of your roof (plate 19).

The shakes were attached to 1 x 4″ boards which had been nailed across the rafters. Because our shakes were so irregular in length, these *purlins* were put on separately as we were ready to add another row of shakes. The shakes were nailed in rows, thick end down, starting at the bottom of the roof. Two shakes were nailed down first, using two shake nails in the bottom and one at the top of each shake. Then a third one was nailed to cover the crack and to cover the nails of the shakes below. The distance

⑰ FROE — TURNING BOLT OVER — PRODUCES WEDGE SHAPE

⑱

⑲

214

COVER CRACKS IN FIRST ROW

3"

⟨20⟩

⟨21⟩

between the first two shakes depends on the width of the one that is to be laid over the crack, but they must not be too close because shakes will swell when wet. The next row of shakes was laid down in the same manner, overlapping the first row by 3″ or so, and the shorter sides were butted directly against the longer one (plates 20 and 21).

If your shakes are uniform in size, they can be nailed at regular intervals eliminating the constant culling and juggling of shakes we were forced to do, and the purlins can also be put on in advance.

Splitting the shakes and roofing with them was an incredibly satisfying experience. The rhythm of splitting is akin to creating music. And there we were, laying down a lovely, brown-red natural roof high enough up for a good view of the fall color explosion advancing down the mountain slope.

Because the roof looked so nice and shaking was such fun, we used the leftovers

to cover the front gable which faces west and gets rained upon. The back gable, facing the mountain was left open for ventilation and to enable the addition of more insulation over the years as settling occurs (plates 22).

(Note: there are several other ways to lay shakes on a roof. This is not the most popular way but if fits our needs. Choose one to fit yours.)

Once the roof was waterproof we drove to the site of a long abandoned mill and scraped off the top dry layer of planer shavings from several piles. We managed to accumulate enough for a measly 6″ layer of insulation before the fall rains destroyed that source for another year. We were about to abandon shavings as our roof insulation material when a neighbor arrived with a pickup load of new shavings, explaining that she had overestimated her need. With hers we gathered enough for an insulation level of 18″.

Prior to adding these shavings we cut a hole in the middle of the ceiling to insert a square box the width of 1 x 6″ cedar boards, long enough to reach above the 18″ of

insulation over the ceiling and extend into the root cellar 2″, 20″ all together. The ends of the box were screened to deny entry to insects and small animals. This screen is a heavy gauge stainless steel screen which was used in a boy's detention home (plate 23). This vent allows air circulation inside the

2 inch board

DON'T PACK FIBREGLASS

24

CHINKING

root cellar's main chamber to prevent mildew. During very cold weather the vent can be closed to protect against freezing. Some vent boxes are built to almost touch the floor of the root cellar. They bring the low, cool air in. Since we have a ground level entrance the cool air can come through the low vents at the bottoms of the doors. Venting a root cellar is dependant upon climatic conditions and should be locally assessed.

The life expectancy of a log root cellar is about 25 years if the logs are protected from gound moisture. There are several methods of waterproofing among which are painting the logs with tar, burning them on the outside with a torch or covering them with a vapor barrier. We chose to cover the walls with building paper, stapling it around the contours of the side and back walls to avoid tearing when the building was backfilled. Once the paper was put on we began the tedious process of bringing the dirt up to the level of the top log in back and under the roof eaves on the sides for maximum insulation. The front was left open.

If a good machine operator exists in your area with a small front-end loader you can eliminate this tiresome task. This summer we plan to hire this modern alternative to a shovel to push the remaining earth into a long gentle slope at the sides. We will then build a retaining wall of logs to keep the dirt in place.

To break the monotony of digging the backfill we finished the inside root cellar chamber. First, we chinked over the fiberglass insulation with 1¾″ triangular surfaced strips which were cut on a table saw. They increased the insulative value of the walls by adding more wood to the thinnest area of the walls. At first we tried stuffing the insulation back into the crack before nailing on the strips but stopped for fear that hard packed insulation does not work as well. Instead we just let the wood push the insulation as far back as was needed, leaving it fluffy (plate 24).

We were now ready to furnish the root cellar. This is an entirely personal matter and depends on what is harvested and what is put up. The number of canning jars and what vegetables and other perishables are stored should determine the size during the initial planning. In our case we resorted to doing the best with what we had to work with. We built a shelf area along the back wall which is 18″ wide for the canning jars and divided it in half for the two families. This solid 2x divider acts as a brace to support the crossing shelves. Along the side walls we bolted shelves of varying dimensions to the ceiling joists. The 2x shelf braces hang from the joists so the shelves could suspend from them and not need to be supported from the valuable space below. The space below is a tall space for winter cabbage which is harvested with its roots. The narrower shelves are for storing tomatoes and other wrapped vegetables. Under these shelves are racks made of 2 x 4s to support bins filled with moist sand for storing root crops.

We wanted to experience a full year with the root cellar before building more permanent bins, so we temporarily stored the potatoes, carrots, and beets in small wooden boxes that are used to transport fruit from orchards. We have now decided that the permanent bins should be unattached boxes, larger than the fruit boxes but small enough to be carried out of the cellar in summer for cleaning, airing and receiving a change of sand.

The entire floor of the root cellar is covered with a sand and light gravel mixture which can be turned over each summer when the building is aired out (a cement floor would have to be disinfected each year).

Now that we know the root cellar is satisfactory we will be growing more storage crops, but the size is perfectly adequate for the two families, provided that we are careful to utilize the space efficiently. This past winter we were able even to offer some space to a neighbor (see plate 1).

The interior work was done prior to hanging the doors so that we had light, though it was still pretty dim and insufficient. If we had used a method other than hanging for attaching the shelves and if the autumn rains had not been rapidly approaching it would have been easier to work inside before putting on the ceiling. As it was Jim had just enough time to stand back and admire his handiwork of the newly hung inside door before he was shoved aside by the rest of us rushing to put jars and potatoes in. This inward opening door is 32 x 72" high (2" shorter than the tallest member of the family) and is made of two layers of

cedar 2 x 8s nailed perpendicular with a vapor barrier of 50 pound roofing paper between the layers. There are stout handles on both sides of the door which are well secured with screws (plate 25).

For the outside door a chalk line was drawn and the logs were chainsawed to create the opening. 2 x 6s were nailed to the top and both sides of this opening to frame the 34" wide x 66" high door. (see plate 5). It is made of 1 x 12 cedar boards nailed perpendicularly to 2 x 8 cedar with the same vapor barrier. The 2x side faces out. The nails come through the 1xs into the thicker outer board, hiding the nail heads from the visible surface of the door. The size of this door was determined by the need to bring animal carcasses in and out which would be hung in the small outer room. Beneath this door is a very shallow air space to supply the inner door air intake holes. A stone step was added in front of this door as a finishing touch (plates 26 and 27).

Our root cellar is now one year old and has proven itself. The only difficulty was the ventilation system was not properly equipped with a sufficient low cold air intake. Mold developed on jars which had not been wiped clean enough and on the boxes storing the root crops. To allow more

air into the inner chamber we drilled 3 holes at the bottom of the inside door (see plate 31). They were closed off with fiberglass insulation when the cold weather arrived. To eliminate using insulation which can be eaten by mice, we will build a sliding panel over the holes.

Last winter was a mild one. An occassional nightime temperature of -5 degrees F. was noted. If this winter is colder we can always leave a pan of coals from the fire to ward off freezing inside the building.

Chapter Five

Railroad Tie Root Cellar

Another simple and quite efficient root cellar design is that of our own root cellar. The first year on our place was filled with the chores of reconstructing a couple of the dilapidated, unusable buildings. There was nothing left of the old barn except what could be salvaged for dry kindling and aged paneling for our kitchen walls. The root cellar was nothing more than a concrete front compost hole filled with well rotted cedar. I shoveled out the old material and redug the hole because I liked this old location. The big question was whether or not to move the ugly concrete front or incorporate it in the design. Since it was already quite late in the year, with some

harvests already in, I decided to keep the front and deal with it later.

It really surprised me to see how decomposed those cedar log walls were. It prevented me from using the same material. I shopped around and asked several friends and neighbors for advice. Soon a friend wanted to borrow our truck to pick up a few loads of railroad ties which he acquired while working for the railroad. He said he could take as many of the discarded old creosoted ties as he wanted for the nominal price of 25 cents each. He asked what I wanted in trade for the use of the truck. You guessed it, a load of ties. Perfect material for the surrounding walls of the root cellar.

CONCRETE FRONT

FILLED WITH SAWDUST

INNER DOOR

TIES ARE TOENAILED AT JOINTS

①

Each tie is 8" x 9" wide and 8' long and is thoroughly creosoted against decay. Each was still in excellent condition even after several years of contact with the ground under a railroad track. I trucked a capacity 3-ton load (about 50 ties) to the cellar site and unloaded them. We put them in five equal stacks on three sides of the hole. One stack went along the back for the back wall and two stacks went along each side wall, making them two ties or 16' long. They were stacked 9 high to make convenient 80" tall walls. many of the ties were toenailed into each other to make the walls more secure. Upright braces spaced along the outside of these ties would have also been a good idea, but didn't really seem necessary since the surrounding soil is very porous and doesn't retain enough moisture to cause much pressure against the walls, even during winter frost.

32" in from the front concrete wall I then built a studded inner wall with a sufficient doorway opening. This wall was 8' long, the width of the rear ties. It consists of 2 x 4 studs with horizontal 1x cedar sheathing. It is insulated with wood shavings that were packed well as the wall went up to insure that there would be a minimum of settling. The inner walls of the cellar were then sheathed with vertical 1 x 8 rough cut cedar. This sheathing completely blocks out any odor from the creosote and adds to the

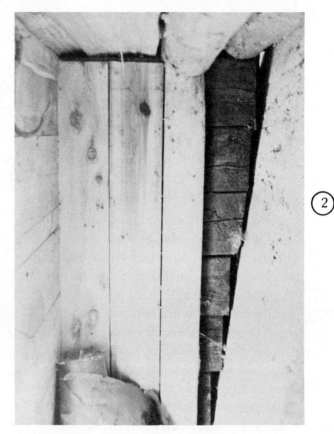

②

beauty of the rest of the rustic inner construction (plates 1 and 2).

The roof is multilayered, consisting of heavy cedar logs, 90-pound roofing paper vapor barrier, 2 x 6 tongue-and-groove cedar, another vapor barrier of black plastic, 24" of dirt and gravel, and finally a gabled cedar-shake roof. The heavy cedar logs were notched and spiked across the top of the

90 POUND ROOFING PAPER

EARTH AND RUBBLE COVERING

③

BLACK PLASTIC VAPOR BARRIER

CEADR LOGS NOTCHED TO SIT ON TIES

④

⑤

walls to tie the whole structure together and to provide a solid primary roof. It was protected by a 90-pound roofing paper vapor barrier to preserve it and keep the moisture off of it. To further seal and insulate the roof, 2 x 6 cedar tongue-and-groove boards were added across the roofing paper, and black plastic was stapled over those boards to protect them from still another roof. This tertiary roof is of gravel and dirt shoveled on at least 24″ thick until it filled the roof space and the surrounding sides.

For an entire winter this was a final roof. We figured with all those layers surely it couldn't leak. But it did. Probably through the nail holes in the roofing and plastic. The water dripped in throughout the winter, causing all the stored meat and vegetables to grow incredible mold because of the dampness.

Come spring we emptied the cellar and cleaned it out. At that point I finally realized another mistake. In my haste to put the roof on I forgot to put in the vent system. Anybody with a little imagination knows

what that meant. Well I got up on the roof, dug a hole in the dirt, cleaned out around the hole and pointed my chainsaw nose down near the rear of the roof, Ahrrahhhrahhh, sputter, sputter . . . cough, cough, in went the tip of the blade and finally an 8″ x 6″ hole was cut for the hot air outlet. A root cellar also needs a low air intake somewhere near the bottom, to let cool air in and a high outlet to allow the rising heat escape. This system provides a proper air ciurculation which is necessary for an efficient root cellar.

After I installed the outlet I extended the 1x cedar vent tube to well above the dirt and gravel roof so it would go out beyond the gabled cedar shake roof which I later put on (plate 3). This vent was then capped with a tiny gabled roof of its own to protect it from direct precipitation entering it and collecting in the cellar (plates 4 and 6). The outlet vent should extend beyond the final roof to provide proper circulation. If the outlet is between two roof layers the rising hot air would not be allowed to freely dissipate

(6)

(7)

outside, but would get partially trapped within the cavity between the roofs where there is little or no circulation.

The intake vent comes in from the outer concrete front wall through an 8 x 6″ cedar tube which extends from that wall to inside the inner chamber. This low vent brings in the cool air (plates 6 and 7). I screened this vent and the outlet vent from the outside with regular gauge screening to prevent rodents from entering but they quickly managed to nibble through the screening and made good their entry (plate 8). I suggest using a heavier gauge stainless steel screen for this purpose.

(8)

The interior is divided into shelf spaces, bins, and floor storage areas. The shelves are on either side of the aisleway in front of the bins. There are three shelves on either side, 16″ apart and 24″ from the floor. They are the width of two 1 x 10's, approximately 19″ apart and are braced by a framework of 2 x 4's which are nailed into the sheathing in the rear and notched into upright log posts in front (plate 9). Below the shelves on the left is a storage space for sacks and boxes; on the right will be a sand pit for root crops to be stored roots down in the sand to help them last longer. The buried root method of preserving root crops makes them feel like they are still in the ground. This keeps them fresh much longer than if they were just placed into the root cellar on shelves or hung from the roof on hooks like the meat (plate

(9)

10).

The three covered 30″ x 30″ bins along the rear wall are for storage of apples, carrots, and onions; three vegetables which should not be in contact with each other because they easily pick up each other's taste and odors. (plate 11). The middle bin is filled with sand so the carrots can feel like they are still in the ground. They stay crisp for a long time when preserved in this manner. The apples should be wrapped individually when stored to prevent "one bad apple spoiling the lot" (plate 12).

The doors were then framed, hung and finished with ornamental handles. This cellar, now that it is properly completed, works great. It keeps a cool 50 to 55 degrees even during the hottest days of summer (perfect place to escape the heat) and remains well above freezing even throughout the winter cold spells. I guess the several layers of roof provide a really fine insulation (plates 13 and 14).

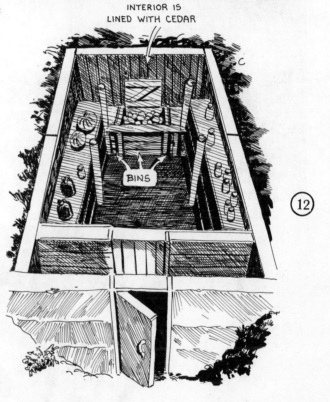

INTERIOR IS
LINED WITH CEDAR

BINS

Chapter Six

Gambrel Roof Root Cellar

We needed a root cellar that was sufficient for two families with plenty of roof space for an out-of-the-way storage area. We didn't want this structure to be incorporated under the same roof as our house or any other building that is heated with wood because of the chance of fire. If it were under the same roof as the wood-heated house a fire could wipe out our home, clothing, and entire winter food supply. I would never want my food supply to be in such a vulnerable spot. Besides, to have a sufficient cellar for two families we would need a large accessible area that could be properly protected from the extreme weather. Such a site should have good drainage and preferably be into a hillside or mountain for protection against frost and direct exposure.

As long as we were building another space we might as well incorporate several uses for it. We needed space for wood storage to keep it dry and to allow it to season. We also requried additional living quarters like a space for guests to crash or a meditation area away from the general order of things (plate 1).

We found the perfect site for this structure within the old rock slide to the east of our house. This slide area contained rock and gravel and didn't contain clay like the rest of our soil. Clay is not very porous, consequently a building constructed in this material would probably rot out within 15 years. A large hole over 10′ in width was dug out in this slide with a backhoe and the floor area was made reasonable level. The first round of logs was then put around the

10′ x 12′ area and was lifted and leveled over hefty rock corner piers.

Because we had only a few heavy logs, all much larger than we needed, we decided to rip them at the site where they were felled. All our material was 80′ long, fire-killed snags which were dry as a bone and still standing. To rip these snags we dogged them in place on skids, raising them 16″ off the ground at bottom so the chainsaw wouldn't kiss the ground while cutting through. We found the top point at either end by holding up a level flush to the end. a chalk line was then snapped along the top of the log and the log was ripped down the center with a heavy duty chainsaw. No guide was used. The cuts were eyeballed, consequently they were not perfectly straight but they were fine for our purposes. After the rip was made each of the half log tops and bottoms were flattened out to create 1½″ shelves for strips of fiberglass insulation to rest on. This insulation seals the spaces between the wall courses (plates 2 and 3).

Since we had a flat surface to work with it was easy to draw the outline for the notch

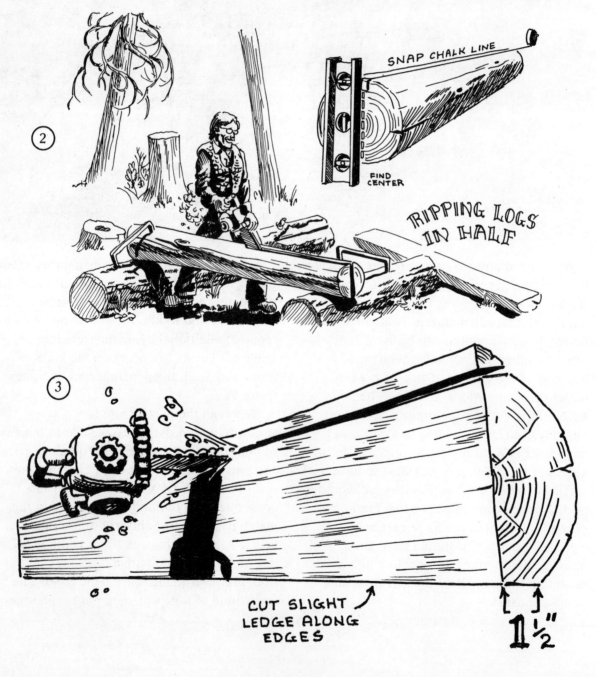

② SNAP CHALK LINE

FIND CENTER

RIPPING LOGS IN HALF

③ CUT SLIGHT LEDGE ALONG EDGES

1 ½″

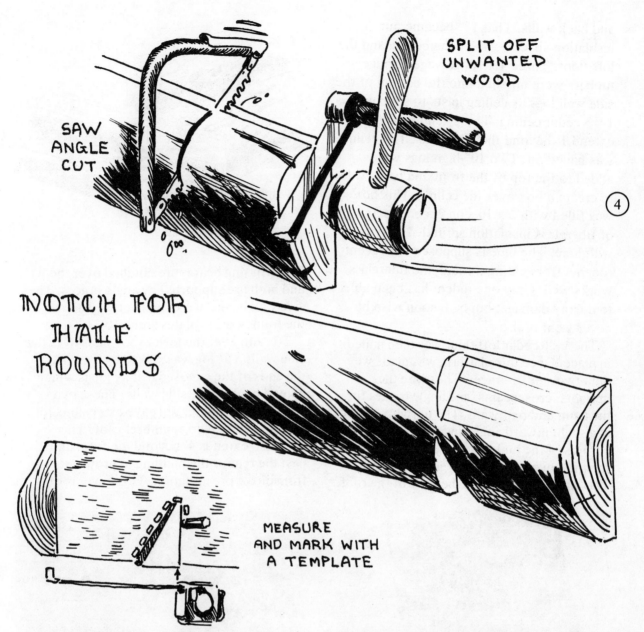

SAW ANGLE CUT

SPLIT OFF UNWANTED WOOD

④

NOTCH FOR HALF ROUNDS

MEASURE AND MARK WITH A TEMPLATE

rather than having to scribe it around a contoured surface. The notch used was a triangular one with a vertical inside line to keep the flat walls plumb. The outside line closest to the end was cut at about a 55-to 60-degree angle, making a sort of triangular *tenon* for the interlocking pieces from the shoulder to the end. The half-round shoulder is jammed against the notch so it can't shift out. For added reinforcement the ends were then spiked through the notch. A simple jig incorporating a straight vertical cut and the angle cut was made. The shape was transferred to the flat face of the log and the notch was cut out with the chainsaw. Two

simple cuts and the notch was done. The walls went up extremely fast with this method (plate 4).

Working with half-round logs provided a few additional structural benefits. The facing walls went up exactly at the same height each course because we put one face of a ripped log opposite the other. This made it easier to deal with the ceiling and roof. The faces also provide a flat surface to hang shelves and fasten bins to (plates 5-8).

When constructing walls with logs that are stagger notched you always end up with two sides higher than the other two sides. The side walls ended up 10" higher than the front and back walls. That 10″ became our insulation space between the ceiling and the loft floor. Three 4 x 10″ salvaged bridge timbers were notched into the bottom of the side wall logs as ceiling joists to support the 1 x 6 cedar ceiling. These ceiling joists extend 1′ beyond the side walls. The ceiling was nailed on. Two 10″-high logs were added to the top of the front and back walls to create a box over the ceiling. This box was filled with 2 x 10's on 2′ centers and 10″ of fiberglass insulation sprinkled heavily with lime. The lime is supposed to prevent rodents from eating through the fiberglass. It works well. Only one rodent has been able to do any damage, but he'll soon wish he never went in there.

The 1 x 6 cedar loft floor was then nailed in place. Once this platform was made we built two sets of braces. These are the uprights, crossbeams, and angle braces for the front and rear walls. The uprights extend at a slight inward angle up from the four corners of the building to create a slight slant for the lower sides of the gambrel roof. This slant complements the lines of the roof.

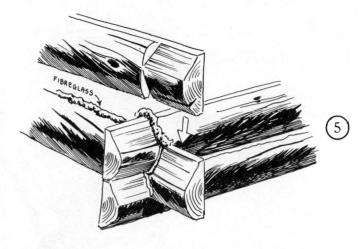

The crossing beams are notched over them and both are supported by angle braces. The side wall beams were then notched across the frameworks (plates 9hmd 10).

To cantilever the lower roof sides over the side walls a 6″ log was spiked over each of the ends of the exposed ceiling joists which extend beyond the side walls. These two poles serve as outer rail eave extensions for the 14″ overhanging gambrel roof. This roof also extends 4′ beyond the front and 2′ past the rear of the building to protect it from direct precipitation. This lower roof

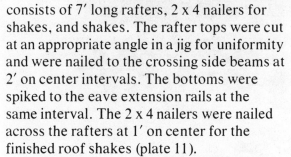

consists of 7' long rafters, 2 x 4 nailers for shakes, and shakes. The rafter tops were cut at an appropriate angle in a jig for uniformity and were nailed to the crossing side beams at 2' on center intervals. The bottoms were spiked to the eave extension rails at the same interval. The 2 x 4 nailers were nailed across the rafters at 1' on center for the finished roof shakes (plate 11).

On the west side of the roof a doorway was constructed as a side entrance for

wood. The gravel in front of that entrance was gradually sloped as a truck ramp so birch wood could be carried up for drying. The doorway is frames with 2 x 6s and the small gable roof extension above it is cantilevered on diagonal uprights (plate 12 and 13).

The upper sections of the gambrel roof were dealt with next. First two 18″ extensions were cut and were notched in over the front and rear cross beams. They raised the loft area to a height of 7½′. A ridgepole was spiked in above the extensions. Rafters were then placed

between the side wall beams and the ridgepole. The front rafters angle beyond the ends of the beams to outline a 5' overhang at the top. Nailers were placed across the rafters and shakes were nailed above them in the same manner as the lower roof (plates 14 and 16).

We have few buildings to store things in so it was important that we design the root cellar to contain as much usable space as possible. The gambrel roof on our root cellar almost goes straight up for the first 6' above the walls. The result being there is only about 6" of floor space on either side that doesn't have free head clearance. The inner area is more than sufficient to store the fresh fruits and vegetables and canned goods for two families. It is comprised of two sections. The 2' x 8' outer chamber is an insulating corridor leading to the inner chamber. The chambers are partitioned off by a frame construction inner wall with a

door. The inner area is comprised of shelf space on the three walls and bins filled with sand on the floor. Some shelves are far enough apart for 2 quart jars to fit snugly on and some are for 1 quart jars. The distances between shelves were figured out accurately so there wouldn't be any wasted space (plate 17).

The root bins are located along the bottoms of the walls. They are filled with sand so roots and root crops (carrots, beets, turnips etc.) could be protected as if they were still in the earth (plate 18). None of the bins were made with lids to separate potatoes, onions, and apples. We didn't feel this precaution was necessary. Our apples, potatoes, and onions were sitting on opposing shelves and they all did well. The apples lasted as late as July and were still crisp and juicy. They did not have even the slightest taste of potato or onion. We ate every one that we stored without having any go bad. The potatoes and onions didn't have any peculiar tastes or odors either. They also kept very well. We attribute a lot of the success of our root cellar to proper ventilation.

A proper vent should have 1″ on a side for every 1′ along the wall of the root cellar. Thus an 8′ x 8′ cellar should have an 8″ x 8″ vent (plates 19 and 20). We should have brought the vents up through the roof before putting on the shakes but we didn't do so. If the vent is extended beyond the roof the air will circulate better especially when the loft gets closed in and used for a room. We didn't want to have to leave a window open all year round for air circulation.

The front door construction of the cellar is unique, neat, and structurally sound. It protects against warpage and is really strong. The door is of laminated pine, planed down to a 2″ thickness. It is reinforced with four 1½″ deep dovetailed fir splines. To cut the

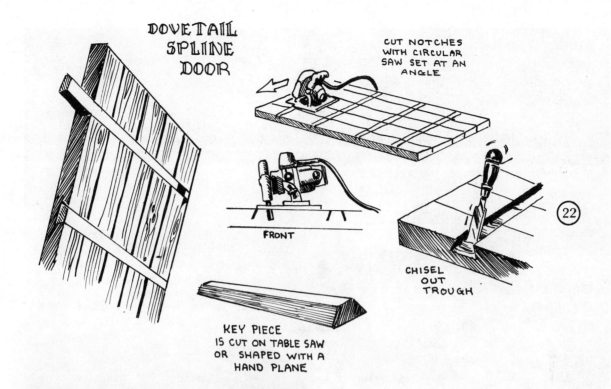

DOVETAIL
SPLINE
DOOR

CUT NOTCHES
WITH CIRCULAR
SAW SET AT AN
ANGLE

FRONT

22

CHISEL
OUT
TROUGH

KEY PIECE
IS CUT ON TABLE SAW
OR SHAPED WITH A
HAND PLANE

23

grooves for the splines I set the blade of the saw to what I thought would be a good angle and put a jig along the door so I could run the saw against it and keep the cut really straight. After that I cut from the other side, making the angle go the opposite direction. The piece between the cuts was chiseled out. The fir dovetailed splines were then cut out on a table saw and were driven into the slots (plates 21-24).

One other thing to note. Be sure to protect your root cellar from spring runoff, especially if it is built in clay or other nonporous types of soil. It should either have drain tile around its foundation or a length of drain pipe down the center to carry off the excess moisture. We have a length of 4″ perforated plastic drain pipe just below ground level in the center of the gravel floor. It has helped to prevent moisture build up and flooding.

BURY OLD 45 GAL.
DRUMS IN
HILLSIDE

STRAW

SAND

CUTAWAY
INTO
EARTH

BARREL ROOT CELLAR

Index